John Stevens Cabot Abbott

The Romance of Spanish History

John Stevens Cabot Abbott

The Romance of Spanish History

ISBN/EAN: 9783337007393

Printed in Europe, USA, Canada, Australia, Japan

Cover: Foto ©ninafisch / pixelio.de

More available books at **www.hansebooks.com**

THE
ROMANCE OF SPAIN.

BY

CHARLES W. WOOD, F.R.G.S.,

AUTHOR OF
"LETTERS FROM MAJORCA," "IN THE VALLEY OF THE RHONE," ETC., ETC.

> " How much of my young heart, O Spain,
> Went out to thee in days of yore!
> What dreams romantic filled my brain,
> And summoned back to life again
> The Paladins of Charlemagne,
> The Cid Campeador!"
>
> *Castles in Spain.*

London:
MACMILLAN AND CO., Limited.
NEW YORK: THE MACMILLAN COMPANY.
1900.

PREFACE.

The following pages were written during the year 1895.

A somewhat wrong impression having been taken up in one or two instances regarding the illustrations to 'In the Valley of the Rhône,' it may be well to state that the following illustrations were drawn especially for 'The Romance of Spain,' and have not appeared, and will not appear, in connection with any other work.

CONTENTS.

CHAPTER I.

PAGE

Gare du Midi—A French drama—The old, old story—H. C.'s ecstasies—Our fellow-traveller—Madame de X.—The next morning—H. C. in despair—An invitation—M. le Comte—H. C. disillusioned—A charming country—First sight of the Pyrenees—Bayonne—Biarritz—A wedding party—Rice and rose-leaves—"Oh, happy fair!"—The *might-have-been*—Fontarabian echoes—Irun—The Fonda de Arupe and its waiting-maid—Bullock-carts—A beautiful people—First sight of Fontarabia—Within the walls—A dream of the past—Wise monks—The *Casa Solar*—Wonderful view—Primitive post-office—Honest post-woman—Human antiquities—Missionary monks—Vain longings—Pheasant Island—On the way to St. Sebastian—Charms of the Spanish ladies—The Bay of Biscay—Rhapsody 1

CHAPTER II.

St. Sebastian—Queen's favourite resort—Disappointment—"The unexpected happens"—Hôtel d'Angleterre—A cold reception—Fine coast—The modern element—Santa Lucia and the harbour—The old gateway—A mixed market—Vespers—Jacob's Ladder—The Carmelite Nuns—A new Beatrice Cenci—H. C. a victim—Lady Maria—A wasted poem—Chiaroscuro—Heavenly music—Almost locked in—Madeleines—Cross purposes—H. C. indignant—The next morning—The Citadel—An English graveyard—Starting for Azpeitia—H. C.'s hamper—"*A bogie!*"—Zaraus—Azpeitia—Plains and Pyrenees—Convent of Ignatius Loyola—House of birth—"Lobo y Olla"—Founding the Order of Jesuits—A sociable guide—Loyola's old home—Pleasant inspection—A runaway donkey—Wasted lecture—Twilight—Silence and solitude—under the stars 32

CONTENTS.

CHAPTER III.

PAGE

St. Sebastian by night—Spanish trains—Uncomfortable travelling—Fine scenery—The Basque plains—Vittoria—Pass of Pancorbo—Burgos—Hôtel de Paris—Uncomfortable inn—Starvation—Disillusions—The cathedral—Night impressions—Santa Maria—Lost—Watchman to the rescue—Cathedral by daylight—Disappointment—Fine cloisters—Cathedral Square—A mediæval gem—The Cid—The old castle—Monastery of Miraflores—Church—A silent monk—Tomb of Don Juan II.—Houses of the Carthusians—Convent of las Huelgas—Past greatness—A vision of Mons—Bare plains—The Cid and his faithful wife—Where they repose—A last visit 62

CHAPTER IV.

St. Esteban—Cloisters—Desecrated churches—San Pablo—A deserted wife—Like Ruth and Naomi—Departed glory—The old watchman again—Happier times—A cruel wind—Last look—A facetious sentry—H. C. as Napoleon—Startling incident—Mortal combat—Landlord triumphant—Embracings—A wise driver—Final impression—At the station—The Carthusian—Exceptional fellow-traveller—Fraternising—An interesting life—Was it all a mistake?—"Good-bye"—A promise—Through the night—Segovia—Fellow-passengers—Half-way house—Roman aqueduct—Town walls—El puento del Diablo—Legend of the fair maiden—Within the walls—Processioning—The old square—Cathedral—Sunrise . . . 94

CHAPTER V.

A dream-city—Why so little known?—A quaint inn—Lordly chef—A slight fraud—An old woman—Peeling potatoes—Noisy argument—Olive oil—Freedom of the kitchen—Mysterious landlord—"Down with the Republic!"—Wonderful old square—The cathedral—A Gothic wonder—Record of the past—Mediæval procession—Monks and convent of el Parral—Interior of cathedral—Maria del Salto—Old-world vision—Troublesome verger—H. C. suggests murder—Circumvented—Delightful old bishop—Harmonies—An aerial flight—The Alcazar—Matchless scene—Historical building—What the students did—The ancient Mint—Cloisters of el Parral—Neglected summons—Death and solitude—The caretaker—Ghost or woman?—Sad life—Earthly paradise 122

CHAPTER VI.

Streets of Segovia—Ancient houses—Juan Bravo—Prison for women—Church of San Martin—San Esteban—Wonderful cloister—Episcopal Palace—View from the old walls—Lower town—A remarkable Calvary—Splendid sunset—H. C. enthusiastic—A strange old woman—Beautiful in age—"One prize worth winning"—Jacob's Ladder—Poverty-stricken thoroughfares—St. Millan—Church of Corpus Christi—Back in the days of the Moors—Moorish nave—Poor Clares—San Miguel—Town-hall—An amiable guide—Polite architect—His picturesque house—Hermit of Fuencisla—Our guide incredulous—Templar Church—Second visit to el Parral—The little old caretaker—Sad history—Back to the river—Segovia behind the times—The chef and the old woman again—More differences—Sentiment not dead yet—The bishop—In the cloisters—What the bishop thought 146

CHAPTER VII.

Last look round—Civil custodian—Wonderful view—Picturesque fountain—Passage at arms—In the lower town—A neglected gem—Friend in need—Mother and daughter—Castilian *versus* Andalusian—Brown-eyed cherub—Birds of prey—Vanity and flirtation—H. C.'s weak point—Like mother like daughter—Antonio—Curious apparition—Mephistopheles—A gossiping Loretta—"Every man to his taste"—An artistic pitcher—Cheating old age—Loretta defends herself—The bishop's right hand—"Happy as the San Millans"—Luisa—A jealous husband—Anticipated revenge—Earthly paradise—Friendly miller—Inspection—Strange sounds—Caretaker of el Parral—Detachment of young monks—Our gentleman monk—Fénélon—Church of Corpus Christi—Service—Hooded figures—Penitential voices—The old priest—Benediction—Goodwill—Ultima thule of nature and art—Freedom of the kitchen for the last time—An avenging power—Processioning through the square—A sleeping world—The dream over . . . 174

CHAPTER VIII.

Crossing the boundary—Mountain ranges—A fruitful land—Old and New Castile—A contrast—Desolate plains—The Castilians—Hardy race—Best seen in the villages—Begging system—Tillers of the soil—Healthy influences—Dining with Duke Humphrey—Overcoming difficulties—The hopeful Castilian—Madrid—Modern in-

PAGE

fluences—Luxury—Historical site—Noisy streets—Last and least interesting capital—Rejected by Goths, Romans and Moors—Trying climate—Extremes of temperature—Rapid changes—Skies that charm—Pandemonium—Shrill voices—So many provinces, so many kingdoms—Religious decline—Discarded mantilla—A woman's voice—The flower-seller—Tuberoses—Sad story—Innocence suffering for guilt—In the dining-room—Babel of sounds—Old Spanish countess and her daughter—H. C. in a fine frenzy—History of attempted elopement—A *billet-doux*—H. C. unhinged—Rapid flight—Madrid's commonplace element—The Prado—Massacre of 1808—Manzanares—Riverside washerwomen—Royal Palace—Armoury—Voices of the dead centuries . . 207

CHAPTER IX.

Madrid—Commonplace atmosphere—Blue skies—Frivolous shops—Modern Spanish art—Fan-language—Wasting the midnight oil—The picture-gallery—Rare treasures—Banished by Ferdinand VII.—Restored by La Portuguesa—Velasquez considered—Murillo—A comparison—"Surrender of Breda"—Raphael's "Salutation"—Spain's debt of gratitude—An early morning journey—Grey skies and mist—Villalba—Eté de St. Martin—Nearing the Escorial—Distant view—Ugly and unimpressive—Spaniards' eighth wonder of the world—In honour of St. Laurence—A monk-king—Philip's rooms—Religious bigotry—Cruelty under the name of religion—Last weeks of life—Mental and physical suffering—The Escorial—Debased architecture—Many destinies—A friendly monk—Splendid library—Halls of philosophy—The church—Magnificent coro—Frescoes—Chapel solemn and impressive—Tombs of the kings—Curious custom at Galapagar—Ghastly ceremonial—A quiet guide—Primitive inn—Within the precincts—Crowd of picturesque beggars—Silence and emptiness—A gigantic tomb—Ichabod . . 237

CHAPTER X.

The Tomb-Palace—Secluded monks—An invisible college—Scene changes—Toledo—A hasty journey—Russian count—H. C.'s successor—Luxury of grief—A choice luncheon—Vision of the plain—Bridge of Alcantara—New inn—Serenade—Spanish love-songs—Lady Maria again—Flirtation—In the dining-room—Shooting party—Curious apparition—Ancient Briton—Drinking healths—Going out in the darkness—First impressions—A late chemist—

PAGE

The great square—Old arcades—Outlines of Alcazar—A *cul-de-sac*—Shudderings—Room of the Secret Inquisition—In front of cathedral—Dim outlines—In the cloisters—Haunted—The archbishop—Deserted streets—Lost again—No watchman to the rescue—Black vacancy—Old square again—Midnight and total eclipse—H. C.'s terror—Toledo by daylight—Disappointing—Wynds and steeps—Moorish traces—Cervantes' courtyard—A bit of Old Toledo—Santa Cruz—Given over to the students—Cells—Young demons—Puerta del Sol—Nunnery of Santiago—Puerta Visagra—Two sets of walls—La Cava—San Servando—Wild slopes of the Tagus—A small hermitage—Bridge of San Martin—A fine view—Departed glory . . . 271

CHAPTER XI.

Toledo—Past history—Present condition—Deserted streets—Closed churches and convents—Cathedral—Rich treasury—General effect—A splendid eagle—Interesting screen and stalls—Capilla Mayor—Cloisters—Religious and domestic elements—Santa Maria la Blanca—Wonderful interior—El Transito—San Juan de los Reyes—Chains and shackles—Old cloisters—Cristo de la Luz—Once a Moorish mosque—Toledo's strong points—Scattered charms—Moorish houses—The fourth Alcazar—Burnt by students—Sacked by troops—Rebuilding—A matchless scene—Stronghold of the past—The song of the river . 307

CHAPTER XII.

Regrets—Early morning—The Escorial once more—Wild scenery—Avila—First view of the walls—A city of the past—Back in the Middle Ages—Melancholy inn—Civil host—Cathedral—Another world—Wonderful interior—A church militant—A 15th century Solomon—San Vicente—A Romanesque vision—Magnificent porch and doorway—San Pedro—Vespers—Dim religious light—An effective choir—Locking up—Overlooking the valley—Convent of St. Thomas Aquinas—Dominican brother—Interesting church—Tomb of Prince Juan—St. Teresa—A freezing experience—Welcome refuge—Philosophic watchman—Heretic also—The last of Avila—Night journey—Salamanca—Sleepy porter—Maddening bells—In the past—Old and new cathedrals—Charm of situation—Famous old bridge—Banks of the river—Washerwomen—H. C. for once resists temptation—General effect disappointing—Curious illusion—

PAGE

Uncomfortable quarters—Strange room—Grinning skeleton—Mocking laughter—Valladolid—Bearish post-office—Old square—Unfinished cathedral—Santa Maria la Antigua—Simancas—Curious little town—Historic plains—Mad Joan—Mediæval castle—Spanish archives—Old custodian—Quaint and original character—Face to face with the past—Golden moments—The imperishable Romance of Spain 334

LIST OF ILLUSTRATIONS.

	PAGE
SEGOVIA	*Frontispiece*
FONTARABIA	9
ON THE WAY TO FONTARABIA	13
FONTARABIA	15
CHIEF STREET	17
FONTARABIA	20
QUIET REFLECTIONS	23
MISSIONARY MONKS	27
ST. SEBASTIAN	33
ST. SEBASTIAN	37
ON THE WAY TO AZPEITIA	45
ON THE WAY TO AZPEITIA	47
CHIEF STREET IN AZPEITIA	49
HOUSE OF IGNATIUS LOYOLA	53
AZPEITIA IN TWILIGHT	59
VITTORIA	65
OLD PALACE, BURGOS	68
CATHEDRAL	71
CATHEDRAL	75
GATEWAY OF SANTA MARIA	79
CHURCH OF ST. NICHOLAS, BURGOS	83
WEST DOORWAY, MIRAFLORES	85
CLOISTERS	87
LAS HUELGAS	89
WALLS OF SEGOVIA	107
AQUEDUCT	111
THE OLD SQUARE	115
BELFRY, SEGOVIA	117

	PAGE
STREET IN SEGOVIA	119
STREET IN SEGOVIA	127
CLOISTERS	133
TEMPLARS' CHURCH	140
DESECRATED CHURCH	142
CLOISTERS OF EL PARRAL	144
SEGOVIA	147
SAN MARTIN	149
ST. ESTEBAN	153
OUTSIDE THE WALLS, SEGOVIA	155
SEGOVIA FROM THE RIVER: EVENING	157
SANTIAGO GATEWAY	161
ALCAZAR AFTER THE FIRE	165
ALCAZAR	175
ALCAZAR AT PRESENT DAY	178
AQUEDUCT	181
OLD ROOFS IN SEGOVIA	186
SEGOVIA	189
STREET IN SEGOVIA	194
EL PARRAL AND THE OLD MINT	197
ALCAZAR	201
OLD NOOK IN SEGOVIA	204
A BIT OF OLD SPAIN, NEAR MADRID	208
NEW MADRID	210
MARKET-PLACE, MADRID	213
CHIEF SQUARE	217
PALACE BRIDGE OVER THE MANZANARES	229
CHANGING GUARD	233
PALACE OF THE ESCORIAL	249
PHILIP'S SITTING-ROOM IN THE ESCORIAL	253
PALACE OF THE ESCORIAL	255
CORO OF CHURCH	259
A SPANISH GARDEN, NEAR THE ESCORIAL	263
ARCHWAY LEADING TO THE ESCORIAL	265
BEGGARS	267
ALCANTARA BRIDGE, TOLEDO	275
STREET LEADING TO CATHEDRAL	281
DOOR OF THE INQUISITION	284

LIST OF ILLUSTRATIONS.

	PAGE
Cervantes' Courtyard	289
Doorway of Santa Cruz	291
Leading to Santa Cruz	293
Puerta del Sol	295
A Patio in Toledo	297
Bridge of San Martin	299
Gateway to Bridge	303
Lower Town	311
East End of Cathedral	317
Cloisters	320
Santa Maria la Blanca	322
Cloisters of San Juan de los Reyes	325
Cristo de la Luz	329
Interior of Cathedral, Avila	337
Bastion and East End of Cathedral	340
San Vicente	343
West Doorway, San Vicente	347
Salamanca from the River	355
House of the Shells	358
House of the Shells	360
Old Houses	362
Market-place	365
Arcades and Dramatic Vision	369
Valladolid	373
Doorway of San Pablo, Valladolid	376

THE ROMANCE OF SPAIN.

CHAPTER I.

Gare du Midi—A French drama—The old, old story—H. C.'s ecstasies—Our fellow-traveller—Madame de X.—The next morning—H. C. in despair—An invitation—M. le Comte—H. C. disillusioned—A charming country—First sight of the Pyrenees—Bayonne—Biarritz—A wedding party—Rice and rose-leaves—"Oh, happy fair!"—The *might-have-been*—Fontarabian echoes—Irun—The Fonda de Arupe and its waiting-maid—Bullock-carts—A beautiful people—First sight of Fontarabia—Within the walls—A dream of the past—Wise monks—The *Casa Solar*—Wonderful view—Primitive post-office—Honest post-woman—Human antiquities—Missionary monks—Vain longings—Pheasant Island—On the way to St. Sebastian—Charms of the Spanish ladies—The Bay of Biscay—Rhapsody.

TIME, ten at night; scene, platform of the Gare du Midi; ourselves waiting for the train to steam out of Paris on its journey towards Spain.

A little French drama was taking place. He, a middle-aged man, handsome and well-preserved; she, quite a young woman, tall, beautiful and distinguished-looking, with the peculiar air that is inherited, not acquired. She was dressed to perfection. Her hat was faultlessly placed upon her well-posed head; the *chevelure* beneath it a magnificent golden, evidently arranged by a perfect maid. There was a tender farewell before she entered the carriage where the maid was already installed amidst all the elegant impedimenta of a lady's travelling gear. He kissed her delicately on both eyelids, evidently not to disturb the bloom upon her cheeks, pressed her gently to his heart. "Au revoir, ma mignonne. Au revoir, sans adieu," we heard him murmur. A charming foot and instep peeped out as she lightly entered the carriage. The door closed, and the train slowly moved away.

They waved their final good-byes to each other, her expression sweet and smiling as she looked at him. But as distance between them increased, the assumed tenderness went out of the face, and she ceased to act a part.

It was evidently the old, old story of a *mariage de convenance*. A young and beautiful woman, especially a Frenchwoman, cannot live without romance, and there can be no romance in middle age. So, when distance made disguise unnecessary, the mask was thrown aside, the sweet expression gave place to a certain hardness. It is possible for man to bind himself with irrevocable chains which so change his whole nature that all the kindness and sympathy once there die out, and he grows harsh and cruel where once he might have been true and tender. What is possible in man is still more possible in impressionable woman.

H. C. was in ecstasies. It was a case of love at first sight. In vain we pointed out that she was not an unappropriated blessing. He took out pencil and sketch-book and reproduced an exact likeness of his divinity—hat, *chevelure*, foot and instep, all perfect with the unerring exactness of his undoubted genius. He gazed surreptitiously through the glazed peephole every French carriage possesses. She was now looking upwards with a Madonna expression in her large liquid eyes. All the hardness had disappeared. Her hands were clasped upon her knees. She seemed sad and melancholy.

"Let me go to her," cried H. C. "She is unhappy, and needs comforting. Her life is sacrificed to that parchment effigy left on the platform. It is a crime."

This was exaggeration. The parchment effigy was handsome and manly, though no longer in the bloom of youth. H. C. grew feverish and excited. Then chaos happened; the maid drew the blind over the lamp; darkness fell upon the vision. H. C. was in despair.

One old gentleman shared the carriage with us. His own romantic days had long been over— were even forgotten. It was possible that, unlike Petrarch, he had never had a Laura to sigh for. He looked at H. C. in wonder and alarm.

"*Votre ami, monsieur, n'a-t-il pas un peu perdu l'esprit, par hasard ?*" he inquired a little anxiously, as he arranged his skull-cap for the night, and placed his pillow at a comfortable angle. Fortunately, H. C. could not speak a word of French, which he professes to despise, after the manner of the fox and the grapes. We assured the inquirer that it was only a harmless insanity brought on by the fair one in the next compartment. He was subject to this sort of attack.

"Madame de X.," cried the old gentleman. "I know her well—who does not? Let him spare his emotion for a better object. She is fascination itself, and has broken more hearts than Cleopatra; but she has no heart of her own. She is now on her way to Biarritz, *pour y faire la pluie et le beau temps. Bonne nuit, monsieur; dormez bien. Que votre ami en fait de même.*"

And the benevolent old gentleman finally settled himself into his skull-cap and his corner, where, undisturbed by feverish dreams of divinities, he soon fell asleep. We followed his example, and H. C. was left to a restless solitude.

The night passed, and early next morning we looked out upon a grey, cold world. A heavy mist blotted out the landscape. The train, rolling on at the rate of forty miles an hour, slackened speed, and the old gentleman roused himself and looked out upon the fog.

"Nous approchons," he cried. "I know it by this horrible mist. Very soon we shall roll over the Garonne."

As he spoke the train rumbled on to the iron bridge, and down below we caught a faint glimmer of the fair flowing water. Then it streamed into the decrepit station of dear historical old Bordeaux, with little of the past about it but its gates. They were about to begin a new station side by side with the old—a sumptuous stone edifice, guaranteed to last through all the ages.

"Il était temps," said the old gentleman, removing his skull-cap, and peering comically at H. C., who had fallen into the slumber of exhaustion. The engine knowing this, maliciously gave a prolonged shriek. The whistle of a French engine is only to be outdone by a German. H. C. sprang up and looked round wildly. "Then we are *not* married?" he cried. "And we are *not* on our honeymoon? And it is all a false, wicked and delusive dream."

"*Effarouché!* It is all one fièvre, Sare," cried the old gentleman. "I do speak a leetle English, and I tell you we are at Bourdeaux,"—so he pronounced it—"where is to find an excellent cup of coffee au buffet that will restore your *ton*. My carriage waits me. Here I depart. Sare, beware of les syrènes. They do not all live in the Méditerranée, but they are all equally dangerous. Ah! j'ai passé par ma jeunesse, moi, for all you think me one old *fossile*."

He shrugged his shoulders, and looking at us with a benevolent twinkle, alighted. On the platform he insisted on shaking hands, and presenting his card, begged us to call upon him if ever the fortunes of war brought us to Bordeaux. "Monsieur le Comte San Salvador Martel de la Veronnière." Merciful powers! what a name to bear in one's memory! And as he departed, we noted that he had just five feet six inches to support this weight of distinction on his way through the world.

As M. le Comte had said, the coffee was excellent and refreshing after the long night journey.

We were no sooner seated than the door opened; the divinity walked in accompanied by her maid, and installed herself at an adjoining table. H. C.'s coffee was forgotten. All his hunger went into his eyes, which greedily devoured this matchless beauty. She passed a roll to her maid, and a bowl of coffee was placed before each. Then occurred the catastrophe of the journey. This resplendent creature took her own roll—a soft *pistolet*—dipped it into her coffee, and absorbed an enormous mouthful of the soaked bread.

It was terribly disillusioning. H. C. turned pale as death, and if we had not had our flask at hand, the heart might have stopped for ever. As it was, he was saved—in more senses than one; and when we returned to the carriage, he was once more sober and in his right mind. "Women, especially beautiful women, should live upon crystallised violets," was all the remark he ever made upon the subject.

We steamed off again. As the morning grew a little older, the mists rolled away, and the southern landscape stood out in all its charm. A succession of forests, of vineyards now dead and fruitless, of small, southern-looking, flat-roofed houses, picturesque with white walls and green shutters, and strings of red capsicums hanging in gorgeous crimson array. About these houses creepers and vines twined themselves with grace and beauty. The autumnal tints were unusually splendid; the landscape a blaze of rich colouring—a dream; tints unknown to English soil. Mile after mile of fir-trees stretched beside the railway; from every tree a strip of bark chopped away, below which a tin cup was fastened to catch the slowly oozing turpentine, many days passing before the cup filled. In spite of this the trees flourish and reach a fair height, straight as an arrow. Down country-roads many a meek-eyed pair of oxen, yoked together, wended their patient way; the heavy yoke added to the burden, causing them infinite discomfort.

We made way through the bare plains, until the Pyrenees appeared, outlined against the blue sky. Few mountains are so beautiful, but here the ranges are less so than those passed on the way to Barcelona. There, especially on a moonlight night, winding amidst the dark impressive outlines, you ask yourself if you are in Wonderland. Rising hills, boundless slopes, solemn, death-like silence, absolute repose, all steeped in the moon's lights and shadows; these form a scene never to be forgotten.

Presently we reached Bayonne, lying amidst the lower ranges of the Pyrenees. It stands out boldly and picturesquely from the station, crowning a hill, upon which its cathedral rises. Below ran the Adour, over which we rolled slowly and heavily. All this country is historically interesting. We know how it was besieged in 1814, when Marshal Soult was entrenched here and resisted the English with much bloodshed; how Sir John Hope was taken prisoner; and how Soult found more than his match in Wellington. In days gone by, this ancient capital of the *Pays de Labourd* was famous for its armourers; whence the word bayonet or Bayonnette.

"I think this is Bayonne," we remarked, recognising familiar outlines as the train slackened speed.

"No," returned H. C., gazing with puzzled expression at a long brick building, destined to imports, and for once determined to be up in his French, "this is *Arrivages*. Never heard of the place before. Hope we're in the right train."

Next came Biarritz, where a group of English were escorting bride and bridegroom en route for Paradise, wherever that may be. Grains of rice and scattered rose-leaves betrayed the secret of the new creation.

"Oh, happy, happy, happy fair,
Thine eyes are lode-stars and thy tongue sweet air,"

sang the best man to the bride, as she looked down radiant with smiles and blushes from the adjoining carriage they had just entered. The lovely old melody, unheard for many a long year, brought back to us memories of the past, when banquet halls, now deserted, were crowded with troops of friends who have all fled to the Silent Land. But under the clear skies of Biarritz, and the bright sunshine, there was no room for melancholy. As the train moved away, even we came in for showers of rice and rose-leaves, misplaced, but deliciously perfumed.

"Coming events cast their shadows before," murmured H. C., applying it all to himself. "I have a presentiment that before long my turn will come. Possibly I shall find my destiny in Spain."

"By the same token there stands your late divinity, Madame de X.," we observed.

She had alighted with her maid, and, at the far end of the platform, surrounded by her impedimenta, looked tall, aristocratic, and certainly beautiful. She too was silently gazing upon the excited little group, and as the faces of the happy pair beamed down upon their friends, reflecting that bliss which comes but once in a lifetime, and then only to the few and only for a while, we fancied we heard a sigh, and saw a tear trembling in the large liquid eyes; and certainly the hands were clasped with that peculiar motion which marks the *might-have-been*. As the train passed out, her tall, motionless figure, crowned by the perfectly posed head and hat, impressed one far more than the frantic wavings of the bridal group or the perfume of falling rose-leaves. Monsieur de la Veronnière had called her heartless, but he was mistaken.

After St. Jean de Luz came Hendaye, the last town on the French frontier, backed by its wild, lofty, solitary mountains, on one of which stood a lonely monastery. Here the sea rolled up into the land in the form of an estuary, in the centre of which rose the town-crowned rock of Fontarabia. Waves for ever dash and break at the foot of the rocks, singing the requiem of the dead past, when the ancient palaces of Fontarabia echoed to the sound of music and laughter, the clashing of swords. It rose like a vision clearly outlined against the more distant hills, its wonderful tones those that only age and exposure to the elements can ever give.

> "O for the voice of that wild horn,
> On Fontarabian echoes borne,
> The dying hero's call,
> That told imperial Charlemagne
> How Paynim sons of swarthy Spain
> Had wrought his champion's fall."

The air seemed to ring out those lines from that prince of novels "Rob Roy."

FONTARABIA.

Then the train stopped at Irun, the frontier town; a new language sounded in our ears; a new type of people met the eye—the "Paynim sons of swarthy Spain," yet more civilised than in the days of Charlemagne.

It was a relief to exchange the train for a Spanish carriage. The driver, young and wild, whipped up his horses, and dashed down the long tree-lined road which separates town from station. These violent means soon brought us to Irun, which has nothing to recommend it beyond extreme beauty of situation and nearness to Fontarabia. But the charm of novelty lay upon all; and the smallest of Spanish towns generally has a certain picturesque colouring about it, though less rich in the north than the south. Much of this is due to the people, especially the women, who wear their bright things with wonderful effect.

We found the Fonda de Arupe quite the type of an ordinary inn in Northern Spain; primitive, but clean. At a small table in the modest dining-room they served us with coffee in large bowls without handles, neither graceful nor convenient. "A Rome comme à Rome," quoted H. C., scalding himself with a hasty draught. The landlord's daughter waited; a very pretty, modest girl, with a charming expression and a good deal of graceful movement; by no means an uncommon type in this district, many of the young peasants possessing a strange refinement of face and feature.

After our coffee-and-bowl experience—served on a bare table, with large spoons to match—we arranged for a conveyance to take us to Fontarabia, and whilst it was preparing, went out to examine the wonders of the town.

They were few and far between. The little place dates far back in the world's history, but few vestiges of antiquity remain. It is probably of Roman origin, and traces of Roman walls and houses still exist, but of little importance. Irun has suffered in times of war, and has on several occasions been burnt down. So to-day it is chiefly distinguished by a modern, unpicturesque element; tall consumptive houses, painted in many colours, with dark interiors and unwholesome atmosphere. The streets were narrow and the pavement was bad, making every mile appear as two. Everything rattled and echoed; and we soon found that the Spaniards love noise. Their voices are loud, harsh and unmusical. Fortunately the traffic was confined to an occasional bullock-cart, and the patient oxen, melancholy and oppressed, were the most characteristic things we saw here. The men drove their cattle with a long stick, gently prodding them—a performance the animals seemed to enjoy.

The carts were often laden with leaves and canes of the Indian maize from which the corn had been taken, serving as fuel and litter. In some of the out-of-the-way country churches they strew the pavement with them and with rushes, recalling far-away houses and cottages in Norway, where, in the evenings of long ago, we have watched them, when work was done, strewing the floors with branches of the scented fir. The church in Irun was fairly characteristic and interesting; its date early sixteenth century, a period when Spanish Gothic had ceased to be always good.

It was a relief to find nothing remarkable in the way of curiosities; no museum, no town hall of consequence, no ancient palaces, one solitary church. But the people were of a good type. Many of the children in the streets were quite beautiful; well-shaped faces, with large

ON THE WAY TO FONTARABIA.

heavenly-blue eyes and cheeks flushed with a delicate damask. Whether it denoted health we knew not, and doubted; but they were charming to look upon. We hoped to find this type almost universal, and were disappointed.

Our equipage did not turn out to be a bullock-cart, but one of those heavy landaus common to the continent, yet the spirited driver did not let the grass grow under his feet.

FONTARABIA.

He whipped up his cattle, and awoke frightful echoes in the narrow streets. Rattling past the old church, we turned into the open country, following the left bank of the Bidassoa— a river whose stone bridge marks the boundary line separating France from Spain.

On either side our road were fields of Indian corn not yet gathered. Amongst this grew huge pumpkins or other vegetable of a rich red tone. The houses were very picturesque; white-washed and ancient-looking, with interesting windows, overhanging eaves, old tiled roofs, and vines creeping about walls and trellis-work. Just beyond a row of these charming cottages the road circled round, and before us rose far-famed Fontarabia.

Nowhere does it look more striking than as you thus approach it. Above the immense rock rise the terraces with their crumbling houses and decayed walls. If the glory of Fontarabia has departed, it has given place to a charm few Spanish towns possess. Skirting the foot of the rock, we suddenly came in sight of the ancient gateway, grey and massive. In the shade of the trees outside the walls, the driver halted; and here waited whilst we walked through the old streets, satisfying our eyes with seeing.

High above this shady avenue stood the dark and massive gateway, outlined against the blue sky. The archway framed in the long street beyond, with its glimpse of old houses, magnificent eaves and grated windows. Above the outlines rose the tower of the uninteresting church.

Passing within the gateway all the beauty of age surrounded us. Great buildings of imperishable stone, once stately palaces; great doorways leading into courtyards sacred to history, which once had echoed with the clash of swords, the tramp of horses; roofs that overhung in wonderful eaves, large and deep; the brilliant sunshine casting long slanting shadows upon the walls. Lights and shades dazzled one with their vivid contrasts. From many a window immense casements of wrought ironwork stood out, examples of an artistic craft now dead to the world; as so much else that was beautiful is dead.

CHIEF STREET IN FONTARABIA.

The streets were deserted. Fontarabia is a dream of the past. And what vicissitudes has it gone through, what fortunes of war! Of its earliest history little is recorded, but with the dawn of the middle ages its romantic name frequently occurs in the Spanish records. It was the frontier outpost of Spain, and, as such, one of the keys to her interior. Milton here places the scene of the defeat of Charlemagne and the death of the Paladin Roland; but history is less definite upon the point. Scott follows in the wake of Milton.

More certain are the records of the sixteenth century; more painful the experiences. In 1521 Francis I. took Fontarabia and held it long. In 1638 the Prince de Condi and the Archbishop of Bordeaux besieged it and were repulsed. In the retreat and confusion, 2,000 French soldiers were drowned in the Bidassoa. In 1794 she was again besieged, and defended by a couple of Capucin monks; worthy recluses, who, when the French commanded them to surrender, under penalty of being run through the body, replied that they preferred life to fame. Lamarque, commanding the French, gave them six minutes for consideration, and they promptly yielded. In 1808, 1813, 1823, and 1837, Fontarabia again went through the chances of war, since which time she has fallen into the repose of old age.

But it is a beautiful old age; worthy the ancient titles bestowed upon her. *Muy Noble; Muy Leal; Muy Valerosa;* the latter given by Philip IV. in 1618, in remembrance of the heroic defence of her brave women for sixty-nine days against a besieging army of 25,000 men. Here Wellington entered upon the last stages of the Peninsular War, the French being hopelessly defeated at Vittoria. But Wellington's successful passage of the estuary in 1813 was partly accidental. The bridges had been broken down, Soult commanded every known ford. Some Basque fishermen, however, told the duke of a ford

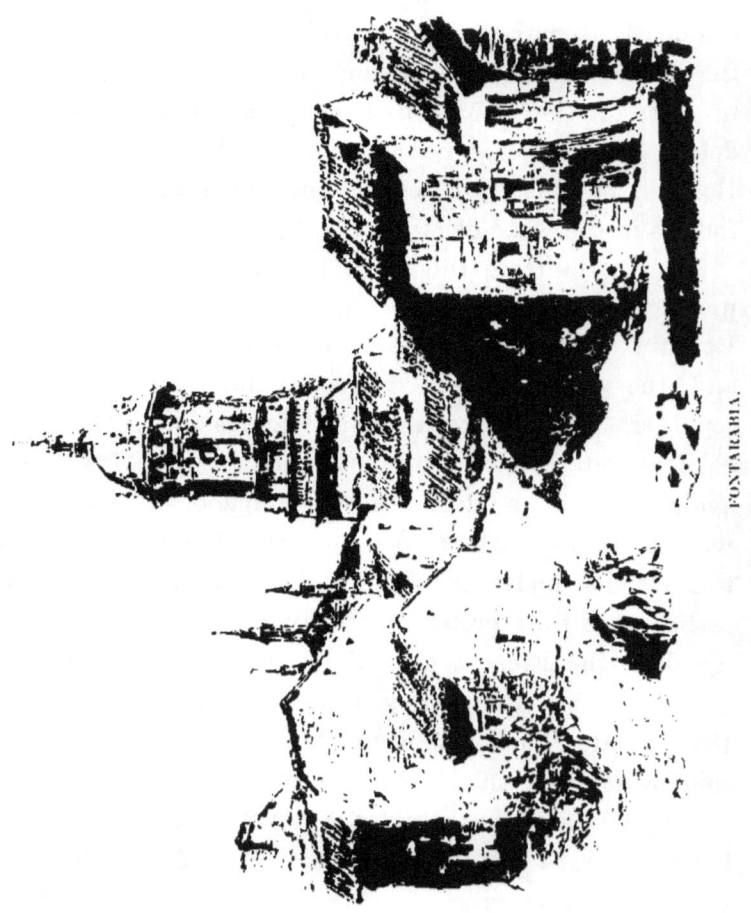

FONTARABIA.

near the sea, known only to themselves, and only to be used at spring tides. Wellington used the information, and on a given day the British troops crossed the wet sands. The French were soon driven before them, and the great war was over.

In the small square of Fontarabia, we found its ancient

palace, now called the *Casa Solar* or Palace of Charles V.; a wonderful old building, of which little remains but the shell. Here Charles loved to linger out days and weeks. The bold plain front, without windows or ornamentation, dates from the latter part of the sixteenth century. The earliest portion was built about the year 907 by the King of Navarre. The part attributed to Charles V. is distinct from this—the Palace of Mad Joan, heavy and massive in its architecture. Nothing remains of the interior but bare walls dividing immense rooms, where dark shadows and ghosts of the past seem to lurk in every corner.

You pass out to the roof and breathe more freely; may well do so, for such a view is seldom seen.

Below reposes the wonderful little town. You trace the narrow streets, the crumbling walls, gates and fortifications, all slowly but surely disappearing: a picture of solitude and desolation. Balconies are untenanted. Behind the splendid gratings of her windows, bright eyes have ceased to look upon gay cavaliers. The courtyards echo no more to the shout of war. In some of the walls you may see the holes made by bullets, every one of which once told a tale of bloodshed. Spanish gipsies now find a refuge in the ruins; but amongst the fortunes they tell there is no place for the prophecy that Fontarabia shall one day return to its greatness.

Farther away Irun reposes upon its slopes, looking almost romantic; encircling all are the Pyrenees in their outlined beauty. The wide waters of the capricious bay spread to unseen limits, blue and ever changing as roll after roll sweeps over the shore and dies away with gentle murmur. At low water the small picturesque harbour lies high and dry, its fleet of fishing boats reposing on the sands.

The town seemed more deserted than ever on returning to it. Here and there women sat sewing in the middle of the road, in front of their houses, undisturbed by any traffic. Once a window was opened, and an ancient cavalier, looking as though he might have taken part in a fifteenth century tournament, stepped out upon his wrought-iron balcony, and gazed in dreamy wonder at the intruders. Who could these strange visitants be, and what could they want?

At that moment we were wanting the post-office, and wandered up and down, looking in vain for sign or token of the institution. The shops were deserted, mournful-looking and closed; we hesitated to intrude upon their sacred solitude and disturb the historical dust of ages. Finding the door of one of them by chance open we went in. The good woman at the counter was actually engaging two other women in conversation—first symptom of a crowd we had seen in Fontarabia.

On asking for the post-office she looked astonished. It did not exist. She sold stamps, and there was a letter-box across the road, and that was all they had in the way of *correos*.

"I assure you it is as I say," she declared. "If you search for a week you will find nothing but a letter-box; and here," she added, producing a portfolio, "are stamps and postcards. I supply the whole town; and the quantity I sell adds little to my fortune."

We were so occupied in working out this problem that we left our umbrella on the counter. In Irun there had been a few drops of rain and we had yet to learn that in Spain this meant fine weather for the rest of the day. Passing through the street half an hour after, we saw the good woman seated in the sunshine in the middle of the road, the umbrella over

her head, for all the world like a Chinese mandarin. When she caught sight of us, she stood up and waved.

"I could think of no other way of attracting your notice," she said. "If I had gone after you, it might only have been a game of hide-and-seek. It is so troublesome to lose umbrellas or purses in travelling," she added. "Fortunately I have had no customers since you went away."

And judging from appearances she would have no more for a month to come. The few women quietly sewing at the doors pointed out various objects of antiquity, as though they knew that we wished to lose no rare traces of the past.

"We also grow antique," said one very aged woman, bending over her knitting, a world of dry humour in her tones; "but we do not become more interesting on that account, like the old houses. It is hard that senseless stones should have the advantage over us."

The hours in Fontarabia passed as a dream, transporting us to the Middle Ages of the world. The town is full of these signs and wonders, and the blue sky with its eternal youth and freshness only added to their charm.

The old gateway once more, our driver resting himself and his horses in the shade of the trees. They take life easily these drivers, and here he would have willingly waited until nightfall. But we had far to go before darkness overtook the shadows, and could not linger. Looking back as he turned swiftly down the road, we thought we had seldom seen a more perfect vision than Fontarabia.

On the right we passed a Capucin monastery, where young novices are trained for missionary-monks to distant colonies. Many go to the penal settlement of New Caledonia. Near this, and close to some charming cottages, we met a long string of these monks, men of all ages, from sixteen or eighteen upwards. They were dressed in Capucin cloaks and cowls, and formed a striking procession in the surrounding scenery. What can be more picturesque and mysterious than a monk, cloaked and hooded, with face concealed, silence observed, and the suggestion of a lonely life? But these had their cowls thrown back, and looked at us with rather sad and longing eyes—or we fancied so—as though they regretted that they too could not wander away and see the world. They had not lived long enough to know that lots are more equally divided than appears at first sight. Yet their special destination was not the cloister but that world itself, for many a long year to come. Those who reach the decline of life often retire into a monastery, devoting their last days to prayer and contemplation.

The young monks filed away, and we went on through the sunny landscape.

On the other side the river lay the small Pheasant Island, which, says Gautier, is no bigger than a fried sole. Why it was ever called Pheasant Island is unknown. Its better name is Ile de la Conférence; and, small though it be, it has played its part in history.

Here, in 1463, the rash and quarrelsome Louis XI. of France, soon after his father had starved himself to death from fear of being poisoned, met the miserable Henry IV. of Castile to negotiate the marriage of the Duc de Guienne. Here came Francis I. after he had been defeated and taken prisoner at Pavia, and signed the treaty of Madrid, leaving his two sons as hostages; sons dear to his heart, as Benjamin to the heart of Jacob. Only five years before he had met Henry VIII. on the Field of the Cloth of Gold, and almost the whole of the intervening time had been spent

OUR MISSIONARY MONKS.

in war with Charles V., that monarch of vicissitudes, whose son married Mary of England, and who ended life by retiring to the monastery of St. Juste in Estremadura, celebrating his own funeral a few weeks before his death.

Irun was reached only to leave it again. As there was nothing to detain one in the little town, with its narrow streets, close atmosphere, and depressing influence, we decided to go on to St. Sebastian—much to our driver's delight. It was a distance of some ten miles, and one sees more of the country by road than by rail.

We turned our backs upon the echoing streets and inquisitive population. An amphitheatre of distant hills surrounded us. In the rich plains reposed houses bright with many colours; white walls and green shutters and red roofs, where, in summer, vine-leaves throw their pencilled, flickering shadows upon the porch; small prospering farm-houses, whose inmates rejoice in the fruits of the earth they cultivate with so much toil. Almost everything under the sun grows in this valley. The people we met on the road were picturesque and fairly energetic, as though they had work to do in life. Women seated on their donkeys were trying their best to urge the cunning animals to a gallop; but the donkeys knew better. In Spain the women do most of the work—the men look on approvingly.

Approaching St. Sebastian, the bustle of life increased; mountains narrowed; houses were perched upon the slopes; factories were in full work. At Pasages the scene, owing to the disposition of the hills, was very romantic, though the place is given up to commerce, and rapidly growing in importance. Many of the wines of Spain go out from here into the world, and the land-locked port is the safest on the shores of Biscay. Houses, looking old and picturesque as the hills themselves, clustered about their base. A narrow, winding strait led to the sea, guarded by a mediæval castle.

Of the bay itself, nothing was visible. But on a still night when doors are closed and work is ended, and people are sleeping, you may hear through the silence and darkness the boom and thunder of breakers about the rocks. In the fearful storms of the Bay of Biscay, many a good ship has gone down in sight of Pasages, trying to make the harbour.

After this came the suburbs of St. Sebastian, where the well-to-do people spend a part of their lives. Fair dames in graceful mantillas went to and fro with easy movement. It has been said that only Spanish women know how to walk; and as they glide along in the charming mantilla, every fold full of grace, one feels inclined to add that only they know how to dress. It gives them an essentially soft and feminine look, adding much to their beauty. A clear olive complexion, a softness of outline, slightly suggestive of voluptuousness when the first youth has passed; a most agreeable cast of feature, seldom too pronounced; eyes large and liquid and almond-shaped; and often a peculiar grey tint upon the skin that is unusual and very artistic: such are the Spanish women.

Passing from all these alluring charms, the towers, steeples and fortified heights of St. Sebastian opened up; a full view of the Bay of Biscay, rolling over a dazzling shore, its waters a transparent emerald. Wave after wave broke into long lines of snowy foam. Far off, a few white-sailed vessels passed on their stately way in the haze of the setting sun. Immense cliffs rose to right and left, against which the rollers broke in showers of spray. A sound of the roaring and surging of the sea goes on for ever, and nature has nothing more impressive than this. As the carriage halted a moment, we felt we had seldom looked upon a lovelier scene.

"Sublime!" cried H. C. in ecstasies of wonder and poetic rhapsody. "After all, these eternal seas and cliffs, these splendours of nature, are more satisfying, more soul-stirring, than even the exquisite but evanescent attractions of the sirens of this lovely land."

"Yes," we replied, like another Mentor. "And in these seas and cliffs which never change, and in the wonderful outlines of her ancient cities which never weary, far more than in the fleeting charms of the sirens, lies the romance, the true ROMANCE OF SPAIN."

CHAPTER II.

St. Sebastian—Queen's favourite resort—Disappointment—" The unexpected happens "—Hôtel d'Angleterre — A cold reception—Fine coast—The modern element—Santa Lucia and the harbour—The old gateway—A mixed market—Vespers—Jacob's Ladder—The Carmelite Nuns—A new Beatrice Cenci—H. C. a victim—Lady Maria—A wasted poem—Chiaroscuro—Heavenly music—Almost locked in—Madeleines—Cross purposes—H. C. indignant—The next morning—The Citadel—An English graveyard—Starting for Azpeitia—H. C.'s hamper—" *A bogie!*"—Zaraus—Azpeitia—Plains and Pyrenees—Convent of Ignatius Loyola—House of birth—" Lobo y Olla "—Founding the Order of Jesuits—A sociable guide—Loyola's old home—Pleasant inspection—A runaway donkey—Wasted lecture—Twilight—Silence and solitude—Driving home under the stars.

ST. SEBASTIAN, like Irun, owes almost everything to beauty of situation. But whilst the one has remained a small frontier town visited by few, and only shining by the reflected glory of Fontarabia, the other has developed into a fashionable watering-place. In summer St. Sebastian is lively and crowded, the Trouville of Spain; for the remainder of the year it is a dead city—deserted streets, empty houses, a general air of melancholy. In the shops people sit with folded hands, patiently waiting for next year's swallows and next year's summer.

When these arrive some thirty thousand visitors arrive with them, and the dead town wakens to life and animation. Every year has come the Queen with the young King, who, humanly speaking, owes his life to his mother's unceasing care, and perhaps a little to the splendid sea air and sands

ST. SEBASTIAN.

of St. Sebastian. It is the Queen's favourite resort, and she has been faithful to it. Earnestness is a part of her nature, a keen sense of her responsibilities, a maternal affection that includes not only her children but her people. Consequently she is very popular. It is charming to hear the terms of universal admiration and reverence applied to her. "But for the Queen we should have had a Republic long ago," was a frequent remark. "And that," they would add, "would be a disaster for Spain--even Republicans admit it."

No wonder that all flock to St. Sebastian who can do so. The sands are white, hard and beautiful; the bathing is some of the finest and safest in the world; the water a splendid green, so clear that quite far out you see the white sand below, where the mermaids dwell. But where the thirty thousand visitors find house-room is a mystery, and the town evidently has unseen possibilities.

To-day there was no evidence that anything of the sort was ever needed. The carriage stopped of its own accord in front of the wonderful bay, as though even the horses wished to enjoy the beauties of Nature, whilst the driver turned his head, delighted with our enthusiasm as we watched the water roll upwards in a long line of white foam that died away upon the shore. The high cliffs were crowned by the Citadel.

The afternoon shadows were lengthening. Most of the houses looked large and modern: a miniature Paris with boulevards, and a disappointing element. Even Irun had been more picturesque than this, for there at least the streets were narrow, quaint and uncomfortable—just what one expected. St. Sebastian suggested luxury and ease, and with the influence of Fontarabia still upon us, looked hopelessly commonplace. We turned to H. C. His face wore a blank expression. "Not even a señorita visible to grace the streets with her soft mantilla and airy footstep," he said, in dejected tones. "This modern element is check the first. Shall we find many more checks in fair Castile?"

"There will be lights and shadows, no doubt," we returned. "Many a place with a great reputation will be hardly worth visiting; others, almost unknown, may prove dreams of beauty. We must take things as we find them."

"And play the part of philosophers," quoth H. C. "It is the unexpected which happens."

Presently we turned into the great gates and garden of the hotel. Shutters were closed, no one appeared at the door, our untimely arrival had awakened no emotion, no train was due, and no one was supposed to arrive by carriage. We rang the bell. After long waiting a woman appeared, gave one glance, and rushed away as though she had seen fiends or vampires. This was not promising. Everything seemed still and dead. But soon a stir and a bustle; half-a-dozen domestics swept down upon us, headed by the landlord and a charming daughter. H. C., who was proposing that we should try to find some hotel facing the sea, stopped abruptly and now declared this perfection. In Spain all hotel-keepers consider themselves ladies and gentlemen; and certainly the daughter of the Hôtel d'Angleterre was ladylike, well-informed, and spoke very good French. Her father was equally accomplished, and at the end of our experiences we thought this the best and most comfortable inn in all Castile.

The first chilling moments soon passed, and we found ourselves installed in luxurious rooms. Our next experience of an inn was just as unfortunate--but we will not anticipate.

We went out before the sun set and the shadows dis-

ST. SEBASTIAN.

appeared, turning instinctively towards the shore. At the end of the esplanade the sea, calm though it was, beat against the stonework with a sound of thunder and fell back in showers of spray. The waters of the bay swept in majestically, roll after roll, gently dying out on the white sands in small waves, clear and brilliant, and leaving long lines of white curling foam. Right and left, the magnificent coast stretched far down, and round the small rocks jutting above the surface the ever restless waters swirled and eddied. We longed for the effect of a storm, but the glass stood at Fair Weather.

So far St. Sebastian has nothing disappointing. But turning from the sea and seeking wonders in the town, we sought in vain. In place of ancient outlines it has modern well-built thoroughfares that are utterly commonplace, whilst the uninteresting churches are not worth even a passing visit.

But no wonder. Much of St. Sebastian has sprung up in the last twenty years, chiefly to accommodate the yearly visitors. Once upon a time it was a small place enclosed in ancient walls and that was its picturesque period. It has a history and a past, in which the English have had their share. At the great battle of St. Sebastian in 1813, the British captured it from the French and burnt the town. Those were sad days. Even Wellington found it difficult to take the almost impregnable fortress; but it fell at length, though with great loss on the part of the besiegers. The English soldiers are said to have been guilty of cruelty, irritated perhaps by a long-delayed triumph. For this reason the ancient town has given way to its new and commonplace element.

On reaching the port we felt that here at last was something picturesque. Few harbours are so beautiful, and it is chiefly formed by Nature.

Before us rose the little fortress-crowned island of Santa Lucia, guarding the entrance. It lies immediately between the cliffs of the mainland, with just sufficient space on both sides for a vessel to pass through. As we first saw it, bathed in sunset, it looked dream-like in its colouring and refinement. Wonderful green waters played about its base; on either side rose the tree-lined terraced heights; sentries guarded the walks and embattled fortifications. Within all was the harbour and basin. At the foot of the cliffs a long row of low white houses stood out in contrast with the green rocks and waving trees above them, whilst here and there amidst the greenery one caught sight of the bright red coat of a sentinel. Small vessels and steamers were moored alongside the quays; work was over for the day, and everything was still and tranquil.

At the head of the quay stood an old arched gateway, within which a few old women sold fish and fruit, a strange medley. This reminds us that the grapes at St. Sebastian were exquisite; large muscatels of purest flavour, to be had for a mere trifle; grapes that are luxuries in England. We found them nowhere else in the Basque country; other grapes in abundance, but muscatels never again, though we sought them diligently. Here the apples and pears were also large and excellent; but as a rule the fruit in the north of Spain is poor and scarce—at any rate in November.

Standing at night on Santa Lucia the reflections of the ship-lights in the harbour dance upon the water. All down the quay the shops are brilliant. In summer the pavement is crowded with people sauntering to and fro, but in autumn and winter the quays are deserted. The few people seen hurry and shiver as they walk; the air, just pleasantly fresh, seems to them ice-laden. Cloaks are thrown round the shoulders, and nothing is visible of the face but eyes and nose.

Long after the sun has gone down to light other worlds, and darkness has fallen upon ours, there is some excuse for thinking the night wind cold as it blows over Santa Lucia. Lights gleam from many a window, but there is no other sign or sound of life. Church towers loom out against the night sky, stars flash silently, and cracked bells mark the flight of time.

These bells are a most intolerable nuisance in Spain, but that first evening upon the quay at St. Sebastian they were happily silent. Vespers were ending. Just to the right a long flight of steps, a perfect Jacob's Ladder, led up to the church of the Carmelite nuns. A few Spanish women in black mantillas, full of graceful movement, were moving up and down. H. C. gazed upon them with all his soul in his eyes. One lovely creature turned at the very end of the flight with a look full of sentiment and expression. She had beautiful black eyes, large, appealing, beseeching; a pale, pensive face that might have sat for a new Beatrice Cenci. He was persuaded the look was for him and clasped his hands in mute appeal. We knew quite well she had only turned to say a word to a passing friend; but then we are not susceptible.

H. C. went up the Jacob's Ladder two steps at a time, not graceful but impassioned. We followed more leisurely, and passed through the portals into the little church, prepared for eccentricities and a remonstrance from the imposing *Suisse*.

It would not be the first time—figuratively speaking—we

had had to take him out of pound, like a stray village sheep, by soothing the feelings of the scandalised verger with a silver charm. Lady Maria, who knew his susceptible weakness, had once hinted that she would be responsible for all fines, a kindly offer we had luckily declined; for once when we showed her the sum total of what had gone in this way during a tour in Brittany, she turned pale and said she would have nothing more to do with him. But Lady Maria is like some of the best people in the world, who bark a good deal, but never bite. The very next day, after solemnly renouncing him, he called with an elaborately prepared apology in verse, which he had sat up all night to compose. It was sweetness wasted on the desert air—rather to his disappointment. No sooner had he entered his aunt's boudoir—she was collationing upon early strawberries and orange-flower water—than she rose, and throwing her arms gracefully round his neck, greeted him with "My dear nephew!" The poem never saw daylight.

As we passed into the church at St. Sebastian, the houri was not visible. A small group of women in mantillas knelt upon the marble floor in penitential but picturesque attitude, full of devotion. All were so much alike it was impossible to distinguish one from another: and not one turned or made any sign.

The church was in semi-darkness: that chiaroscuro so striking and effective. A few lights gleamed here and there with pale and sickly rays. A perfume of incense was perceptible. The altar was slightly lighted up, and a priest was officiating. Behind a grating we caught sight of the motionless kneeling figures of the Carmelite nuns. Suddenly the organ commenced a melody, and from behind that grating a nun's voice rang forth in some of the sweetest, most silvery tones ever heard. In the world it would have made fame and fortune. We stood entranced, wishing the pure and beautiful voice would go on for ever. But after a few minutes of rapture, during which we felt lifted to paradise, the voice ceased, the organ died away, the priest turned and gave a benediction ; all was over. The nuns disappeared as silently as though they had been shadows from spirit-land, not mortal women ; lights were extinguished, the altar was left in darkness. The graceful penitents rose from their knees, and one by one, touching the holy water, filed out into the night air.

We turned to H. C., expecting him to follow. He was leaning against a marble column, pale, emotioned.

" Let us go," we said. He did not move.

" That voice," he whispered. " I feel as if it ought to have been my destiny. Is my life to be a blighted blank after all ? "

A sound of locking up brought him to his senses. Blighted life is charming for contemplation, from a melancholy point of view, but mere sentiment can never take the place of " wholesome faring." For a heaven-born poet, H. C. realises this truth in a wonderful manner. He has no sympathy with Lady Maria's refined collations, and always declines them; much to her surprise.

The jingling of keys restored him to the world and a substantial frame of mind. We too passed out of the church, and the old Suisse locked the great doors upon us.

Twilight was passing into darkness : the evening star trembled in the sky, large and luminous, a liquid, silvery point. Extremes meet. As we passed down the quay, a confectioner's displayed its dainties. Our coffee-and-bowl experiences at Irun seemed to belong to the last century ;

we might be said to have fasted for twenty-four hours. The temptation was too great for H. C., who is not a St. Anthony. "Nature abhors a vacuum," said our poet. "We don't dine till eight o'clock. I cannot lose this opportunity." And he turned in to the displayed snares.

"Will you have the goodness to give me one of those," he said to the amiable woman behind the counter, pointing to some small cakes in the window.

"Ah! Monsieur désire une madeleine?" she asked, for she did not understand English.

"Magdalene!" cried H. C., blushing to the tips of his ears; "certainly not. I don't approve of them. What do you mean by asking such a question?" And without further parley, he walked round the counter and helped himself to one of the cakes under discussion. "Really," he added, turning to us, "these people in St. Sebastian must very much need the Lord Chamberlain, or the County Council, or Prowling Prudes, or whoever looks after the moral welfare of Spanish society."

We explained the matter, but he was not satisfied at all. "The sooner they change the name of the cakes, the better," he said, helping himself to his fourth. "They are excellent."

Meanwhile madame behind the counter, looking at H. C. as though she thought him an eccentric gentleman, entertained us with a history of the place. In winter it was worse than a monastery; it was a desert; but in summer it was paradise. The Queen? Ah, la belle dame! she came every year, and really helped to make the fortune of St. Sebastian. No one so amiable, no one so good. The young king was delicate, but everyone hoped he would develop into a strong man by-and-by. Thirty thousand people visited St. Sebastian every year, and the season was a series of fêtes. She frequently had her shop so full of people that there was not room to move. Often it happened that when they closed at night there was neither cake nor comfit left in the place.

So she ran on; but by the time H. C. had helped himself

ON THE ROAD TO AZPEITIA.

to his eighth madeleine we grew anxious, and settling the account, departed.

The next morning found us again on the port, looking, in the early sunshine, less dreamy but quite as picturesque as under the evening sky. Jacob's Ladder was there, leading up to the Carmelite church. The church was open, but no lovely voice rang through the aisles; all was silent and deserted, with the exception of a solitary kneeling figure on the flags, and a fair penitent in the confessional box.

The quays were more lively; a few vessels were preparing to put out to sea; Santa Lucia looked glorious. We attacked another Jacob's Ladder, and ascended the citadel. The sentries were at their posts, and we envied their perpetual outlook. A winding path led round to the front, with nothing before it but the ever-sounding ocean. The heat was intense in spite of autumn; the sky had not a cloud.

Soon we came to a spot full of sad interest. On the slopes was a little English graveyard, resting-place of those English officers who had fallen in the wars in the early part of the century. Small graves, white crosses, railed-in tombs, stood out against the green embankment. Some of the names and records had become almost illegible. One was to the memory of Sir Oliver de Lancy; another to Colonel Tupper; a third to the young wife of Staff-Surgeon John Callander; a fourth to Lieutenant Henry Backhouse, who died valiantly; a fifth to Colonel F. C. Ebsworth. All had fallen in the way of duty. Some had died in the flower of youth, and their records were especially sad. But a more lovely resting-place could not be imagined, and scarcely a more fitting, for above them the walls of the citadel crown the heights, and not far off, sentinels for ever keep guard; the sea sings them a perpetual requiem, and round them in winter the wild birds wing their flight. Vessels for ever pass to and fro amidst the uncertain waters of the Bay of Biscay, gliding into the west at sundown, as though they too had set out upon their eternal voyage. We stood far above the sea, and now looked down upon Santa Lucia with its white lighthouse. Few towns are so gloriously placed as St. Sebastian.

One brilliant morning we started on a long drive of nearly thirty miles to Azpeitia, the birthplace of Ignatius Loyola.

A light victoria and strong horses had been provided by our attentive landlord, who had every appearance of keeping the hotel for pleasure rather than profit. It was one of those days in which mere existence is a delight, and all we

ON THE WAY TO AZPEITIA.

ask is to bask in the sunshine and blue skies, breathe the pure air, and gaze in silence and repose upon the laughing beauties of earth.

A substantial hamper had been packed under H. C.'s direction, including a supply of his favourite olives to bring out the flavour of a special bottle of Lafitte, all for his own private consumption; for with us luncheon found no place.

Lady Maria would have fainted at the long list of dainties. Thus laden, we started in the early morning, the landlord impressing speed upon the driver, and arranging to send post-horses to meet us half-way on the return journey. The day had been purposely made for us. Every step of the road was full of interest; there was no monotony, and no time for the mind to rest from delightful impressions.

On leaving the town we passed a church from which a stream of people were coming out. They were on H. C.'s side, and at the moment we were studying a map. "What a crowd!" cried he, after we had gone by. "What service can have been going on? A mass for the dead? They are all in black, and every one carries a *bogie!*"

"A *bogie!*" we echoed, startled at the ghostly suggestion, and looking up; only to find that, like H. C.'s poem and Lady Maria's anger, it was wasted emotion. The bogie proved nothing but a *bougie*, and once more H. C.'s attempt at French had failed. There had been a funeral, or a requiem mass, and this was the conclusion; a picturesque procession, the women gracefully draped in veils and mantillas, each carrying a long white candle, all bound on a penitential visit to the cemetery.

Ordinary civilisation was soon exchanged for the beauties of nature; lovely fertile valleys; trees rich in autumnal tints colouring the landscape with rainbow hues; to our left a deep and silent river, its steep banks covered with ferns, wild flowers and bracken. Here and there a bridge spanned the stream, grey with age, picturesque with Gothic arches. Occasionally a large gabled cottage, adorned with vine-leaves and rich creepers gave life to the scene.

Now the valley narrowed and closed in, now widened into fair plains bounded by the undulating Pyrenees. Then

CHIEF STREET IN AZPEITIA.

came Zaraus, a fashionable sea-bathing place, where the Spanish nobles have their summer villas. To-day everything was closed and silent as late autumn could make it. A small town with narrow streets, one of them containing a curious fifteenth-century house with a half-ruined tower, and a church in no way remarkable. The charm of Zaraus lies in its sea, rolling over smooth sands, wide and expansive. Far down, mile after mile, stretched the splendid outlines of the rocky coast.

The horses started off again, fresh and vigorous after their long halt. The character of the scenery continued much the same; plains and valleys, villages that looked like dreams of romance, so remote are they from the world, so snugly do they repose under the sheltering hills. Then, between four or five hours from the time we left St. Sebastian, we reached Azpeitia.

The town was picturesque with narrow streets and overhanging eaves, lively with crowds of people dressed in many colours: some driving heavily-laden donkeys. We had expected a "dead city"—and found it large, bustling and thriving. The old-fashioned market-place, strewn with the artistic pottery in daily use, was a gay scene and noisy, for it was market-day and the country is well populated. The church tower with its open belfry was very curious, and opposite to it was a interesting old house with an Moorish façade. There was, indeed, a good deal of the Moorish element about Azpeitia, to add to its interest. As our driver rattled through the streets the people flew right and left, and nervous donkeys took possession of the doorways.

We passed through the town into the open country again; a great plain surrounded by the Pyrenees; a broad valley shut in by the mountains. Through this ran the little river

Urola, crossed by quaint old bridges, where Ignatius Loyola fished for trout in the days when he had not exchanged his sword for a cowl. A mile away, on the southern slopes, the monastery rose amidst the hills, its great dome standing out in prominent outlines.

It had been a long drive and rapid, and we were not sorry when it came to an end. Down the straight white road the horses went with a will, and we drew up at the foot of a long flight of white steps, above which rose the solemn dome, poor in architecture, yet imposing; partly, no doubt, from the halo of romance and antiquity surrounding the spot. The dome was the church, and the wings of the monastery extending far down on either side, had nothing special about them: one could only regret Fontana's choosing the Roman Pantheon for his model. The interior of the church, though in bad taste, is decorated with costly marbles, and its vastness, silence and solemnity make it effective. One feels the remoteness, the solemn silence and solitude of its exquisite situation on the Pyrenean slopes.

The house in which Ignatius Loyola was born in 1491 forms the nucleus round which the convent is built—the only interesting part of the immense pile, with its small arched court and venerable façade. Its upper portion is of small red brick, with charming windows. The family of Loyola was ancient and noble. Over the entrance are the remains of the family arms, dating from the tenth century: a device consisting of a camp-kettle swinging from a chain between two wolves: and the motto: "Lobo y olla;" a play upon the word Loyola: a wolf being the badge of the Spanish nobility.

Loyola was born in eventful times. It was the year in which Columbus set out to discover new worlds, and

Ferdinand and Isabella sat on the throne. He was christened Iñigo, but called himself Ignatius, after the martyr-Bishop of Antioch. His father was severe with his children; his mother was a woman of great piety and gentleness. The history of the saint is well known; how, inclined to wild gaiety at the commencement of his career, he during an illness read the fathers with such effect that

HOUSE OF IGNATIUS LOYOLA.

on recovery he decided to devote himself to a religious life; gave up writing love-sonnets to fair ladies, threw aside sword and armour, and became a monk, eventually establishing the Order of Jesuits. But they presently became a very different sect from that he had founded, and to-day bear very little resemblance to the original institution. There seems ever to have been something chivalrous and generous about him, and the history of his life at court, characterised by some of the gallantries of the times, reveals a fine mind, high aspirations, and a bias towards the better things of life. It only wanted a period of inaction and reflection to turn his views to the extreme of asceticism.

Passing through the small arched court of the original house, we rang the convent bell. The door was answered by a lay brother in a soutane, with head uncovered. Asking for one of the fathers, to whom we bore an introduction, we were admitted to a large waiting-room, where in a few minutes he came to us. He was tall and thin, spoke excellent French and English, had seen much of the world, and seemed to have nothing bigoted or narrow-minded about him. They are not monks here, but fathers, neither cloistered nor spending their lives in gloomy cells. The Jesuits are never cloistered. It is more especially a convent for students, of which there are one hundred, whilst there are only twelve fathers. There are also a number of lay brethren.

Our guide, who proved very sociable and quite a man of the world, conducted us over the immense building. The convent was founded in 1681 by Maria Anna of Austria, wife of Philip IV.—perhaps as an expiation for the weak reign of that imperfect monarch. The corridors were plain, bare and white-washed, endless in number and extent; and with the exception of a student or lay brother here and there hurrying along were deserted. The doors of the students' rooms each bear the name of its occupant; and on leaving he has to indicate to what part of the building he is bound; otherwise, if suddenly wanted, in this great labyrinth he would never be found.

We went into one of these rooms. It was barely furnished

with necessaries: a rush chair, a hard bed, round which white curtains were drawn; a small deal table at which the student sits and works.

But the walls were white, everything was clean, and in at the open window came a flood of sunshine. The glorious view lay beyond, including a quaint garden full of fruit, flowers, and vegetables. In a large refectory the bare tables were spread in readiness for the evening meal; and as we passed through the kitchens men-cooks were preparing a mountain of fish for supper. It was large, light and airy; a kitchen in which you might roast an ox, and like everything else about the monastery was the perfection of order.

An old, exquisite staircase belonged to the original house, into which our conductor admitted us by a private door.

At once we were in an ancient and picturesque world; the low rooms in which Loyola and his people lived, full of charm and containing many treasures; but only a few of these rooms remain. From one of them a door led into the private chapel. Here he recovered from his wounds, for which reason it was afterwards consecrated. In a recess beneath the altar an effigy of the saint studying the Scriptures may be seen on the spot where his bed was placed. The walls were decorated with carved incidents taken from his life. The portion in which we found ourselves was separated by iron railings from the larger and outer portion, to which the public are admitted. One solitary woman knelt in prayer.

But in seasons of pilgrimage to this *Santa Casa* crowds assemble. The greatest is the 31st of July, on which day, in 1556, St. Ignatius died at Rome. It is made a public festival, and is worth attending if one happens to be in the neighbourhood. The Zorzico—that curious Spanish performance—is danced in the Plaza on the first day; on the second there is a bull-fight, indispensable to the Spaniards' enjoyment; on the third the *Inego de Pelota*—Spanish tennis—brings the whole to a conclusion.

That visit to the convent left pleasant recollections behind it. When over we walked back to Azpeitia to examine its points more leisurely, our amiable conductor accompanying us some portion of the way. Had we wished to remain the night, they would have given us hospitality, we should have made one with them at their frugal board, and probably have slept none the worse for hard beds and scanty fare.

A plantation of pollard trees grew at the foot of the steps. Passing beyond into the charming valley, our guide took a friendly leave of us, hoping we might meet again in England, which he shortly contemplated visiting. We went on our way towards Azpeitia, reposing at the foot of Mount Itzarriz. Turning, we watched the tall slight figure, taller and slighter for its black soutane, slowly ascend the long flight of steps and disappear within the convent walls. He might have been passing away from the world for ever, so still and remote is the whole place, such a death in life does it all seem. On we went through the wonderful valley. Beside us ran the little river; right and left hills rose in beauty of outline, hill behind hill. Country people passing greeted us with a Good-morrow in Spanish patois. The sun gilding all was sensibly declining, yet our day was by no means over.

Crossing the stream by a narrow bridge, we entered the town near the quaint market-place with its arcades. The pottery had disappeared, the crowd departed, streets were deserted; magic seemed to have been at work. It now resembled our imagined city of the dead; but the picturesque element remained; perhaps more forcible for the contrast. The bells of the quaint church, with its eighteenth-century Doric façade, struck the hours; the old Moorish house bore witness to the rolling ages. Outside many a door sat an industrious inhabitant making rope shoes, much worn by the Spanish peasantry, which they sew together with a long needle and strong thread, not too particular as to an exact imitation of the human foot. It is not picturesque work—like lace-making, by which many of the Spanish women gain a livelihood—but it keeps the wolf from the door, and the men, earning their daily bread, are happy and contented.

We realised that afternoon, if never before, that much seeing is a weariness to the flesh. Before we turned our backs upon Azpeitia for the second time, we felt we had earned the rest that was still distant. Even the Moorish remains began to lose charm as we passed once more into the broad valley towards the convent. On each side the great building, almost like a dependence, was an hotel; its existence due to the Santa Casa.

At one of these reposed our equipage: a large, gloomy, prison-like, greystone building.

Towards this we went down the long white road. A frisky runaway donkey, far ahead of us, seemed to thoroughly appreciate his liberty, as legs and tail described circles and squares in the air. Behind us hurried an excited woman and two boys. One boy carried a stick with a pin at the end, the free application of which had caused the donkey to take the law into his own hands. But he evidently knew how far he might carry his joke, for he presently stopped and looked round with an air of affectionate remonstrance.

Next we all found ourselves in a group together; the donkey's fallen sandbags were replaced, and one of the boys mounted him, sitting just in front of his tail. A lecture upon cruelty to animals was well taken but probably wasted, and finally we parted very good friends. The donkey understood the whole matter, and, had he been gifted with speech, would no doubt have returned thanks. Instead of that, he went off with a flourish of the tail, whilst we, crossing the bridge, made for the grey inn and collapsed into the first seat. "Had you taken some lunch and half that bottle of Lafitte," said H. C., "you would be equal to doing all this over again. For my part I feel as if I could jump over the moon, or write a sonnet to My Lady's Eyebrows."

"Which lady?" we asked, for their name is legion. But he was silent.

Asking for tea, they brought us a decoction of chopped hay in large bowls. Nevertheless it was refreshing and dissipated all fatigue. We sat in front of the inn, at a little iron round-table, the great convent building, the wide valley with its chains of hills before us. The scene was all poetry and romance, depth and mystery. Near us the small stream rippled on its course. In the distance the setting sun gilded the houses of Azpeitia with a special but fleeting glory. The shadows were dying out in the twilight, and the pale evening star shone in the sky.

"We shall have a night-drive home," said H. C. "It will be splendid under the stars. But," in a more melancholy strain, "there will be no dining until ten o'clock, and too much fasting is bad for digestion."

Down the long white road once more, the horses fresh as ever. The convent stood out mysteriously in the evening light with its background of hills, the essence of repose and solitude. No wonder there are men who, storm-tossed and weary, at last seek refuge and oblivion within a monastic

AZPEITIA IN THE TWILIGHT, WITH CONVENT OF IGNATIUS LOYOLA IN THE DISTANCE.

cell; ending life in at least a semblance of peace. On we went, dashing through the quiet streets of Azpeitia; the eternal cobblers at their doors pausing in their work to look after the retreating cavalcade. Then darkness set in, and a chill night air, which made rugs and coats, despised in the morning, very acceptable. Through plains and valleys, up mountain passes and down zigzag paths we journeyed, surrounded by a cold, heavy, damp mist, which wrapped the whole country as in a shroud.

Then Zaraus, where fortunately we had not to wait. Post-horses met us, and in a few minutes, with a fresh driver, we were once more on the road. The new man was twenty years younger than the other, and if we had gone fast before, we now flew over the ground. Presently the mist cleared away, we passed out of the marshy region, and rejoiced in the dark outlines of the hills and the flashing stars.

At last the lights of St. Sebastian began to glimmer upon the slopes. A turn, and the lamps of the port grew visible with their watery reflections, the dim outlines of graceful Santa Lucia beyond them.

A few minutes, and we had reached the hotel; the landlord came forward and congratulated us upon a rare and perfect experience; a day of sunshine and blue skies, marked by an especial brightness that even a cloudless day may be without. The charming daughter stood just inside the hall, and as we passed up to prepare for a well-earned repast it was now half-past nine—we left H. C. in the seventh heaven of delight, expatiating in the most enthusiastic poetical-prose upon the beauties of nature, and the privilege of composing a sonnet *au sourire de Mademoiselle*: a subject that, for him, was certainly included in the ROMANCE OF SPAIN.

CHAPTER III.

St. Sebastian by night—Spanish trains—Uncomfortable travelling—Fine scenery—The Basque plains—Vittoria—Pass of Pancorbo—Burgos—Hôtel de Paris—Uncomfortable inn—Starvation—Disillusions—The cathedral—Night impressions—Santa Maria—Lost—Watchman to the rescue—Cathedral by daylight—Disappointment—Fine cloisters—Cathedral Square—A mediæval gem—The Cid—The old castle—Monastery of Miraflores—Church—A silent monk—Tomb of Don Juan II.—Houses of the Carthusians—Convent of las Huelgas—Past greatness—A vision of Mons—Bare plains—The Cid and his faithful wife—Where they repose—A last visit.

TEN o'clock had long struck, the whole town was in repose, streets were empty. Under the stars we traced the long white line of foam as the waves broke upon the beach. Round the rocks the waters plashed and surged in the dark night. Far away stretched the black wide waste of ocean. Here and there gleamed the lights of a vessel passing westward. Above us rose the outlines of the coast, crowned by citadel and fort, and amidst them we pictured that little handful of graves sacred to the memory of those who had fallen in the service of their country, where they alike " in trembling hope repose."

St. Sebastian was certainly more interesting by night than by day. Down on the port everything was still; outlines of vessels and masts were just discernible, their lights throwing long trailing pathways upon the waters. Santa Lucia flashed her warning over the wide Bay to vessels passing east and west - a warning little heeded to-night, when all boisterous elements were at rest.

The next day we left the old town. The lady who served the delicious madeleines gave us a bow as we passed her tempting window, whilst her lips framed " Au revoir, messieurs ; revenez avec les hirondelles et les beaux jours." H. C. slightly coloured as he remembered a bygone passage-at-arms. We passed on to the railway station, and the train steamed away.

In Spain the trains do everything slowly and deliberately. It is the worst system in Europe, and its officials are the least civil and obliging. Carriages are uncomfortable ; every compartment is free to smokers. They are bound by law to have one compartment for non-smokers, but honour the law in the breach, not in the observance. The long lingering at every station is horribly wearisome. Very few trains run in the twenty-four hours. The lines are in the hands of private companies—in some cases, a private individual ; they do not pay, and energy and enterprise have consequently no encouragement. As the country is large, it happens that through many of the towns the solitary train passes in the dead of night. More often than not we found ourselves at a junction at midnight, walking the platform for a couple of hours, waiting our train onwards.

On leaving St. Sebastian for Burgos we had a long journey before us, being due about nine o'clock. For some hours the scenery was magnificent. We passed through the western extremities of the Pyrenees, now losing the mountains and sweeping through vast plains ; now returning to their very centre. There were moments when granite walls of colossal size, reaching cloudland, as it seemed, surrounded us. But to-day there were only a few snow-white vapours sailing along like angels' wings.

We skirted many a village in the plain, often gazing down from a giddy height as the train climbed a mountain pass. Wonderful red roofs, looking a thousand years old, harmonised with the great green stretches. Many a small stream reflected the village upon its banks. These wide plains of the Basque country are very fertile, and better cultivation would yield rich revenues. The country of the Areria was especially lovely and productive; we looked upon endless forests of oak trees, chestnuts, and walnuts; the autumn tints still rich and flaming.

So it went on until we reached Vittoria, capital of the Basque province of Alava, with its mediæval walls and streets narrow and winding, after the manner of Toledo. The town commands the surrounding plains; its market-place picturesque with ancient houses and Moorish casements, and its twelfth century cathedral of Santa Maria, with magnificent Gothic portals and a long flight of steps; a church with wonderful red roofs and an interesting belfry. On market-days the scene is lively and animated; men and women flashing about in their bright colours, and the stalls groaning with the fruits of the season. Near here was fought the famous battle under Wellington against the French, so decisive in the annals of the Peninsular War. The town is divided into three distinct parts—upper, old, and new—surrounded by lovely walks and gardens that make Vittoria an agreeable sojourn at all times.

The afternoon shadows were lengthening when we steamed leisurely away again. As the sun neared the horizon, gorgeous colours filled the sky; white clouds

INTERIOR OF BURGOS CATHEDRAL.

turned into flaming swords; deep orange and red marked the west; the peak of many a hill seemed blazing with fire. In the vast plains rocky hills uprose like mediaeval castles, shooting forth tongues of flame from the reflected sunset.

Just before the gloaming, we entered the famous Pass of Pancorbo. Giant walls of rock with sharp peaks, towered heavenwards; perpendicular surfaces of granite; enormous mountains with material enough to build the cities of a new world. We rolled over wonderful bridges and looked into thrilling depth; viaducts spanned laughing valleys and sparkling streams; and so on through strange sunset effects.

When night fell, the grandeur of the scenery was for the most part over. We had nothing to regret with the darkness. Wide, bare, desolate plains, to which the lingering light in the west alone lent charm and mystery. Far off, one fancied it possible to trace the outlines of the once splendid and wealthy monastery of San Salvador, reposing in its rich valley, watered by four rivers. Here for long ages the Benedictines rejoiced in a peace only to be found far from the madding crowd. It was founded in 1011 by Count Don Sancho, as a burial-place for himself, hoping, perhaps, to secure in death a repose he had never found in life. In 1835 the monks were turned out; for a time the monastery was transformed into barracks, and the soldiers injured the tombs and destroyed much that was beautiful. In days gone by the monastery was much visited, but the railroad has deprived it of that small glory. Travellers rush past Briviesca on their way to Burgos or Madrid, and few think of making a pilgrimage to the tomb of Don Sancho. The solemn silence of the plain is broken only by the sound of running waters.

Nine o'clock was striking when the train steamed into Burgos station, and we looked out into the darkness for sign or outline of the cathedral; but the station lies outside the town, and nothing appeared.

OLD PALACE, BURGOS.

The magic syllables thrilled us as they were called out by the officials. For years Burgos had been one of our dreams, and we expected a wonder of the world. Its cathedral was supposed to be matchless; an Ultima Thule of charm and genius in architecture. Visions of splendour, refinement, and mediæval remains had long haunted us. The town was surrounded by a halo of marvellous legends; it was the home of the mighty Cid. No wonder we hoped much from this ancient city reposing in the barren plains of Castile.

A rattling omnibus took its way down a long straight road lined with trees, beside which ran the Arlanzon: a deep, silent stream that could tell of many a deed of horror, many a life secretly disposed of, from the days when the Goths first inhabited these vast plains, to the less barbarous but not less treacherous times of Rodrigo the famous Cid, Spain's favourite hero.

Soon we came to the lights of the towns; not the picturesque oil-lamp swung across the street, sacred to antiquity and the romantic watchman with his glimmering lantern, but electric globes blazing upon the boulevard facing the river. In a few minutes we had reached the Hôtel de Paris, and wondered whether we should find it as pleasant as the inn at St. Sebastian.

It did not promise well to begin with. No attentive host came out to greet us; no charming daughter smiled upon H. C. A shabby porch and neglected staircase, and no one to show the way. Above we found the unprepossessing host, least agreeable of all Spanish landlords. Already we had begun to learn that all the courtesy and gallantry placed to the credit of the Spaniards generally, is more or less mythological, and belongs exclusively to the upper classes. The lower classes, in this respect, might shake hands with the Germans.

No inn could be less comfortable than the Hôtel de Paris at Burgos, and when the hour came for leaving, we sang for joy.

Once upon a time a charming hotel stood facing the cathedral: an old house with wonderful carvings and quaint passages and a mediæval atmosphere. It was worth while going to Burgos only to put up at that inn. The host, distinguished for his old-world courtesy, was really a host, not merely a landlord. You might stand at the casements with their leaded panes and gaze for hours upon the wonderful façade, upon spires and pinnacles rising in Gothic beauty and refinement; a vision to make you forget the passing of time, measured by the bells in the tower — cracked and unmusical, like many of the bells in Spain.

But that wonderful inn has disappeared and the ideal landlord is no more. So far the glory of Burgos has departed, and with the present infinitely wretched accommodation, travellers do well to avoid the town.

On arriving, after many hours' fasting, it provided fare that not even the most ascetic monk would have accepted. Everything was done with a bad grace, and we were glad to escape from the ungenial atmosphere, where we were mentally and physically starved. The town, we thought, would prove its own reward, and we hopefully passed down the neglected staircase into the street. Opposite was one of the town barracks; lights gleamed from the windows, sentinels paced to and fro. We turned away, never doubting that magnificent traces of antiquity would meet us at every step. Alas, for the castles in the air we build all through life!

We turned towards the cathedral; our narrow street opened on to the boulevard facing the river, and worthy of a modern French town. Every house was new; large cafés were brilliant with electric light, fragrant coffee sent

CATHEDRAL, BURGOS.

forth its aroma, waiters hurried about. All this in dignified Burgos, with its history, legends and traditions! Why does one always expect these ancient towns to stand still?

We soon discovered that Burgos was not what we had pictured it. The ravings of past writers were a delusion. Even under the night sky, which softens and beautifies, it was evident that we must prepare for vexation of soul.

A cracked bell rang out the hour. A few moments more and a sudden turn brought us face to face with a building that for many a long year we had dreamed of as a wonder of the world. In some respects it is so.

Face to face with the building, or rather a fragment of the building; for it is so surrounded by houses that one can only see a little at a time, which is much to be regretted. To the small square we made our way.

It was quite a walk to get round to it and the west front, where we at last gazed upon our long anticipation. Under the night sky the effect was singularly grand and solemn; silence reigned; a sense of mystery hung over the cathedral; the scene was full of beauty and charm. The massive façade stood out in all the light and shadow that the night loves, so that sight scarcely reached to the deep, mysterious porches with their pointed outlines. Above them rose the splendid world-famed spires crowning the bell towers; bells that rang out the quarters as we looked and lingered in this enchanted spot. Beyond these outlines rose the pinnacles of the lantern, and beyond that again the splendid pinnacles and roof of the chapel of the Constable. Nothing could be more impressive. We went up to the great centre doorway, hoping that for once the *Suisse* had neglected his duty. One longed at this witching hour to trace arch and vault and flying buttress, and make one with the shades of the departed. But bars and bolts were fast, and there was no one at hand to loosen them.

From all this we passed to the old gateway of Santa Maria, attached to the city walls and guarding the bridge over the ancient moat—a massive fifteenth-century structure; finally wandering into the streets in a vain search for antiquities. The town lay in silence and slumber; all lights were out.

Thus seeking for beauties that would not come, keenly disappointed, illusions melting away like snow in summer, we forgot that we were in a strange land, lost ourselves, and kept returning to the same spot. "I feel like the Babes in the Wood," said H. C.; "but if we lie down in the street, there are no birds to make us a winding-sheet or sing us a requiem."

The air was sharp and clear, and the prospect he conjured up made one shiver.

Presently, at the end of a long street we saw a moving light, and hope revived; the hotel people had sent the town-crier to our rescue; a voice broke the silence in the air; evidently we were causing a sensation.

We went towards the midnight apparition; a substantial ghost, but friendly. Not the town-crier, but a watchman calling the hour, guarding the city. In the darkness, he looked colossal; Gog going forth to battle. Magog was not far off, as we saw by another outline and another moving lantern. These threw weird lights and shadows about, making the streets mysterious. The men had deep sonorous voices, and did not spare them. We went up to the first, confessing our state. "Lost, stolen, or strayed," he replied, "all one if you cannot find your way back to the

BURGOS CATHEDRAL.

inn. It is not easy to do so in a strange town—for I perceive that you are visitors. In Burgos one has a way of going round in a circle, and returning to the same point. But I will be your guide. You are within a stone's throw of your inn."

He led the way through a maze of small streets and turnings; a very long stone's throw. As he went he swung his lantern, and still the weird fantastic shadows flitted about. His double bass now called the hour, now made a passing remark, asking where we had come from, whither bound. His seven-leagued boots awoke echoes in the quiet thoroughfares. It was the most old-world, picturesque moment we spent in Burgos.

Almost with regret we found ourselves at the hotel door, just as the cathedral bells chimed and the solemn solitary stroke of ONE rang out upon the night air; but the old watchman would not leave us until the porter appeared on the scene. Then he departed, his deep tones calling the hour as he went back to his beat; perhaps to generously divide the spoils with Magog, and call for a loving cup where ecclesiastical bars and bolts were unknown.

The next morning we made straight for the cathedral, and as we went we saw that Burgos was indeed terribly disappointing. The prevailing element was modern. All the charm of antiquity existed for the most part in theory. Here and there an ancient house or palace stood out amidst its new surroundings; gems in a false setting. These were the exception; the remains of the picturesque age are few and far between.

We hoped the cathedral would more than atone, as we once more stood before it, and how confess to a certain disappointment in face of some of the greatest judges of architecture? And yet, standing in the little square we acknowledged that it rose a vast and wonderful pile, though blocked up and crushed in by its surroundings.

The church is of many dates: the earliest portion going back to 1221. Then came additions and alterations in the three following centuries. The later portions are the most conspicuous, and to some extent overwhelm the earlier and severer features. The western spires are late fifteenth century: roofs and pinnacles are of rich Renaissance work, and with the crocketed and perforated spires, rising 300 feet high, give an effect of singular beauty and refinement, outlined against the blue sky.

This outline, taking in the west front, is the most striking feature of the cathedral. Many would consider the Renaissance portion the least meritorious and artistic, and look beyond this at the more thoughtful thirteenth-century work. As a rule we should agree with them, but in Burgos Cathedral we do not. There was a time when, untouched, unrestored, it must have been far finer than now; when lovely, deeply-recessed portals had not given place to a sort of Greco-Roman barbarism. Its picturesque approach has been in great part destroyed; the bishop's palace cut down; the three western doorways, though still very beautiful, modernised. Above the centre is a magnificent rose window with exquisite tracery, but no fine ancient glass.

It was the interior that chiefly disappointed us, though of vast proportions and full of perfect work. The separate details were exquisite. Arcades, triforia and clerestory were once scarcely to be surpassed, but much has been altered.

The early pointed work of nave and aisles possesses a coldness one never finds in Norman architecture, however

GATEWAY OF SANTA MARIA, BURGOS.

plain and unadorned. Where this has been improved upon by ornamentation, the effect is not satisfactory. The columns supporting the central octagon are Renaissance, and the triforium is formed of wide bays, each having five or six lights.

The chapels are late Perpendicular or Renaissance, excepting two of early fourteenth-century work. Gorgeous the chapel built in 1487 by John de Cologne for the hereditary Constable of Castile: octagonal at the east end and square at the west, with richly traced vaulting. The pendentives are very fine, with semi-circular arches, the masonry below radiating in the form of a fan. The windows are flamboyant and the stalls are in an angle of the chapel. In the centre are the tombs of the Constable and his wife in Carrara marble, splendidly designed and sculptured. This chapel is one of the principal features of the cathedral both within and without, for its roof is as conspicuous as it is beautiful.

With all these advantages, the general effect of the cathedral fails to charm. The proportion of stained glass is small, and there is too much light, making the whole tone crude and unsatisfying. It may once have been perfect, but the craze for whitewashing and scraping effectually destroys all that beauty of colouring which the past ages understood so well. The interior of Burgos seems in some way to have been secularised; it raises no religious emotion —or emotion of any sort, excepting the wonder that a vast and magnificent building always produces. We feel how much more there might be and ought to be. With all its possibilities, the truest and best effect is lost, for it is wanting in repose and mystery—the very first conditions of all religious structures.

G

On first entering, the eye is arrested and offended by the great choir which has been brought down into the nave and obstructs the view; an unfortunate and later arrangement never dreamed of by the original designers of this cathedral, which ought to have been one of the most perfect in the world. But the barbarism also exists in other cathedrals of Spain.

We did our best to persuade ourselves into thinking the interior of Burgos a wonder of the world. We examined it from every point of view; essayed a hundred different effects and combinations; saw details not to be surpassed. We tried to work ourselves into an architectural rapture. In vain. It was a beautiful structure without a soul.

The cloisters, on the other hand, were admirable in their early fourteenth-century work. They are of two storeys, the lower plain, the upper much ornamented. Beautiful also was the early fifteenth-century sacristy, with an exquisite groined roof, whilst the chapter-house was remarkable for its Moresque ceiling. High up on the north wall of the ante-room was a most interesting relic—the coffre of the Cid, with iron clamps: the trunk that he filled with sand and sold to the Jews for six hundred marks, as full of gold. Later, when he became rich and powerful, he redeemed the act by paying them back principal and interest.

The small cathedral square was a gem in its way: an ecclesiastical corner. At right angles with the west front, on higher ground, was the little sixteenth-century church of St. Nicholas, with a rich and wonderfully carved retable. Beside it was the fourteenth-century church of Santa Agueda, in which the Cid compelled Alfonzo VI. to take an oath that he had not murdered his brother; an oath taken upon a silver lock, the model of which, in iron, is placed over the doorway.

One of the most interesting features of Burgos is its connection with that same remarkable character, the Cid, who so strongly influenced his times. His career has been

CHURCH OF ST. NICHOLAS, BURGOS.

the theme of poets and historians of all countries. The house in which he was born in 1026, below the walls of the cemetery, was demolished in 1771, and a pillar and two small obelisks bearing shields mark the spot.

Above the cemetery are the ruins of the old castle that

also played its part in history. It dates from the ninth century, and here lived the early Kings of Castile. In 959, Garcia, King of Navarre, was confined a prisoner by Gonzalez. Here Alfonzo VI. was imprisoned by the Cid. Here in 1270 Fernando received Santa Casilda, daughter of the Moorish King of Toledo, who was converted to Christianity. Here the Cid married his wife Ximena; here Edward I. of England espoused Eleanor of Castile; and here Pedro the Cruel was born. It was destroyed by fire in 1736, and the French built strong fortifications around it, which played their part in the siege of Burgos in 1812. Wellington approached it in his advance into France with a force of 32,000 men, the enemy within the castle being only 12,000 strong. The siege began on the 19th September, and on the 18th October Wellington raised the siege and retreated towards Madrid. The following year, on June 14, 1813, the French destroyed the fortifications on hearing that Wellington was again marching upon them; and his second attempt was successful.

We paid two interesting visits outside the town; one to the Cartuja de Miraflores, a Carthusian church and monastery; the other to the convent of Las Huelgas.

Miraflores stands on rising ground, two miles away; miles of barren, uninteresting country, where neither fruit nor flower is ever seen, so that its name is a mystery. Crossing the river, we reach the open stretches beyond. The church from its elevated position is a prominent but not picturesque object, something in the form of Eton Chapel without decoration. At a closed gateway sat a number of beggars, waiting the doles distributed by the monks.

The great door was closed, and a peal of the bell awoke

the echoes. A lay-monk admitted us into a large quadrangle or cloister, at the further end of which was the Perpendicular west doorway of the church. It was locked, but the keeper hurried into regions invisible, and presently the great door was swung open by a cloistered monk,

WEST DOORWAY, MIRAFLORES.

dressed as a Carthusian in brown hood and cowl, a long rosary at his side, a girdle round his waist. He was tall and grave-looking, with eyes subdued by fast and vigil. His black hair was turning grey. It was evident that he had the vow of silence upon him, for on speaking he only smiled—a sad repressed smile—and placed his finger on his lips. Then he left us to find our own way about, and gliding like a shadow into a pew, fell upon his knees, buried his face in his hands, and seemed lost in prayer.

The church is divided into three portions; outer for the people, centre for the lay-monks, innermost for the priests. As a building it was not very interesting, but was once rich in monuments, which have been nearly all removed.

One, however, remains; one of the finest monuments in the world; the tomb of Don Juan II. and his wife Isabel of Portugal. Octagonal, of pure alabaster, nothing more richly carved, more splendidly and minutely executed can be conceived. On the tomb are the recumbent figures of Juan and Isabel, the one holding a sceptre, the other a book. At the corners sixteen lions support the royal arms; scenes from the New Testament filling up the sides. At the four chief angles are the figures of the four Evangelists, and there are many effigies of kings and saints and the Virtues. This monument alone would repay a visit to Burgos.

On leaving the church the monk did not even look up, but remained motionless as one of the marble figures. We went round into the precincts inhabited by the Carthusians, many courts and quadrangles. The houses have two or three rooms below and two above, with quaint entrances. Beside each door was a small hatch through which the food is passed into the rooms; and here the monks live out their solitary days.

Straight from this we passed to the other end of Burgos and the convent of Santa Maria la Real de las Huelgas, founded by Alfonso VIII. and his Queen Eleanor, daughter of Henry II. of England: a convent commenced in 1180, and in 1199 established as a house for Cistertian nuns.

It soon rose to great distinction, and became one of the first institutions in Spain. Kings were crowned before its sacred altars, and many of the early Spanish kings were buried here. Church and cloisters are very fine examples of early

CLOISTERS, MIRAFLORES.

pointed Gothic. The outlines are beautiful but severe, and without trace of Moorish influence. The monastery buildings are well guarded, for its precincts include the village, to which the great gateway admits one: a hideous village of small houses, in the centre of which rises the church and convent like a beautiful dream.

The cloistered nuns must belong to the nobility of Spain, each bringing a dowry. In days gone by it was fabulously rich and enjoyed exceptional privileges. The abbess was a princess palatine and ranked next to the queen; was mitred and invested with powers of life and death. Here once were cloistered Berenguela, daughter of St. Ferdinand, and Maria of Aragon, aunt of Charles V. Visitors are admitted to the transepts, but a strong iron railing separates the nave devoted to the nuns; a basilica, fitted up with richly-carved stalls. At the further end we saw and heard the nuns chanting their devotions; and even from a distance they all looked graceful and dignified, moving with refinement and repose as they glided about the aisles, silent as shadows and almost as insubstantial. Beyond the ironwork we could not penetrate, and unfortunately could not be admitted into the chapter-house and exquisite Romanesque cloister. Lady visitors may enter on rare occasions, but a command from the Pope would hardly open the door to one of the perfidious sex. The church has many interesting relics, including a richly-embroidered banner taken from the Moors at the Battle of the Navas de Toleso.

The plains surrounding this charming building are bare and desolate. As we looked back on leaving, it stood out in the evening light in picturesque outlines, a calm, quiet atmosphere. We wondered how women born to luxury and all earth's gaieties could be found to accept this death-in-life existence, with its narrowing round of duties that never end and never vary. For the convent is not what it once was. It has lost its privileges, a great part of its

LAS HUELGAS.

revenues. No longer is the abbess a princess palatine with power to condemn to death or reprieve. No longer are kings knighted, crowned, or buried within the walls. Its glory has departed with the glory of Spain; but it is still a refuge from the world for those whom the world has failed.

A keen wind was blowing, and we realised that Burgos in the depth of winter must own a climate to be avoided.

Beside us ran the river, here and there crossed by massive stone bridges; a dark, deep, silent stream. In the near distance stood the town. Above the houses rose the towers, spires and pinnacles of the cathedral, a lovely vision outlined against the clear sky and visible from every point of the surrounding country. We crossed in front of the old gateway of Santa Maria, one of the comparatively ancient landmarks of Burgos, yet in part modernised; its massive stonework, bulwarks and battlements defying Time itself. The front, though striking and remarkable, was semi-Italianised by Charles V., whose statue is conspicuous, surrounded by other statues, including that of the Cid.

A strange being, that Cid, half real, half mythical, whose record dates before William the Conqueror. Bold and unscrupulous, victorious in war, a dread name he made for himself. Yet he was capable of generosity at times, and was affectionate towards his faithful wife. Feared and honoured, he came to a better end than many, though dying of grief, in the fair city of Valencia, which he had taken from the Moors, a people over whom he was more than once victorious. It was they who gave him his name "Seyyid," or lord, corrupted to Cid. He stands out in a strangely romantic halo as one of the most remarkable figures in the world's history; as a marvellous warrior;

as Spain's greatest and most favourite hero; a man who, from being a soldier of fortune though of noble descent, became one of the most powerful and wealthiest conquerors of his time. For all this he did not wander far from home, had no ambition to subdue the world. His world lay around him, and there he found sufficient occupation for a long and laborious life. For many ages his bones had no permanent rest. The body was first interred in the convent of San Pedro de Cardena, near Burgos, and in the convent chapel the empty tomb may yet be seen. They were removed by Thiebault, the French general, who, it is said, kept them long in his room from a superstitious feeling that they would inspire him with invincible courage. Now they repose in the Town Hall—as much of them as could be gathered together—in a room that has been turned into a chapel; and his wife sleeps beside him.

The shadows of evening were falling when we found ourselves again before the west front of Santa Maria la Mayor, and entered the Gothic doorway. The vast building was almost deserted, the far end hardly visible. We stood in front of the three naves, but even in the twilight the choir rose offending. The beauties of the lantern, which Philip said must have been built by angels, not by men, were hidden. We tried to believe that aisles and arches were haunted by a sense of mystery, a spirit of devotion. It would not come; the impression remained cold, unsatisfying. Yet strange to say, taken in detail the points of beauty are numerous enough to fill a volume. Why then is the general effect a failure? To us it was nothing less. We noted the lengthening shadows, the darkening windows; a silent figure here and there flitting ghost-like across the wide nave with noiseless step and disappearing beyond the portal; time, the evening light, everything was in favour of the vast, magnificent building; yet we remained untouched. With a keen regret, we too crossed the wide nave and passed through the doorway.

In the gathering gloom we once more looked upwards at the towers and spires, pointed roofs and pinnacles, that rose like delicate lacework against the sky. Here at least, in this gloaming hour, we were not disappointed: our sense of the beautiful was satisfied. All that was wanting of perfection was lost in the shadows of evening. And here again, we declared emphatically, we stood face to face with that which contributes to the true ROMANCE OF SPAIN.

CHAPTER IV.

St. Esteban — Cloisters — Desecrated churches — San Pablo — A deserted wife — Like Ruth and Naomi — Departed glory — The old watchman again — Happier times — A cruel wind — Last look — A facetious sentry — H. C. as Napoleon — Startling incident — Mortal combat — Landlord triumphant — Embracings — A wise driver — Final impression — At the station — The Carthusian — Exceptional fellow-traveller — Fraternising — An interesting life — Was it all a mistake? — "Good-bye" — A promise — Through the night — Segovia — Fellow-passengers — Half-way house — Roman aqueduct — Town walls — El puento del Diablo — Legend of the fair maiden — Within the walls — Processioning — The old square — Cathedral — Sunrise.

The chief interest of Burgos lies in its churches. As we have just said, street after street has been spoilt, houses have been taken down, the romance of its domestic architecture has vanished.

Opposite the fortifications, round the ruins of the old castle - from which you have so splendid a view of the whole length of the cathedral in all its refinement -- stands the ancient church of St. Esteban. The west doorway had some very good sculpture about it, but the closed doors looked in the last stage of existence.

We found entrance by small but lovely cloisters built about the year 1300, now falling to ruin through neglect, open to the mischievous boys of the town, a sad, abandoned air about them, as though no one cared for their dying, yet still full of charm. The tracery is destroyed, and many of the windows are blocked up, but one sees what has been. The groining is excellent, the whole cloister refined and delicate.

The interior of the church, in spite of mutilation, is beautiful, simple and dignified, but spoilt by an abominable yellowwash. Here, also, was some very good groining. Light came only from windows high up in the clerestory, and in some respects the planning of the cathedral has been imitated. A small western gallery was charming, but of later period, about the year 1450. Two ambons projected like pulpits at each end of the balustrade with admirable effect; and the choir was placed here, a frequent arrangement in Spanish churches. Organ, organ-loft, and pulpit, were of Plateresque Renaissance work: a style introduced by Berengueti and so called from its delicate detail in relief.

This church of St. Esteban, like many other buildings in Burgos, will disappear for want of attention. Some have become devoted to secular uses, like the convent of San Pablo, now a cavalry store, but founded by San Pablo, a Jew converted to Christianity; and here his monument may still be seen. He endeavoured to convert his wife also, and failing, discarded her, though she was the mother of his four sons and daughter. But though the brave wife suffered desertion rather than change her faith, she bore him no enmity, and rejoiced in his success.

To enable him to enter the priesthood, he dissolved his marriage, and in due time, at Valladolid, became Bishop of Burgos. The whole town went out to meet him when he made his triumphant entry into the city: his mother, Doña Maria, and his wife, Joana, waiting in the Episcopal Palace to offer him their good wishes. A strange meeting this, between wife who was no wife, and Bishop who in the sight of heaven was no bachelor. There must have been mixed feelings on both sides. Doña Maria, though proud of her son's success, no less sympathised with her daughter-in-law, whose claims had been so easily set aside. Both were Jewesses, and like Ruth and Naomi, clung to each other. Five years after his triumphal entry into Burgos, Joana died. The Bishop survived her fifteen years, living to the good old age of eighty-five.

The exterior of this desecrated church has been ruined, but the interior, with its fine proportions, vaulting, lancet windows, clerestory circular windows and choir traceried windows, is very fine.

Such remains make this ancient capital of Castile and Leon interesting. It is surrounded by a halo of romance and historical association, of which so few traces exist that one has to draw strongly upon the imagination for the influence of the past. Yet something is still to be found beyond mere tradition. Here lived St. Ferdinand the Good and Alonzo the Wise; and it is impossible to mention the name of Burgos without conjuring up visions of the mighty Cid, with all his dramatic power and activity. But it existed before his time, for it was founded in 884 by Diego de Porcello; a small town that paid tribute to the kings of Leon, and later on asserted its independence under Gonzalez, first Count of Castile. Then followed many years of prosperity, until Toledo arose and became the Castilian capital; so mighty and flourishing that the glory of Burgos departed after three centuries of struggling jealousy and internal dissension.

We had decided to leave Burgos that night. The train started about ten o'clock—an uncomfortable time, but the only available train in the twenty-four hours. A night in the train would be far pleasanter than another night in the wretched hotel, whose landlord grew more churlish as our departure drew near. It was simply his nature to be disagreeable; he could not help it. Such people exist, and are not confined to Spain.

We sauntered through the streets for a final impression, a last good-bye, just in time to see the old watchmen turn out with their heavy coats and lanterns. Our guide of last night recognised us, and evidently wished we had again lost our way.

He was interested in hearing we were about to leave; that, so to say, we were being driven from the place for want of decent accommodation. The old watchman shook his lantern angrily, and a thousand fantastic shadows sprang up against this inhospitality. He sighed, and what a gigantic sigh it was! The very bells of the cathedral seemed affected by it, for at that moment they struck out the hour in melancholy tones: requiem to a departed host. For the watchman was telling us how he remembered the ancient inn opposite the great church of Santa Maria. How comfortable and happy everyone had been there; what a right royal master the old landlord was; how many a time as the cathedral clock chimed midnight, he had in wintry weather, when snow lay upon the ground and icicles hung from the beards of the stone images upon the old gateway, with his own hand administered to the watchman a potion hot and comforting, then bolted and barred, whilst the fortified Diogenes had gone his way, crying " Past twelve o'clock and a wintry night. Oh, ye warmed and housed, pity him who keeps watch and ward through the dark hours. *Il Sereno!*"

It blew keenly enough to-night in this ancient city, three thousand feet above the sea-level, but the snow season had not yet arrived. It was not a white world, suggestive of Christmas, torchlight processions, and midnight skating parties. The plains of Castile are wide, bare and unprotected; over them the wind sweeps with harsh, penetrating force, with melancholy moan, as though mourning the past glories of Castile, when the Cid went forth conquering and to conquer; when Fernando the Good sat upon the throne of his fathers; when Belchides built the old castle ere yet nine hundred years had rolled over the Christian world: that castle where Edward of England espoused Eleanor of Castile with an array of pomp and pageantry rare even in that imaginative land. Days of mighty works and deeds; when glorious structures, such as the world sees no more, rose stone by stone, vast in size, perfect in form. And as we walked, there presently appeared against the sky, clear-cut, refined, dream-like, the outlines of Santa Maria la Mayor; yet more beautiful then than now, when its exquisite roof had not been removed, or restoration interfered with the original design.

To-night the wind blew keenly across the plains, and rushed through the streets. The starlit skies shone down upon a dark world. The watchman, substantial as one of the old walls, evidently had a mind for our company, for as we wandered on, he deserted his beat and wandered also. We were glad of the picturesque figure in our last walk, who would be for ever mixed up with our impressions of this otherwise inhospitable city. A man of humble rank, yet removed from the commonplace.

We halted in front of the Town Hall, and he threw his light upon it. The shadows playing in the old archway might have been shades of the old Cid and his faithful

Ximena, whose bones rest within, dancing the Dance of Death.

Again the melancholy cathedral bells chimed a quarter, and we shall never think of Burgos without hearing them. Once more, and for the last time, we gazed upon the wondrous outlines beneath which those bells reposed. The lights and shadows of the watchman's lantern could not reach these; they were too far away, too near the skies. The west front uprose majestically; the porches in deep shadow looked weird and mysterious, portals leading into a sacred, silent world.

We had to turn from it all; to say farewell to the old watchman; to bid him remember the lost wanderers whom he had safely piloted into harbour—a cold and cheerless harbour notwithstanding. Then he passed slowly from our sight for ever.

We turned towards our inn. The omnibus stood at the door, waiting our pleasure—a pleasure, indeed, to pass out for the last time from this cheerless mansion. The sentry guarding the opposite barracks presented arms as we entered the gloomy depths of the ancient equipage. As well, perhaps, that his commanding officer was not looking out from an upper window, as he had been a few hours ago, or his little joke might have cost him an extra drill.

Or perhaps he meant it in sober earnest, taking H. C. for a great general from beyond the seas. For he is a strange mixture, this H. C., and now looks like a love-lorn poet writing sonnets to my lady's eyebrows, and now like another Napoleon going forth to conquer worlds. We can only explain the apparent contradiction by the fact that there is a duality in every man's character. To-night he wore the Napoleon type. That sentry was probably a reader of character, even in the darkness, and so presented arms, perhaps in spite of himself. He recognised greatness when he saw it. This argued that he himself might one day be great, if it be true that we can only understand Shakespeare by the Shakespeare within us.

So we passed away from the inhospitable quarters.

We slightly shivered as we entered the gloomy depths of the omnibus. So did H. C., though it was quite beneath his Napoleon spirit to do so. But the east wind was keen, and blew across the river and over the housetops, and rushed through the streets with a moaning, searching sound. It would have no pity upon this inhospitable city. In kindly St. Sebastian, we had midsummer heat and laughing sunshine; here we froze. The elements were consistent and knew what they were about.

We were not alone in the omnibus. On the point of starting, two or three darkly-clad figures came quickly out of the hotel. They were evidently commercial travellers, and explained the mystery of the mountains of luggage on the roof. These men rushed into the road like a whirlwind. After them rushed the irate landlord. Whether they had refused to pay his bill, abused his commissariat department, offered to embrace his wife, or to run away with his daughter, supposing him to possess these unmerited blessings, we never discovered. Whatever the offence, it was mortal, and in mortal combat we thought they would engage in the middle of the road, that dark night in the streets of Burgos.

The glimmering hotel lights threw their pale gleams upon the raging faces of the four men. The landlord was without his hat; his hair was wild, his eyes glared. Their voices rose above the shrieking of the wintry wind, and the sound was far more terrible—caused us a keener shivering. The sentry, wise man, made ready to fire, in case they should attack him in their madness. A wise general is always prepared. The Napoleon type in H. C. retired into the background. It may have been fancy, but we thought we heard teeth chattering; after all, the wind was bitter.

Then suddenly the tempest of sound, the raging torrent of words and gestures and loud voices, ceased.

We looked, expecting to see four men dead upon the ground, instead of which they had suddenly made it up and were embracing all round. There was a gleam of gold in the landlord's hand; on his face an expression of fiendish triumph. He had conquered—supreme will against brute strength, mind over matter. "An ounce of tact is worth a hundredweight of force," murmured H. C.

The sentry was quietly withdrawing his cartridge with a smile of derision that would have made his fortune upon the stage. He thoroughly appreciated the situation, and probably stored up a lesson for future use.

The three warriors stumbled into the omnibus; its darkness swallowed them up. We retreated to the furthest corners and barricaded ourselves with our traps. H. C. spread his rug and held it ready to throw over the head of the first one who might show signs of violence. At last, after long detention, we rattled off, almost fearing to lose the train. The driver evidently thought so too, for he went like the wind.

He had not gone two hundred yards before the reconciled men suddenly repented, wanted to return and have it out all over again. They bombarded the roof and rattled the door and shouted to the driver to stop. He was too wise, whipped up his horses and went on faster than ever. Having caged his lions he kept them.

*

We rattled down the promenade with its new houses, brilliant electric lights, and modern cafés that looked so warm and comfortable in comparison with our present quarters. Then came the fine old gateway of Santa Maria, whose stone images seemed to bid us a cold, unfriendly farewell; for the last time we heard the cathedral bells ring out the quarter, and felt their want of harmony was not out of place. We thundered over the bridge, beneath which ran the silent river, and looking upwards saw, dim and shadowy, the wonderful outlines of the cathedral rising into the dark dome of night.

It was our final impression, and the best we could take away with us. In a few moments we had reached the station, and the three men tumbled out as they had tumbled in. They began their argument all over again, one with another, not quarrelling, but proving their case. The offending landlord was happily absent, or this time his life would probably have been taken. A human life more or less in Spain does not count. It is not half so precious as revenge. We left them to it, and never knew whether in their grievance they lost the train.

It was a dark night. The station was feebly lighted. Passengers were few, in spite of there being only this one train in the twenty-four hours. The signal was down, and in a few moments we saw lights approaching out of the darkness.

We hoped for an empty compartment, but hoped in vain. When the train came up most carriages presented the usual night appearance—here a party of noisy smokers blowing clouds and playing cards, there a few sleepy travellers who had made themselves comfortable. If we opened the door upon these, a wild and matted head looked up and frowned as if we had been fiends incarnate. We had no wish to disturb them.

"Eureka!" cried H. C., taking a rapid survey of windows. "Here is a compartment with only a monk inside—a picturesque monk. The very thing. We could desire nothing better."

But we hesitated.

"Is there not some risk?" we asked. "Is it not a part of their religion never to wash, and never to change their things until they drop to pieces?"

"Oh! this is a gentleman, or he would not be travelling in a first-class carriage," returned H. C. "There can be no danger."

"Would not the gentleman be lost in the monk?" we asked, unconvinced.

But H. C. had not stayed for further parleying. Opening the door and springing in, he began settling our traps. The decision taken out of our hands, we followed humbly, giving the monk all possible latitude. The shield was over the lamp and we saw things indistinctly, but he was certainly a picturesque object, as H. C. had remarked.

When we first looked in he was lying down; even monks make themselves at home in travelling; but on opening the door he got up, adjusted his cowl, and moved his seat. He was habited in a brown cloak, the order of our favourite Carthusians.

We uncovered the lamp. Had we observed his order at the first moment, we should not have hesitated to enter, risk or no risk, glad of his company even though he might have been too sleepy or absorbed for conversation. His image brought back a thousand recollections coloured with the bitter-sweet of the past.

As the train moved on, our traveller's cowl fell back from a black head of hair closely cropped. The head was well shaped, the face unmistakably that of a gentleman; an extremely handsome face, with large, dark soft eyes that seemed clouded with sadness. The face was pale, and a well-trimmed, short dark beard and moustache almost concealed the mouth and chin. When he opened his mouth he disclosed a set of white and perfect teeth, and when he spoke his voice was soft and musical. He might have been thirty-five years old.

What had induced him to forsake the world and bury himself in a monastery? It seemed a thousand pities. Had his heart broken before taking the vows? Had some fair woman's heart broken also? For such a man many a woman's heart would beat fast. What was the mystery and romance?—for evidently his life had had to do with both. Everything about him was refined. Even his cloak and cowl seemed made of finer stuff than that generally worn by monks. Was this due to nothing but his higher instincts, or had he still some lingering remains of vanity?—still some little love left for self, and beauty, and refinement, and the eternal fitness of things? Did the world possess still a little of his heart?—a fractional desire to stand well in the eyes of his fellow-men, as in days for ever past? The thought was painful; as to some extent pain was mixed with the whole impression he produced.

We spoke to him. He was a Spaniard, but spoke French as a native, and we could meet on mutual ground. Possibly there was something in our voice which betrayed interest; its tones, it may be, awoke some familiar strain of the past — the lingering echo of a brother or close friend. Certain it is that he immediately responded. His eyes lost their sadness and brightened up almost with fire and fervour. His attitude gained energy. He leaned forward and looked into our face as though he would learn whether curiosity or something truer had intruded upon his meditations. Apparently he was satisfied. Instead of a brief reply, an adjustment of the cowl and a return to self-absorption, he grew animated, entered freely into conversation. Perhaps he felt there was between us the subtle, indefinable link of sympathy.

The train rolled on and the moments seemed to fly with it. Gradually he spoke of himself, alluded to his past. For an instant there was a tremor in his voice; again that cloud of sadness in his soft and beautiful eyes. We were keenly interested and showed it: hinted as delicately as we could that the little we had heard made us desire more. Finally, he opened his heart and gave us his confidence—a complete outline of his strange eventful life.

The train stopped at Medina. Here, as fortune would have it, we both changed; both had to wait nearly two hours for incoming trains.

In the darkness we paced the long platform to and fro, whilst the great outline of his past expanded and we listened with unwavering attention. Some day we may record the history; here we have neither time nor space to give to it. It was crowded with human interest—a strange experience. The two hours passed, and it seemed so many moments. We had lost count of time; in his graphic descriptions had entered a new existence.

And now he had done with that existence. Ere the prime of life had matured he had turned his back upon all that to most men makes life worth living. The love of woman, domestic happiness, social pleasures, these were never to be his. Solitude, penance, the monk's cell, monk's fare, this to a great extent would now be his portion. It was full of regret, a mistaken zeal; not zeal at all, we thought, but a morbidness that would die out, leaving him high and dry on a lonely strand. Then his eyes would open to his mistake, disappointment would eat into his soul.

Every word he uttered proved that unconsciously he still hungered, not for the fleshpots of Egypt but for the stirring, wholesome life of what is a wholesome world to all who choose to have it so.

We made some such remark—a half suggestion—putting it more in the form of a problem than a prophecy, lest we should awaken him to a consciousness of an evil for which we had no remedy. But there was a remedy. "It is not too late to return to the world," he said. "I have taken vows for five years and may then, if I please, lay aside cowl and cloak, and once more buckle on sword and helmet, cease to be Brother Antonio, and assume the pomp and splendour of Il Conte——. I can do so; it is possible that I may do so; but I have a conviction that I shall not change. And if by that time I still feel that a monk's life is the life for me, it will prove that I have not made a mistake, and shall not be unhappy in the retirement of the cloister."

He sighed deeply as he spoke. We felt that his argument was based on philosophy, not conviction. He was persuading himself against his better judgment.

Our train came up first, and he saw us comfortably settled in our compartment.

"Good-bye," he said, with a sweet, sad smile, clasping our hand with very unmonklike warmth. "But it is not farewell. Something tells me we shall meet again. I have known you not hours, but years. I shall picture you taking

SEGOVIA.

your part in the world, filling in the details of life; gradually rounding to that far-off event which happens to all. You will think of me as passing more and more into the ascetic monk; the years bringing no change; youth and comeliness disappearing under the influence of watchings and fastings; a denial of the appetite which does not exist; a penance for sins never committed."

Again he sighed and again we felt that he knew he was cherishing a false persuasion.

Taking a small note-book from the inner pocket of his monk's cloak, he hastily wrote down two names and addresses and gave them to us.

"Such was I in this gay world," he said; "such I am now in religious retirement. That is my present cloister. You will never pass near me, whether in the world or out of the world, without finding me out. Promise me that."

The promise was given, and then we parted. He remained on the platform, gazing after the train that was taking us wider afield: a solitary, silent, picturesque figure, whose grace and comeliness the monk's dress could not conceal. We saw him draw his cowl over his head, as though he would shut out the world and its memories. His outlines soon faded in the dark night, and our last glimpse of him showed his hand pointing upwards; whether registering a fresh vow, or wishing to intimate to us as a final impression that all his thoughts must henceforth be directed heavenwards, we knew not. Two minutes afterwards the train passed us that was to carry him into solitude.

We went on in the dark night. Mile after mile was a slow progress through the barren plains of Castile: especially bleak and desolate in this autumn weather, with an east wind blowing. Yet the wind was less searching and unkindly than we had found it at Burgos, or seemed so.

The hours passed, and when a faint glimmering of the dawn broke, we reached Segovia.

It was about five o'clock, and still too dark to discern much beyond immediate outlines. A small omnibus waited at the station, capable of holding six people. Exactly six passengers appeared, but none of them were of those who had thirsted for the life of the Burgos landlord. These were quiet men and peaceful. One, it is true, carried a gun and a sword, but otherwise looked very unwarlike.

No signs of the town were visible, and it was evident that we had a drive before us. Every instant the light increased, lovely colours began to show themselves in the east. From the moment we approached the town we felt we were entering upon a rare experience. As yet we had seen nothing like it. Presently we came to straggling, crumbling walls; detached houses; then a view of the town itself with massive town walls full of age and picturesque romance. Over all, a splendid tone; an eastern glow; a warm tinge of yellow that seems reserved for lands of strong sunshine, as though the sun had thrown its gold permanently upon all.

From the first moment we loved the place, felt at home in it, and knew we should leave it with regret. We could not have arrived at a happier hour.

At a sort of half-way house, long before entering the town, the omnibus stopped in front of a large stone building, closed and shuttered. We wondered whether this was the inn, and if so, whether, like the hotel at San Sebastian, visitors were not expected. But only our warlike friend got out with his gun and sword, clanking down the omnibus steps and across the road with a martial sound which made

AQUEDUCT, SEGOVIA.

one realise all the blessings of peace. Still the house remained silent and dark. As he reached the door it mysteriously opened without summons, and closed upon him. The keeper was in police or military uniform, so evidently our mysterious house was an official residence.

The omnibus went on round the walls, and suddenly came in view of the wonderful Roman aqueduct, stretching across the country, sharply outlined against the morning sky. As we have just said, we could not possibly have arrived at a better moment; all the lovely mysterious light of early dawn glorifying earth and heaven.

There was the aqueduct built centuries ago by the Romans, who, we know, occupied Spain two hundred years before and four hundred years after the Christian Era. It is generally attributed to Trajan, and has been in use ever since, the most perfect now in existence. Strangely romantic and imposing it looked in that pale early light, a far-off chain of low, undulating hills circling beyond.

In thought we went back to days when we had first made acquaintance with Rome, and down the Appian Way, beyond the tombs and monuments, first saw the wonderful remains of that other Trajan aqueduct stretching across the Campagna towards the Alban Hills. But those were fragments only; at Segovia the aqueduct was still in its glory: useful, substantial, time-defying as the day it was built.

Of course it has gone through vicissitudes; but constructed in the manner most used by the Romans has survived hard blows and unkind treatment. Nothing could be more simple and enduring; one enormous stone of granite laid upon another without cement or mortar. The country people call it El puento del Diablo; and according to the legend, the devil, in love with a fair maiden of Segovia, offered to do anything in the world for her if she would accept him. The maiden's hardest daily task was to carry pails of water up and down hill. Weary of this, she agreed to be his if he would build an aqueduct in one night. No sooner said than done. The next morning the wonderful "Devil's Bridge" was seen stretching across the country, and pure water flowed freely to the upper town.

The maiden was in despair; her vow must be kept. Was there no loophole of escape? At the last moment it was found that the aqueduct was not completed; the devil had forgotten to place the last stone. So the Church held the maiden free from her promise, and she married a fine and flourishing Segovian youth who had long been her heart's idol. It is recorded they lived happily ever after, and brought up a large family of sons and daughters, which perhaps was more than she deserved—only that we all get more than we deserve.

So much for romance. Reality brings us to the Romans; and it is quite possible that many a fair maid of Segovia gave her hand to many a handsome and stalwart Roman builder, but about this history is silent. It is certain that the women of Segovia have not inherited the Roman type, like the women of Arles.

We only know that the aqueduct is there, stretching in front of one of the entrances to the town like a huge triumphal procession of arches, than which nothing can be more striking. It was much wanted. Segovia stands high upon a bold rocky knoll, some three thousand feet above the level of the sea, magnificently commanding the surrounding country; the far-reaching plains and barren hills beyond. Small rivers encircle it, some of them full of delicate trout; all charming and romantic to look at. But the waters are

not good for use; whilst ten miles away, in the Sierra
Fonfria, also a barren chain of hills, there runs a lovely
supply of pure and sparkling liquid—the Rio Frio. To
bring this water to the town the Romans built the
aqueduct, and it has been used ever since.

In 1071 it was injured by the Moors of Toledo, when they

THE OLD SQUARE, AND EAST END OF CATHEDRAL.

sacked Segovia, and in their jealousy would gladly have
brought it to the ground. But the old town, like the
Phœnix, rose with fresh life from its ashes.

The ruined portion was not restored for four hundred
years, when, at the instigation of Isabella the Good, a monk
of the recently-founded convent of el Parral took it in hand.
This Juan Escovedo was a man of sense, and feeling that he

could not improve upon the Romans, let well alone. Soon the aqueduct was once more perfect; one could not tell the new from the old. Then Juan, adjusting his girdle and sandals and drawing his cowl, set out for distant Seville; and thought the journey harder work than repairing the aqueduct. At Seville he found the Queen, who received him with honour, and as payment for his labour gave him all the scaffolding used in the restoration. Whether Juan was satisfied, history does not say, and probably love for the work proved the greater part of his reward.

Our glimpse of the aqueduct that early morning was sufficient to show us what a mighty work it was. But the omnibus rattled on, and slowly ascended the hill.

Within the walls our vision narrowed, but we asked for nothing better. Every step revealed the fact that Segovia was a town of towns; a rich storehouse of treasures. The ancient element abounded; the tone upon everything was exquisite; outlines everywhere were marvellous; it was a true city of antiquity. The omnibus suddenly came to a standstill, and we found ourselves in the great square. Here everyone got out; our fellow-passengers went their several ways; none for the hotel.

We looked up, but saw no signs of an inn. Round the ancient and picturesque square were arcades, one side in decay; arches that stood out solitary and crumbling adding to the general effect—like another Roman ruin.

The inn was on the opposite side of the square, and in the early morning light we streamed across, a small procession. The stars had gone in, the pale sky looked coldly down upon us. Half-a-dozen hotel people accompanied us. No one else was abroad; a small, still, sleeping world; making our procession all the more solemn and conspicuous. Why the omnibus could not deposit us at the door we never knew; the same thing happened on leaving.

The short walk was delightful; the air fresh, keen, and bracing. Everything looked ancient and time-honoured under the grey lights and shadows of early morning.

To our right, most splendid object of all, reposed the

OLD BELFRY, SEGOVIA.

cathedral, in beauty of architecture, richness of decoration, an infinite variety of detail. Peaks and pinnacles rose heavenward; a magnificent dome sharply cut the early sky. There was something gorgeous and eastern in the general effect as it appeared in all the grace and charm of the florid Gothic. Its tone was rich and warm, the east end full of exquisite detail and decoration. Above the houses and arcades rose the square tower with its cupola.

After the disappointments of San Sebastian and Burgos we felt that here was a rich reward. Yet the world does not rave about Segovia. One hears of Burgos and Toledo; a thousand voices proclaim their honour, a thousand tongues their wonders; but little is said about Segovia. Not one person in a hundred who visits Spain goes to Segovia. It is all a mystery. If we were asked which town in Spain, if not in the whole world, we would place above all others for beauty, interest and charm, we should unhesitatingly say Segovia.

This we realised even in that first early-morning impression. Arrived at the inn we felt we should not be cradled in the lap of luxury. It was more primitive than Burgos, but proved much pleasanter.

Here, too, we had to ascend—the hotel quarters were on the second floor. The staircase was poor and shabby; the unenterprising inn people still slept; the boys who brought up our luggage hardly seemed to belong to it and no one knew what to do. At last we were given rooms, and the view from the windows was charming.

Before us was the square we had just crossed. We looked upon quaint old roofs which might have been untouched for centuries; slanting red roofs in which dormer windows were set like wonderful eyes. Far below us were the quaint arcades, the ruins standing out with an effect that might have been designed, not accidental; only that the good folk of Segovia do not study artistic effect. Nature and a bygone art have done everything for them; that and the comparative poverty of the present, which has happily kept them from exchanging their ancient landmarks for modern horrors.

STREET IN SEGOVIA.

To our left rose the cathedral, lovely in its warm colouring and singularly graceful outlines; tower and dome, peak and pinnacle and flying buttress.

Then up rose the sun behind us, gilding and glowing everything. In the sky the colours were magnificent; fleecy clouds sailed across the blue, touched with gold and crimson. The town was beginning to awaken. We almost looked for a second procession—heralds announcing the new day with silver trumpets: instead of which the bells of the church clashed out upon the air, telling the world it was time to be up and doing. Even these, if we could not say very much in their favour, were better than the bells of Burgos. Doors opened, people appeared, the business of the day was being taken in hand. As yet it was of a domestic nature: dust-carts, and sleepy maidens, and early greetings in the market-place; a general taking down of shutters and shaking of mats; unromantic details, but necessary.

And hovering round the towers and domes of the cathedral, and above the quaint roofs of the houses, and over the head of the wonderful aqueduct bringing its sparkling water to the town; and across the far-reaching valleys, and over the tops of the barren hills, a thousand voices seemed to proclaim, not the break of day, not a summons to work, but the words, infinitely multiplied: "Romance, romance! Behold here the infinite ROMANCE OF SPAIN!"

CHAPTER V.

A dream-city—Why so little known?—A quaint inn—Lordly chef—A slight fraud—An old woman—Peeling potatoes—Noisy argument—Olive oil—Freedom of the kitchen—Mysterious landlord—" Down with the Republic !"—Wonderful old square—The cathedral—A Gothic wonder—Record of the past—Mediæval procession—Monks and convent of el Parral—Interior of cathedral—Maria del Salto—Old-world vision—Troublesome verger—H. C. suggests murder—Circumvented—Delightful old bishop—Harmonies—An aerial flight—The Alcazar—Matchless scene—Historical building—What the students did—The ancient Mint—Cloisters of el Parral—Neglected summons—Death and solitude—The caretaker—Ghost or woman?—Sad life—Earthly paradise.

COULD artist or writer ever do justice to Segovia?

Our impression from first to last was of a dream-city that would presently fade and disappear, like the fabric of a vision. Every hour added to the enchantment.

"Where will disappointment begin?" we asked each other. "And where will shock the first come in?"

But there was neither shock nor disappointment; no delusion, disappearance, or rude awakening. The town overflows with antiquity; with the picturesque as it is seldom seen; wonderful outlines meeting the eye at every turn. Its situation is perfect and matchless; full of charm and delight, crowded with exquisite points.

Yet little is heard or read of Segovia, and how are we to account for the strange silence and neglect? Here is a gem amidst the cities of the world, and its overwhelming merits are unknown; it is easy of access, yet unvisited. The world rushes to Madrid the commonplace, Burgos the inhospitable, Toledo the disappointing; but Segovia lies lonely and neglected, dreaming of the past.

Never had she greater glory and beauty than to-day; never her charms more evident; never did she more fully repay ardent lover for devotion. Why, then, we ask again, is she neglected?

That first morning the cathedral bells seemed full of sweetness and melody. How could it be otherwise, wafted over such wonderful outlines? The whole town might have been sleeping for centuries, everything was so consistently old and charming.

Even the inn was conducted upon ancient lines. Here also there had been no progress for a hundred years. It was curious and primitive, with rooms not very uncomfortable, the sanded passages long, narrow and dark, a plain, sanded dining-room at the back looking on to a series of old roofs and quaint chimney-pots; casements adorned with simple flowers, birds that sang in cages, and fair Segovians that gazed down upon us from their dormer windows singing their siren songs.

The chef was the most modern and civilised-looking object connected with the hotel. He went about in a grave and lordly manner, with a spotless white apron and cap, official and business-like.

Yet he was a slight fraud and imposition. A little less of the official bearing, a little less of the Barmecide element in his preparations would have been agreeable, for we fared very badly. His kitchen was close to the dining-room; and like himself was the most official-looking part of the house—capable of great things.

An enormous stove sent forth its roaring flames up the chimney. Walls were covered with brass and copper pots and pans that shone like mirrors and were charming. On a broad table great dishes of milk reposed, on which the cream had risen. On another table a heap of vegetables had been thrown in picturesque confusion.

The first time we entered, an old woman was seated near the roaring fire peeling potatoes.

She was distinctly Segovian in point of antiquity. Her face, once smooth and comely, was now wrinkled and hag-like. Her hands, once fair and rounded, now resembled birds' claws, as they dipped and fished a potato out of the pan of water. Yet it was amazing how deftly she did her work; one long strip of peel after another falling beside her as potato after potato splashed into the second pan of water prepared for them.

The monarch of this picturesque room—the cook himself —was indulging in a moment's recreation, reading the paper. He was deep in a political article, and we gathered that his views were Republican. Every now and then he came to a specially exciting passage, and read it out for the benefit of the old woman.

Then for a moment the hands would stop peeling, the head shake in protest. No Republican she, but a good old Royalist.

"I have not lived to be near ninety," she cried in a voice that quavered with age, "without discovering what is best for the world. I have not gone through life with eyes closed and perverted mind. And I tell you that I hate all Republics; and if you know when you are well off, you will keep to your kings and queens, and honour them and be loyal to them. But not you! A Republic, you cry; anything for a change; even though you fall into the hands of thieves and robbers. For that's what a Republic means, you poor weak-brained, short-sighted mortal!"

This was too much for the equanimity of the chef, and a red tomato went flying through the air, directed at the old woman's ancient head-dress. The head-dress was expert enough to avoid it, and the tomato hitting a brass pan, a sound like a tocsin joined in with the old hag's derisive laughter.

It was such an old, quivering, quavering voice! Yet there was in it a ring of wisdom and experience; one heard, as it were, the echo of ninety years.

All this was the most interesting part of the inn. The chef made us welcome in the kitchen, and asked comparisons between his cooking and the cooking of England. But here, as everywhere, when his work was in progress, there was the overpowering smell of rancid olive oil.

The oil for the English market goes through refining processes; in Spain they simply crush it out of the olive, and use it in its natural state, with a result only to be known by experience: a smell that would destroy a hunter's appetite. It insidiously creeps up passages and through closed doors until every room is filled with the sickening influence. In this also Spain is a hundred years behind the age.

But though we were presented with the freedom of the kitchen, it was by the cook and not by the landlord.

The latter was a mystery—we had almost said a myth. We asked for him in vain: he would not appear. Where he hid himself we could not imagine. Only at the moment of leaving we caught sight of him, when he suddenly came upon the scene like a ghost, tall, grim, grey, with cadaverous face and diaphanous body; made a profound bow, uttered not a word, as though he had been deaf and dumb, and vanished. We had no time to investigate the enigma. He crossed our path like a meteor, and as quickly died away.

Altogether the hotel furnished us with diversion; with food for speculation and wonder—there was little else in the way of food; but though still more primitive than the inn at Burgos, it was infinitely more interesting.

Even that first morning we felt this, as we turned away from cook and kitchen, and the singular old hag seated amongst her pots and pans, who seemed to have been brought into the world for the express purpose of peeling potatoes: for we never saw her doing anything else. A goodly quantity must have passed through her hands in ninety years. No wonder her claw-like fingers handled them dexterously.

As we went off, she nodded her old head with quite a motherly gesture, wished us a happy morning, and good appetite for déjeuner. On our way down the long passage we heard her giving a parting shot to the cook, who was going marketing in his cap and apron.

"Down with the Republic!" she cried in her ninety-year-old voice. "Learn to know when you're well off, you poor weak-brained, short-sighted, deluded mortal!"

He turned and another tomato went flying through the air, and again the tocsin and cackling laugh told that it had once more missed its mark—no doubt purposely.

We looked about us in the square and felt in a delightful dream, in which the Arabian Nights and everything that was wonderful had come to pass. Aladdin had been at work, conjuring up impossible outlines and combinations.

A FOUNTAIN, SEGOVIA.

Turning the corner we should see him coming up with his lamp, his dazzling raiment flashing with gold and jewels.

We crossed to the centre of the square. The world had awakened; people went to and fro; not a great crowd, but sufficient to animate the scene. For the most part they were not equal to their old buildings; had no special beauty or refinement; no particular costume to separate them from the rest of the world. But that did not matter. Amidst such vestiges of the past, we could dispense with the men and women of to-day.

The old arcades surrounded us. On the north side the ruined arches stood out conspicuously. In front of us the east end of the wonderful cathedral rose in all its charm. The warm colour of the stone was admirable. An Eastern feeling and atmosphere distinguished the dome that crowned the centre, and the cupola that rose above the tower. Although one of the largest cathedrals in Spain, yet it is little known. Architects have raved over Burgos and Toledo—a few words have sufficed for Segovia. Nevertheless it appeals most strongly to the imagination, one's sense of grandeur, dignity and repose. The more we study it the more we become impressed with its merits.

It is one of the last of the pure Gothic cathedrals of Spain; built when the influence of Renaissance art had not yet fallen upon Segovia; most modern of its mediæval buildings, but most important. Its plan was supposed to be founded upon that of Salamanca, but Segovia is infinitely the finer of the two.

The foundation stone was laid with great pomp on the 8th June, 1522. Bishop Diego de Ribera, proceeding in procession, conducting the ceremony at the west end.

Segovia was then in all the glory of its mediæval charm.

K

Though it had already lost much of its prosperity, owing to the rivalry of Toledo, it was still a town on which the gaze of all Spain rested.

The care of the work was given into the hands of one of the Canons of Santa Clara, Juan Rodriguez, who remained at his post forty years, yet did not live to see his work accomplished. He left behind him an interesting record which is kept in the archives of the cathedral.

"On Thursday the 8th June, 1522," he narrates, " it was agreed to commence the new work of the said church, to the glory of God, and in honour of the Virgin Mary and All Saints. On that day the Bishop ordered a general procession with the Dean and Chapter and clergy, and all the religious orders. Solemn mass was said in the great Plaza and there was a sermon, absolution and general pardon to all who had erred. From there the Bishop, Dean and Chapter, clergy and religious orders, went in procession to the part where was the foundation of the principal wall of the foot of the holy church, and in that place where the principal door was to be, which is now called ' del Pardon.' And the Master of the Works (Juan Gil de Hontañon) and the officials being there with stone and mortar, the Lord Bishop placed the foundation in the middle where the said door had to come. Giving first his benediction on the commencement of the work, he put a piece of silver with his face on it, and others of metal with certain letters, and upon them placed the stone and mortar. The workmen then raised the building."

We can easily imagine that mediæval procession. We see them in the middle of the old square, surrounded by the arcades—not so old and interesting then as now. We hear voices raised in solemn mass; the crowd taking up a thanksgiving hymn to the dedication of the work in hand. All eyes are turned towards the empty space, where presently that splendid church shall rise stone by stone, to charm the centuries to come. The Bishop lifts his hand and pronounces a general forgiveness of sins. A great Hallelujah goes up to heaven, followed by a solemn benediction. The crowd rises from its knees, and the procession moves on towards the great empty space that has been chosen for the site of the new cathedral.

The clergy come first, followed by Dean and Chapter and Bishop. Then follow the religious orders, amongst whom the hooded monks of el Parral are conspicuous. Lastly the crowd of laymen. The ceremony of laying the stone takes place, and the solemn procession winds through the streets of the city and disbands; bishop and clergy returning to the sacred precincts of Santa Clara. The long train of hooded monks wend their way down the steep incline, pass through the ancient Moorish gateway of Santiago, which lies northward of the town, and streaming down the long descent in the blazing sun, reach the convent of el Parral and disappear within its walls. The great ceremony is over, the great work begun; but it will take years to accomplish, and few present will see its conclusion.

Those were days when they built for posterity. Every stone was a monument carefully placed and considered.

Entering the west doorway, one is at once struck by the grandeur of the proportions; a solemn dignity and repose, a sense of expanse and loftiness: effects altogether wanting in Burgos. Here, too, unfortunately, the choir has been brought down into the nave; but it interferes less than might be supposed with the general outline and arrangement of the interior.

This interior is noble and magnificent, and if there are any architectural defects due to its late date, they are lost in the splendid general effect. The tone is subdued and good; the windows are filled in with excellent stained glass, so that a dim religious light is thrown over all. It is not very ancient glass, and the design has no special merit, but it has great richness of colour.

Simplicity is one of the charms of Segovia Cathedral, and adds much to its grandeur.

There is no triforium, but a traceried flamboyant balustrade in front of the clerestory takes its place with good effect. Behind and above this rise the subdued windows. Above all, in nave and aisles, are the beautiful pointed roofs and arches.

To the right a dark heavy doorway, kept securely locked by the ever watchful vergers, led into the cloisters, where we found ourselves in a new world.

These cloisters originally belonged to the old cathedral of Santa Clara, and were taken down and rebuilt as cloisters to the new cathedral in 1524, by Juan Campero. Nothing could be more perfect. In style they are flamboyant, the rich tracery and pointed arches dominating all.

To the west of the cloister, in the chapel of Santa Catalina, is the tomb of the infante Don Pedro, recalling the child's unhappy history. The pride and hope of his father, Enrique II., at the age of three his nurse let him fall from a window of the Alcazar into the awful depths below. This was in 1366. Whether the woman died of grief, or was put to death as a punishment, has not been made quite clear. Tradition says that, horrified at the catastrophe, in the madness of the moment she threw herself after the child and perished with him. Not far off lies the beautiful Maria

CLOISTERS.

del Salto, a woman frail as lovely : a Jewess by birth and profession, but in reality a Christian. As a punishment for her sins she was ordered to be thrown from a rock into the shuddering depths, where a torrent rushed over its rocky bed. At the moment of leaping she prayed to the Virgin to save her. Whereupon the Madonna appeared, visible to all, and taking her gently by the hand, placed her safely beside the stream. The penitent Maria was immediately baptized publicly under the name of Maria del Salto, lived many years the cloistered life of a saint, and died in 1237. In the S.W. corner of the cloister a roughly executed picture represents the scene, and the spot where the leap took place is carefully pointed out by the devout Segovians.

These cloisters were most beautiful and refined. The centre was laid out as a garden, and mingling with the exquisite tracery of the pointed windows, were small cypress and other trees ; whilst out of a profusion of tangle, beautiful in its wildness, rose an old well which must have been there for centuries, adorned with antique ironwork. Whilst we looked, a woman entered through the iron gates into the garden, drew water from the well, and with her pitcher passed away into unseen regions ; probably a dependant of the bishop, drawing water for his dinner-table ; round this ran the beautiful arched passages, over whose flags, bishops, priests and deacons, cowled monks and uncowled novices, have paced to and fro through succeeding centuries.

We gazed long at this exquisite old-world vision, and went back to it many times. Like everything else about the place it was surrounded by a dream atmosphere.

We longed to enjoy the arched aisles in solitude, to wander about the little garden and study the traceried windows, all the wonderful outlines, undisturbed by the presence of the verger; but it was impossible to get rid of him. He would not leave us, though it was clear that we could not run away with cloisters and chapels.

At last H. C., who has yet to learn the philosophy of patience, grew desperate.

"This man is an intolerable nuisance!" he cried. "I cannot bear it any longer. I have no dynamite about me; let us throw him down the well."

"That would be murder. They would put us to death in return."

"Not at all," returned H. C.; "dead men tell no tales. They would never look for his body in these sacred boundaries."

"Things have an awkward way of turning up unexpectedly. Trees whisper secrets, and birds of the air carry tales. Suppose the bishop's handmaiden came to the well to draw water?"

"I see," pondered H. C. "The bishop would detect a flavour of verger in the water. That would be awkward. We should be betrayed; then hung or beheaded, whichever may be the Spanish way of performing capital punishment."

So the man's life was spared. Yet he must have understood something of what went on, for he turned pale and shook with fright and rattled his keys, and placed himself outside the little iron gates.

The next time we visited the cloisters, as he saw us coming he fled, and another but equally attentive verger took his place.

One morning we watched a procession of priests and acolytes coming from the choir and filing round to the sacristy, headed by our timid verger, who cast us a look as he went by which seemed to say that he was still living and had circumvented us. He wore a scarlet robe on this occasion, and marched with a far more consequential air than the bishop, who was present and walked behind his clergy quite humbly, with subdued footstep and bowed head.

They had performed some special mass, and we had listened in silent enjoyment to the great organ. The diapasons had thundered through the building; wonderful harmonies, now loud and crashing, now soft as whispers, had vibrated through aisles and arches. This full harmony of sound, this picturesque procession, fitted perfectly with the dignity of the building.

The procession disappeared into the sacristy, and we saw them no more. The organ went on for a few charmed minutes, then died away in faint whispers. There was a sound as of closing the instrument, and all was silent. The building was left to its normal element: repose, dignity, a certain sense of mystery.

Outside, pinnacles, buttresses and parapets all lent their charm to the scene. In the centre over the crossing rose the great domed lantern; beyond this the east-end sloped downwards in fine Gothic gradations. A lovely warmth of tone blended well with the clear atmosphere and the blue of the sky. It was a picture to dream about for the rest of one's life.

But all this was only a part of the charm of Segovia.

Let us take flight across valleys, precipices and hidden depths to within a few feet of the famous Alcazar—itself one of earth's greatest and most impressive sights—and look around.

A matchless scene—almost bewildering—almost unearthly.

If demons built the aqueduct, surely angels wrought upon the town.

It is difficult to say what the impression and what the effect of this view, which for us stands unrivalled before all others in the world.

At our feet was a deep romantic ravine, its silence broken by the sound of running water, caused by the meeting of two rivers, one washing the north, the other the south walls of the town; and here the valleys also meet; so that Segovia is protected not only by ramparts, watch-towers, ancient bulwarks, and massive gateways. These streams run through the country, adding much to its beauty.

In the broad noonday glare the first impression is one of a radiant atmosphere, throwing its eastern tone upon all. The blue skies are growing pale and molten, effect of a burning sun approaching its meridian. The month is November, yet the heat is almost tropical. Wherever the sun catches the water a myriad jewels flash and flame.

Crowning a rocky precipice looking into the running waters, are the massive walls of the Alcazar.

Beyond this, ancient walls surround the town, warm in colouring and picturesque with towers, bastions and occasional gateways. They look half ruinous and crumbling; the dust of ages has fallen upon them; they have borne the burden and heat of many a long day, many a century, shaken with the tread of armed horsemen; the steel blades of Toledo have flashed from their battlements; yet they will stand the test of many a century to come. Far down we see the gateway of Santiago, the only one left possessing Moorish traces: even from here we observe the beautiful outlines of its horse-shoe archway. All is in keeping with the eastern atmosphere and outlines.

Above all, the marvellous outlines of the cathedral rise, like a vision of paradise, on the very summit of the dazzling height. It seems almost ascending heavenwards, as it stands out against the clear sky; the cupola, rising between four great pinnacles, challenging the admiration of the world.

Many degrees lower than the cathedral, perched upon its immense rock, far above the level of the plain, rises the matchless Alcazar.

Imposing though it be, it is modern. The building was originally Moorish, and one of the charms of Segovia lies in the fact that if the Moorish element has in great part disappeared, the Moorish influence is everywhere visible. The Alcazar dates back to a very early age. In the 14th century Enrique IV. restored, embellished and fortified it. Here he lived and kept his treasures; an impregnable kingly residence.

It has played its part in history. In 1474 Beatriz of Bobadilla went forth in stately pageantry, and was proclaimed Queen of Castile. Two years later the unruly Segovians rose against her husband, Andrez de Cabrera, who had managed to displease them. Whereupon the queen rode out amongst them alone, and dispersed the unruly mob; her beauty and charm, no less than her bravery, captivating the people.

From time to time the monarchs of Spain have given thought to this wonderful Alcazar. Charles V. especially did so, and his son Philip II. followed his example. Philip V. converted the tower into a state prison, and here Ripperda, the Dutch premier, was confined. Here, too, Gil Blas spent some of his days in confinement—a much more interesting personage. Here our unhappy Charles I. stayed and was fêted, and he, who, whatever his weaknesses, was a lover of the beautiful, must have revelled in a scene and a residence he had never seen equalled. Here he spent the night of the 13th September, 1623, and it is recorded that "he supped on certaine trouts

TEMPLARS' CHURCH, SEGOVIA.

of extraordinary greatnesse," taken from the river flowing below, where the descendants of these trout may still be found.

Time passed on, and in this century the castle was used as a military college. Disaffected students lodged within its time-honoured walls, with little reverence for antiquity.

On the 7th March, 1862, out of revenge for what they considered too stern a discipline, they set fire to the ancient Alcazar. It was burnt to the ground, and one of the glorious monuments of the world disappeared for ever. The same fate overtook the Alcazar of Toledo, in 1886.

Some of the outer walls remain, of enormous size and thickness. The Alcazar has been nobly restored, somewhat on the old lines, and once more rises a magnificent though modern monument. Extinguisher turrets, battlemented towers and slanting roofs rise with great dignity and matchless effect.

Loopholes from the castle walls keep watch and ward upon the surrounding country; a vast plain, bounded by the Guadarrama mountains. In the immediate neighbourhood, everything is luxuriant and romantic. Sparkling streams flash in the sunlight.

Reposing not very many yards away is a wonderful old Templar church, one of the few round churches in existence—small, curious and beautiful, one of the most ancient buildings of Segovia, dating back to the year 1205. It lies below the great rock of the Alcazar, and the very shadow of the castle falls upon it as the sun creeps round towards the south.

Not far off, in the lovely river-watered valley, on the left bank of the stream, embowered in greenery, is the ancient Mint, founded by Alonzo VII. Its grey roofs and turrets are overshadowed by trees that whisper their secrets to the murmuring waters. The building is now a flour-mill.

Again, beyond this, looking from the loopholes of the Alcazar, you see the ancient, once rich and flourishing convent of el Parral. We saw its monks assisting at the laying of the cathedral foundation stone in the Middle Ages.

Now its glory has departed. It has become a convent for Franciscan nuns; but they are not rich, and much of the convent has fallen to decay; a sad, abandoned air enfolds it; melancholy marks it for its own.

DESECRATED CHURCH, SEGOVIA.

On visiting it, we came to a great closed gateway with a heavy knocker, and sounded a bold alarm, but no one came to our bidding. We noticed a bell-handle and rang a peal that echoed through the quiet air. All to no purpose.

We took up the knocker again, it turned in our hands, and the gate slowly opened.

In a few moments we found ourselves in the half-ruined cloisters of the ancient convent, where the monks in the centuries gone by paced to and fro in prayer and contemplation. Now silence and desolation reigned. The roofs were lichen-stained, windows were barred or broken, arched doorways looked as though they had been closed for ages. Rank grass grew tall and coarse upon the pavement.

But it was beautiful in its decay. The sun threw lights and shadows within the quadrangle, so that the pillars looked doubled in their dark reflections. Once it was all very different; vines and fig-trees grew in the luxuriant gardens and gave rise to the proverb: "Las huertas del Parral, paradiso terrenal." Now all has turned to death and solitude.

As we looked, a woman came out of a dilapidated door on the upper floor. So unexpected was the sight of a human being that we half mistook her for the ghost of a Franciscan nun. A little old woman, with white hair and pale face and dark pathetic eyes that seemed to have looked much upon sorrow, so mournful was their expression. Wrapping a grey shawl round her shoulders, and armed with official-looking keys, she came towards us, intimating her willingness to show us over the church.

"You are the guardian here?"

"Yes," she replied, in a voice pathetic as her eyes.

"And do you live alone?"

"Quite alone."

"Have you no fear?"

"No fear for the living, and I have too many beloved ones in the other world to fear the dead."

"You have seen much sorrow," we remarked, for that expression of patient suffering could not be mistaken. We felt she had had a strange eventful history.

"My life has been one sorrow," she said. "But it is far

CLOISTERS OF EL PARRAL, SEGOVIA.

off now, and the worst has long been over. I once had only a desolate life before me; now I have a blessed hope of reunion to look to. It may come any day at my age."

She looked frail and fleeting; no fitting inmate for these gloomy walls. A ghost seemed to lurk in every shadow; at night the silence must be appalling.

"Surely you are not alone during the dark hours?" we said. "The solitude might almost turn your brain."

"It might turn that of others," she quietly answered; "but it is just what I love—this solitude. I can think of the past and no one disturbs me. Everything from the outer world brings back that world to which I once belonged."

"Have you been here long?"

"Many, many years. I was quite young when I came as guardian to these cloisters and the church. No one cared to take the sad, solitary office, but I was thankful for it. The nuns are good to me, too; we are all friends together. Yes, this has been called a death-in-life, but that is what I am, and so I and these cloisters are well matched. Will not the señores like to see the church? I should have pleasure in conducting them."

There was something infinitely appealing in the face, and we wondered if we should ever hear its true history. We said no more, and presently, passing from these depressing yet lovely precincts, turned our faces once more southward, again and again astonished and arrested by the view.

Before us flowed the river. Above it rose the ancient walls of the town, crumbling yet still substantial, and the Moorish gateway of Santiago; beyond, the splendid Alcazar crowned its huge precipitous rock; whilst far above all, the magnificent, amazing, overwhelming outlines of the cathedral, sharply pencilled against the blue sky, still seemed ascending heavenwards.

Here, indeed, was an earthly paradise. And here, more than ever, we felt, in the charm of antiquity, the splendour of Gothic refinement, the gorgeousness of Moresque influence, the stupendous work of the Romans of old, dwelt the true and wonderful ROMANCE OF SPAIN.

L

CHAPTER VI.

Streets of Segovia—Ancient houses—Juan Bravo—Prison for women—Church of San Martin—San Esteban—Wonderful cloister—Episcopal Palace—View from the old walls—Lower town—A remarkable Calvary—Splendid sunset—H. C. enthusiastic—A strange old woman—Beautiful in age—" One prize worth winning "—Jacob's Ladder—Poverty-stricken thoroughfares—St. Millan—Church of Corpus Christi—Back in the days of the Moors—Moorish nave—Poor Clares—San Miguel—Town-hall—An amiable guide—Polite architect—His picturesque house—Hermit of Fuencisla—Our guide incredulous—Templar Church—Second visit to el Parral—The little old caretaker—Sad history—Back to the river—Segovia behind the times—The chef and the old woman again—More differences—Sentiment not dead yet—The bishop—In the cloisters—What the bishop thought.

IF we come to the streets of Segovia we find them a succession of splendid pictures and glorious outlines—hilly and irregular, after the manner of towns built upon a rock; narrow, as streets exposed for many months of the year to the scorching sunshine; whilst exquisite old casements added to the eastern influence of which we were so often reminded. Here and there, round arches crossed the streets, framing a lovely view beyond; an arch of blue sky, against which, at an open window, the radiant face of a Segovian maiden looked down wonderingly at the bewildered wanderers, beyond all, sharply pencilled, a Moresque or mediæval tower.

Some of the old houses had been palaces centuries ago, and built of massive stone looked as though they had lived for two thousand years and meant to live two thousand years more. Heavy gratings barred many of the casements. A few *patios* or courtyards were interesting, but these are not the strong points of Segovia.

One house, Florentine in character, was ornamented with

SEGOVIA.

immense diamond-faced stones. Not far off, in another interesting house, Juan Bravo, one of the five chiefs of the Comuneros, was said to have been executed in 1512. A further tradition declares him to have been executed in the village of Villalar, with those other brave leaders, Padilla and Maldonado. One thing is certain—that he stood upon the walls of Segovia, defending the town, one of its long-suffering inhabitants.

Near this was another house, large and square, dark and gloomy, to which an interest attaches, human but not romantic: one of the few prisons in Spain exclusively devoted to women. Its windows are closely barred, bars behind which no face is ever seen, no sound ever heard. The great gates only open to admit a fresh arrival of prisoners or to discharge others. Some are there for life, with no hope this side the grave. Admission is possible, but we would not enter merely to gaze on misery we could not lessen. Rather we turned the other way—to meet one of the most enchanting views of a city where enchantment abounds.

This was the church of San Martin, standing, like the prison, in the centre of the town. From many quarters its tower, with small pointed roof and pinnacle, may be seen rising in outlines.

A still more perfect tower was that of San Esteban, with five storeys or arcades, exquisite windows, both blind and open, some with the pointed, others with the Romanesque arch—one of the eighteen churches of Segovia possessing distinct Romanesque traces. Many other steeples have the same curious arrangement of the rounded angle, with a shaft ending in a sculptured capital delicately inserted into the slant, an unusual detail, giving grace and finish to the tower, whose outlines against the background of sky are soft and clear. The roof, with its little dormer windows, above which rose a heavy moulding ending in a small turret or spire, was an excellent termination, though not architecturally correct.

But the most remarkable feature was a small cloister attached to the south-west walls of the nave. This ran

SAN MARTIN.

from the steeple and crossed at the west end—a gem of rare description, with Romanesque arcades refined and beautiful. We first saw it in the strong lights and shadows of the sun, with charming, long-drawn reflections of rounded arch and fluted pillar traced upon the inner walls and pavement, above which rose the tiled slanting roof.

Opposite to this was the Episcopal Palace—an ancient stone house ornamented with curious reliefs of Samson. Prison, churches and palace formed a remarkable group.

A little below this was another point of a very different nature, but equally attractive.

Leaning against the old town walls we looked upon a far-stretching valley and a sea of houses, many apparently ready to fall with age and decay; houses with wonderful walls and roofs. Through the centre of this lower town ran a narrow stream between tortuous streets formed without plan or design.

Above the houses rose the steeples of a few ancient churches, their tone a warm amber mellowed by age, to which the wonderful red roofs were a splendid contrast; all harmonising with the blue of the far-off sky.

No sound came from the vast area. Poverty-stricken to the last extent it also looked, but was not. The people of Spain are poor for the most part, but it is a contented poverty, in which there is seldom absolute want.

To the left, beyond this vision of houses, stretched the Roman aqueduct, its double arches framing the blue sky beyond. In the distance, in faint and fading undulations, reposed the beautiful Guaderrama hills. The vast intermediate plain, like so much of Castile, is bare and barren. Romantic in name and famous in history, it is too often cold and inhospitable.

But we are still leaning against the old town walls overlooking that sea of roofs and houses. These cease, the slopes pass out clear and barren, and in the distance a strange sight meets the eye.

Standing up cold and naked against the sky are three huge crosses: a Calvary to which the townspeople bend their steps in pilgrimage—a remarkable vision full of silence and repose, with sharp black outlines clearly defined. The distance surrounds the crosses with a mystic atmosphere. In the early morning the sun rises behind them, and the eastern skies are glowing and glorious. Against all this splendour they stand out in dark, strong relief. Towards evening, when the sun sinks westward, its glory is thrown upon them, and they seem turned to gold, warmed into life.

It so happened to us on a certain evening. One moment they had looked cold and frowning, the next, the sun touching some particular point suddenly glorified them. Deep crimson and gold overspread the sky, and the crosses stood out in splendour of colouring. As though the centre cross were crowned with metal, there appeared to go forth above it a dazzling reflection, as of the sun upon silver, and we thought we traced the outlines of a crown.

"No cross, no crown!" cried H. C. involuntarily. "What a scene! And what a background for the Crucifixion of one of the old Masters—if we could only transport the whole effect to that mound beyond the Damascus Gate of Jerusalem."

Attached to the walls against which we leant were the long flights of steps leading to the lower town. Whilst this sunset vision was going on, an old woman came up the steep street to our left, and stood at the head of the stairs. She

ST. ESTEBAN.

must have seen at least eighty years of life; her form was bent, but her face was still comely and her dark eyes sparkled.

OUTSIDE THE WALLS, SEGOVIA

She paused, overcome as it seemed by the vision; her hands clasped and her lips moved; an expression of almost divine love glowed upon her fine old countenance. Probably she felt how close she was to the end of her own pilgrimage; how all these signs and symbols were about to pass for her into realities. She was nearing her own sunset—or shall we say sunrise? Such a face was the evidence of a good life. Many a pilgrimage, no doubt, had she taken to that distant calvary.

Then she turned and saw us narrowly watching her. There are moments which bring strangers into touch with each other. Such a moment was this. She raised her hand and pointed beyond the valley.

"A wonderful vision of all the love and suffering endured for us poor mortals!" she murmured. "Ah! senores, you have many years of your lives before you. Mine is over. Take the experience of an old woman. There is only one happy way in the world; one prize worth winning; one thing to bring peace at the last. There you have its emblem."

She gave a long-drawn sigh, this singular old woman, which seemed a mixture of pleasure and pain. Probably life had been hard; she may have endured chastening, seen a succession of sorrows; and adversity had opened her heart to paradise.

Her little sermon finished, she slowly passed down the steep stone stairs with hands clasped, disappeared within the sea of houses, and we saw her no more. We felt as though we had parted from an old friend, and knew the old woman was of those who are faithful unto death.

Sunset was over all; the towers of the old churches shone out in the warm glow. Presently twilight fell, the glory departed; the crown disappeared, the cross remained; once more the outlines of the calvary looked dark, mystic and mysterious against the purple sky beyond. A solitary pale star shone in the west.

Still we watched, forgetting for the moment that we

SEGOVIA FROM THE SOUTH-WEST BANK OF THE RIVER: EVENING.

formed part of the work-a-day world. Twilight deepened; the houses below were blotted out; the calvary became invisible; the broad outlines of the Roman aqueduct grew faint and shadowy; lights here and there marked a wakeful inhabitant; otherwise it seemed a sleeping enchanted world.

One morning we trod in the footsteps of the old woman, passed down the stone staircase—a Jacob's ladder—and acquainted ourselves with the old thoroughfares. Even here they seemed fairly poverty-stricken and thinly populated, but crumbling and ruinous and picturesque as they appeared, they are good for many an age to come.

The old churches were gems in their way. That of St. Millan is thought by some to be the finest of the early churches of Segovia, with its small exquisite cloisters on either side, but not crossing the west front as in San Esteban; making them less striking, but leaving exposed all the beauty and rich ornamentation of the Romanesque west doorway. The cloisters have more solidity but less grace than those of San Esteban, whilst the shafts are coupled and the capitals elaborately carved. The edge of the eaves-cornice is cut in a delicate interlacing tracery of ivy-leaves, exceedingly beautiful and refined, of later date than some parts of the building, though not earlier than the thirteenth century. The north and south doorways were both good, solid and substantial, like the rest of the church. Solidity rather than grace was an effect aimed at by the early Spanish architects.

The interior is very fine, and though modernised is still grand in many of its outlines and details and in the untouched parts. Nave and aisles terminate at the east end with early Spanish apses, engaged shafts and round windows; a low square lantern at the crossing. The prevailing tone was disappointing; all its antiquity had disappeared; in spite of the dim religious light all sense of mystery and devotion was lost. But in its unrestored state the Romanesque grandeur must have been striking, and much of it still remains.

The date of the church is uncertain. It probably goes back to the twelfth century, with its semi-circular arches, but is said to have been founded as early as 923; a period of which there seems to be no architectural trace. Without doubt it is one of Segovia's finest examples, and probably largely influenced the church architecture of the town.

A most curious and interesting church of the upper town is that of Corpus Christi, which we discovered by accident, hidden from the world in its small unsuspected corner.

Passing through a pointed arch into an open courtyard, in the further angle a lovely ecclesiastical doorway caught our attention. No one went in or out; it appeared deserted. Crossing the courtyard, which was closely built up by houses, we opened the doorway and found ourselves in a wonderful trace of the past: a small church with a Moorish nave; exquisite horseshoe arches supported by octagonal columns with fir-cone capitals. Above was a blind triforium. The walls were painted white, and still the obscurity was profound.

We stood charmed beyond words, transported to the days of the Moors; at once surrounded by an Eastern atmosphere, a sense of mystery.

The windows with their latticed panes looked on to a small enclosure where no foot ever seemed to fall. At the west end of the church opposite the altar was a large open grating, with chairs and benches behind it lost in gloom. The church belongs to an institution. What it originally

SANTIAGO GATEWAY.

was, we did not discover, but it is now a nunnery for Poor Clares; and behind this grating black-veiled figures steal in to their devotions; silent, motionless, for whom one feels a strange compassion.

There are nunneries in the world surrounded by the pure air of heaven; gardens in which the cloistered women walk and gaze upon the ripening fruit and rejoice in the opening flowers, blue skies smiling over all. But this nunnery is in the most crowded part of Segovia, and within its walls, sun and sky, fruit and flowers are things only to dream about.

Not far off, the Gothic fifteenth-century church of San Miguel stands on the brow of the rock, overlooking the wonderful city walls, the river flowing beneath, the vast country beyond.

Its fine tower is visible far and near, and the Gothic cloisters and arcades white and dazzling in the sunshine are very striking. It looks down upon the remarkable little Templar church, which, one sunny morning we felt we must visit. But the doors are always locked, and the key was said to be religiously kept at the town-hall. So to the town-hall we went.

This official building was opposite the hotel. Crossing the square we passed under the ancient arcades and mounted to the second floor of what looked like an ordinary house. There, however, we found civil people; but all the people of Segovia are civil, hospitable and obliging. We then found that the key was in possession of the town architect.

One of the officials offered to pilot us to the house, but on passing out of the arcades, we came upon the architect himself. Matters were explained, he bowed politely, placed himself at our disposal, and as he could not at that moment accompany us, if our guide would proceed to his house the key should be given to him. Wishing us a pleasant sojourn in fair Segovia, pointing out that the city was crowded with charms, hoping that we might meet again, he smiled and hurried away as if another great cathedral or aqueduct were in process of construction.

Turning into the narrow streets—endless joys for ever—we reached the house we should never have found without our amiable guide. It was picturesque, with a little covered courtyard full of evergreens and a wide shallow staircase leading up to the living-rooms; a servant came to the door, and the key was handed over.

The morning was lovely; a brilliant sun and radiant atmosphere. We reached the old Moorish gate with its horseshoe arch. The river ran its flashing course and beyond it rose the grey picturesque roofs of the old Mint. Lower down the stream we crossed an ancient bridge, on our way to the Templars' Church. Towering above it to the left was the Alcazar crowning its precipitous rock.

Beyond the bridge a grove of trees led to the Ermita de Fuencisla, where a spring of fresh water for ever runs. Here in days gone by lived a hermit whose years were supposed to equal those of the Wandering Jew. His food consisted of dry bread, seasoned with herbs which grew around him; he drank the clear cold water of the spring. This maintained life until he became bowed and grey-headed, his long white beard swept the ground, senses waned; all but the keenness of his mind, which was never brighter or more serene and rejoicing than on the day of his death.

Our intelligent guide recounted the legend as we went along the white dusty road, but he was evidently a nineteenth-century production, who wanted strong evidence

ALCAZAR AFTER THE FIRE.

before he could accept anything outside the ordinary laws of nature. The miraculous history of Maria del Salto was received with caution. He was more practical than imaginative.

"What would you?" he laughed. "We live in a practical age; and my prosaic work at the town-hall—helping to adjust the rates of the parish, and trying my best to make five out of two and two—does not enlarge one's fancy. I find that two and two only make four, try as I will; and I place as much faith in the appearance of the Virgin to Maria del Salto, as I do in the legend that il diabolo built the Aqueduct. There stands our Templar Church, and I know that we shall enter, for here is our evidence," holding up the ancient ponderous keys.

The little church crowning a slight ascent stood in the blazing sun, strongly outlined against the north sky. High up in the walls were small windows, one in each angle, just above which the eaves of the tiled roof projected. Above this roof in the centre was a small pointed roof of great beauty, terminating the central chamber. The colouring of the whole was mellowed to an exquisite tone.

The west doorway was a lovely Romanesque arch, richly moulded. At the south-east angle of the church, rose the tower, with its open windows in the belfry, a tiled roof and projecting eaves. But the bells have long been silent, for it is many an age since the church was used. The Templars were suppressed in 1312, and became nothing more than a theme for poets and historians; a dream of the world. The little church, as far as the Templars were concerned, had barely a century of existence, for it was consecrated about the year 1205. Close to the bend in the road was a large grey-stone cross.

After a little trouble the rusty locks gave way and the ancient south doorway slowly opened. Few visit it now. To the townspeople it means nothing, and strangers in Segovia are few and far between.

The interior was very peculiar. One's first impression was its forlorn appearance, a ruin in everything but the walls. This perhaps was inevitable. The church is round, the nave dodecagonal, or twelve-sided. In the centre is a small chamber of two storeys solidly built, on the model of the Holy Sepulchre at Jerusalem. Round this runs the vaulted nave, forming a circular aisle. A flight of steps leads to the vaulted upper storey, and here still stands the original stone altar, beautifully wrought. Seven small windows opened to the aisle. The room below was domed, the arches round the aisle were pointed. The chancel and two chapels at the east end formed stiff apses, where we found remains of extremely rich decoration. A great deal of fine moulding was still apparent; and the small pillars with their sculptured capitals supporting the pointed arches were very effective in a building otherwise remarkable for its severity. It was a gem yielding the utmost pleasure and delight; carrying one back to those old days of the Templars as few of the remaining churches can now do.

We were so near the ancient convent of el Parral, that a visit seemed imperative. Under the escort of our friendly guide—who appeared glad for once to put aside his parish taxes—we followed the course of the river, passed under the shadow of the old Mint, and mounted the little ascent to the gates.

Once more we looked upon the forsaken cloisters. Ruin, decay and neglect met one on every side. The sun still threw his lights and shadows upon the inclosure, trying to quicken a dead world into life. Again the pillars seemed doubled. Again the silence might be felt. And again the little old woman in the grey shawl came out of her room in the upper floor. This time we knew she was not a ghost, but flesh and blood; dried up and withered, it is true, but mortal. As before, she advanced with her keys, and this now seemed to be the one occupation of her days. She evidently knew our guide, and greeted him by name.

"Poor thing!" he said to us aside; "hers is a melancholy history. She was once well-to-do; had a house in the town; husband and children. I have heard that she was comely, this piece of antiquated parchment, and of course she must once have been young. No one in Segovia was brighter, happier, more active than she. Then in one sad month all was changed. Husband and children died of an epidemic; not one was left to her; but she, who would have died with them, escaped. In that short time she lost all traces of youth; her hair turned grey, her face white. All her living went with her husband. 'I have done with the world,' she said; 'have nothing left to live for. I will go to the nuns of el Parral. Perhaps they will take me in.' But they could not afford to do this, for she had no money, and they are poor. They were sorry for her, and did the best they could—offered her this post; to live in the cloisters, keep the keys of the church, have the care of the church itself. She gladly accepted—and what a desolate existence! Still, the people around are good to her; those who do not remember her history, know about it. But all this happened years ago, and I think she has pretty well reached the end of life. She will soon have a successor here, who may be younger, but won't be half so interesting."

Escorted by the old woman, we passed out of the cloisters

and made a short pilgrimage to the church, curiously planned, but fine in effect. The western end is almost without windows, and the gallery stretches half over the nave. On first entering, the impression is one of solemn gloom and repose. The east end is lighted with twelve enormous windows, their jambs ornamented with statues of the apostles. Here, as in other old buildings, lights and shadows play their part in the element of mystery. The exterior of the church has little to recommend it.

When we passed out again, the little grey old woman religiously locked up and departed with the keys. The great cloister gate closed upon her solitary existence and we saw her no more. So pathetic a figure we had seldom found, or so sad a history.

Back to the river side, the ever-marvellous outlines of the town—ancient walls, church towers, and great cathedral. To the left the aqueduct stretched away towards the undulating Guaderramas.

At the foot of the old bridge we parted from our guide. Segovia, he confessed, was behind the times, and had no professional escorts, therefore he should be happy to be of any further use in his power. We went our several ways—he to return the keys of the Templars' church and take up again the question of parish taxes at the town-hall—we round by the south bank of the river with its unrivalled view.

We crossed the old bridge and skirted the town walls, the old battlemented south gateway, above which rose the cathedral outlines. A steep ascent amidst quaint old houses—evidently a poorer part of the town—brought us again to the cathedral and the arcaded square. Our stay was drawing to a close, and the thought of leaving Segovia was difficult to face.

We said as much in the picturesque kitchen where the old woman was still peeling potatoes. The chef could not sympathise with us. He had no eye for the picturesque. Thank goodness he was not a Segovian, and hardly knew what evil fate had prompted him to spend two years of his life in the place. Madrid was his earthly paradise, and to Madrid he hoped one day to return.

"And I," chimed in the old woman, "tell you there is no place like Segovia. If you are not happy here, you will be happy nowhere, poor deluded, dissatisfied mortal, with your Madrid, and your republics, and your love of change."

"What do you know about it?" returned the chef. "What have you seen of the outside world?"

"Nothing," returned the old fossil. "In all my ninety years and more I have never set foot outside Segovia; never even went to Madrid. Here I was born, here I married and saw my children grow up, here I buried my troublesome old husband—all men are troublesome, for that matter—and here I hope to die. Segovia is my world, and you will not find a better. Ah! you may pelt me with tomatoes if you like, but I tell you that when you go back to your world you will regret Segovia. Hark to that music!" as the cathedral bells at that moment rang out. "Many a time have I listened to it from the roof of the Alcazar, when my husband was keeper there. I have heard it pealing across the valley, right down the river, right up into the mountains, and with my baby in my arms it has sung many a cradle song to hush it to sleep."

So the old woman really had some poetry and sentiment in her after all. She had not always been ancient and witch-like; even now was only so outwardly. The spirit had not withered with the body. We left her to her potatoes and her recollections, and went out to listen to the bells.

Once more we passed into the cathedral. The afternoon shadows were lengthening; a dim religious light made aisles and arches beautiful and mysterious. Inexpressibly solemn it seemed in its solitude. We were alone in the great building. Nothing broke the silence but the echo of our footsteps. No mass was going on, no organ sent forth sweet sounds; the bells had ceased.

Suddenly a dignified figure issued from a doorway and crossed our path, bowing as he passed. It was the bishop. We watched him open the cloister door and disappear, leaving the door ajar. The temptation was too great. O for a last look at those wonderful outlines, not personally conducted by a verger! We followed in the august footsteps. Could one do better? The bishop was in the centre of the garden, looking round at the splendid architecture, now putting on all its mystic atmosphere in the evening light. How well his figure harmonised with its surroundings.

He approached us with quite a paternal smile.

"I see that you are attracted by these influences," he remarked in French. "I do not wonder. They are indeed beautiful, and seem to bring us nearer to that world to which I trust we are all travelling. You love all this as much as I do—is it not so?"

We readily assented. How could it be otherwise? What would life be with no love for the beautiful? "It glorifies everything," we said, "and gilds all one's days. And where will you find such beauty as in Segovia? We have lived in a dream ever since we entered it, and we sorrow to depart. Amidst such treasures as the town possesses, such scenes as these ancient cloisters, those wonderful cathedral outlines, dwells, it appears to us, the romance of Spain."

"True, true," murmured the bishop. "You may listen to love-songs under the moonlight; I have heard there is intoxication in the flash of love-lit eyes; but all that passes away; it may appeal to the senses, but can never satisfy the soul. As you rightly observe, it is in such scenes and influences as these that you must look for the true ROMANCE OF SPAIN."

CHAPTER VII.

Last look round—Civil custodian—Wonderful view—Picturesque fountain—Passage at arms—In the lower town—A neglected gem—Friend in need—Mother and daughter—Castilian *versus* Andalusian—Brown-eyed cherub—Birds of prey—Vanity and flirtation—H. C.'s weak point—Like mother like daughter—Antonio—Curious apparition—Mephistopheles—A gossiping Loretta—" Every man to his taste "— An artistic pitcher—Cheating old age—Loretta defends herself—The bishop's right hand—" Happy as the San Millans "—Luisa—A jealous husband—Anticipated revenge—Earthly paradise—Friendly miller—Inspection—Strange sounds—Caretaker of el Parral—Detachment of young monks—Our gentleman monk—Fénélon—Church of Corpus Christi—Service—Hooded figures—Penitential voices—The old priest—Benediction—Goodwill—Ultima thule of nature and art—Freedom of the kitchen for the last time—An avenging power—Processioning through the square—A sleeping world—The dream over.

THE hour came for leaving Segovia.

We had revisited all our beloved haunts for the last time—had gone to the wonderful Alcazar, rung the great bell, found admittance, and once more wandered through rooms bare and cold, without chair or table from end to end. The castle has been rebuilt, but remains untenanted. In days to come, when a king reigns in Spain, perhaps it will once more take up its old life of romance and reality. The empty rooms echoed to our footsteps; rooms well restored and beautiful in their way, without stain or blemish, but hopelessly modern. More than ever we regretted the fire that in a few hours had destroyed the beauty of centuries; more than ever wished the girdle of St. Anthony or the gridiron of St. Lawrence had ended the career of those

THE ALCAZAR.

terrific students. But not at all. Many of them still live and flourish like green bay-trees.

The custodian, civil and obliging after the manner of the Segovians, took a pride in showing us how everything had been in the days gone by, where restoration had departed from the original. He was well acquainted with his subject; opened casement after casement, disclosing wonderful views, and had something to say about all.

Far over the plains one traced the winding course of the great river. Its old bridges stood out boldly, their round arches hoary with age—a dark, deep grey stone, moss-grown and lichen-stained. Beyond the last bridge to the right stood the convent of the uncloistered monks, and yet beyond it the convent of the barefooted Carmelites. Further on, the Ermita de Fuencisla, where the old hermit had lived a cheerful life for a hundred years, and fared sumptuously upon dried herbs, barley bread and fresh water.

From the battlemented roof of one of the towers we traced the unbroken outlines of cathedral and town, overwhelming in their splendour.

The ancient walls, with bastions and towers, encircled the vision. Far down the long white road stood the Moorish gateway of Santiago. Round about it were avenues of trees that in summer form a shady and popular walk. The sun shines with tropical force, even when the afternoon shadows throw chequered lights upon the white roads, and in the gloaming the walks are most frequented—when the sun travels westward across the plain, and sinks, a great red ball, below the horizon, and gorgeous colours flush the sky. The silver crescent of the young moon sinks westward too. Darkness falls, and nothing is left in the sky but the stars, large and flashing.

Re-entering the town, we presently found ourselves in front of a picturesque fountain under the shadow of the Roman aqueduct. It was attached to the wall of a garden, and creepers and hanging roses, the gay nasturtium and

THE ALCAZAR AT PRESENT DAY.

graceful convolvulus, fell above it in rich profusion. Water flowed abundantly into broad troughs; group after group of women came up with pails and pitchers; group after group of mules and donkeys took their turn, and the fountain was broad enough for all. The drivers were more aggressive than the animals, their polite attentions to the fair drawers of water being a little too pointed. Many a passage-at-arms ensued. In one instance, a bold kiss was followed by a sousing that ought to have cooled the most ardent flame. Shouts of laughter made the very arches of the aqueduct ring with astonishment, and every one appreciated the situation —excepting the unfortunate hero of the drama.

We were now on a level with the outer town, on which we had so often looked from Jacob's Ladder. Strolling through it we discovered a small church which had escaped us—a Romanesque treasure. But the door was locked, and there seemed no sacristan at hand. As we lingered, an old woman with a white but kindly face appeared at the open window of an adjoining house, and asked our mission. We explained that we had no mission, but that H. C. was a great poet, who would write a sonnet to her eyebrows if she would open the church to us.

The old woman smiled and blushed, even at her mature age.

"You are making fun of me," she said. "My days of beauty are over—but I have had them."

This was quite possible, for she had a smooth and comely face in her old age, a rare feature amongst women of her rank and country. To this her pale colour and white hair added a certain refinement. But the pathetic element was wanting; there was no suggestion of suffering in her dark eyes. She had had no great sorrows in life.

Her figure, framed by the window, was very picturesque. She smiled at H. C.'s compliment, and declared she was not to be bribed. She had had her day.

"Nevertheless, I can help you to get into the church," she said. "No, I am not the sacristan. I should make a bad keeper of keys, for they would always go astray. But I can find the sacristan for you. He lives round the corner, and my daughter shall call him."

Her voice penetrated to distant regions, and a far-off voice replied. Next, a woman appeared, some thirty or forty years younger than the mother; no white hairs, a rosy colour in her cheeks, soft blue eyes. She might have been an Andalusian. We said so to her.

"My father was one," she replied, "and always declared the Andalusians worth all the rest of Spain put together. But I don't know. I have never been outside my own province; and feel that the country to which my mother belongs"—with an affectionate glance at the older woman—"cannot be excelled."

"That is all very well," laughed the mother, "but the keys, the keys of the church. Compliments are very pretty, but they will not bring the sacristan."

At this moment a child appeared upon the scene: a third generation; the son of the younger woman, with dark eyes like the grandmother. The heavenly-blue eyes of his mother had passed him by.

"His father is a Castilian," said the mother fondly, who seemed made up of human kindness, "and he takes after him. It is just as well. The Castilians are stronger than the Andalusians, and fight their way better through the world. My husband is head verger of the cathedral—an official person," she laughed. "It is respectable, and sure and safe. We know where we are and what we can do."

H. C. turned a shade paler. Was it possible that her husband was the man he had wished to throw down the well? Had he nearly made this fair woman a widow and

AQUEDUCT.

her children orphans? There was remorse in his tones as he asked:

"Does your husband keep the keys of the cloisters, sometimes wear a scarlet gown, and occasionally head the processions?"

"Oh, no," she laughed. "My husband is chief of all. You don't often see him. He never loiters about to conduct people over the cathedral—birds of prey, I call them. He has more important work to think about, and attends very much personally upon our good bishop."

All this time the sun was pursuing his steady upward course and the moments were flying. In this lower town one felt in tropical regions.

"Are you going for the sacristan or not?" cried the old grandmother from the casement—for the daughter had joined us in the little open square, and we stood at the top of the flight of steps which added so much to the Romanesque outlines above them.

The younger woman laughed. She had seen H. C.'s admiration in his eyes, and, fair-woman-like, was not above gratifying her vanity by a slight flirtation. But now she turned to her mother with a laugh, and with a friendly nod to H. C., caught up her child's hand and rapidly disappeared down the steps, beyond the church.

"She is a good daughter, good wife and mother," said the old woman, "but I doubt me thinks too much of her fair face."

"An inherited weakness?" suggested H. C.

"You bad man!" she retorted, laughing. "I was ever bashful and retiring; and should never have discovered I had beauty if I had not been told so."

A statement one might fairly doubt without disloyalty.

"What do you expect to find in the church, that you are so anxious to enter?" she continued. "You will be disappointed. The exterior is fine, the inside poor and plain. Ah! here comes Antonio. Now you will see for yourselves."

A young man, looking like a gnome or a Cornish miner, for he was bright browny-red of face and bright browny-red of dress—a most curious apparition—came flying up the steps keys in hand, and greeted us with a grave salutation.

"If the señores would follow him he would have the honour of showing them the church." And applying his keys to the locks, the great door creaked on its rusty hinges.

"Mephistopheles!" said H. C., pointing to our strange conductor. "Nothing but horns and tail wanting—just like that scene in *Faust*. But where is Gretchen? Poor Gretchen! Is she not a beautiful character?"

We looked doubtful and wondered what Lady Maria would say to such a sentiment; but perhaps he was only thinking of her punishment, repentance, and triumphant ending. So, making no reply, we followed Mephistopheles into the church. The old woman had spoken too truly—we had our waiting for our pains: a miserable interior without redeeming point. One glance at the cold, white-washed, ill-favoured outlines and we went back to the sunshine.

"I told you so," said the old woman—that terrible sentence that so often rings in one's ears from the world's comforters. "I told you so"—marking our disappointed expressions. "It is an old barn of a church inside, and not worth the fee you bestow upon the sacristan. But, poor fellow, it won't come amiss to him. He works hard to supply his daily wants."

"What makes him so red?" we asked. "He might almost have painted his face, and looks half a Zulu."

"Nobody knows why he is so brown-red or red-brown—which is it?—one can hardly tell," she laughed. "His father and mother were not so, but were ordinary worthy Castilians. We think he must have had a Moor in some far-away ancestor who has come up again in him. That is not impossible in Segovia. He has a brown-red mania upon him and never wears anything but brown-red clothes, summer and winter, Sundays and week-days. But he is industrious, and lives at peace with his neighbours. He is quite sane too, for if he has a twist in the brain, it amounts only to wearing these clothes which match the colour of his face. That and jealousy for his wife. For he has a wife, and two lovely children, not a bit brown-red like himself. The Moorish ancestor wisely retired into the background—for we do not like the Moors in Spain."

The good old woman little knew or appreciated how much Spain owed to the Moors, and how she would have lost half her romance but for that strange and little-understood people. At this juncture the sacristan re-appeared on one side, and the old woman's daughter with her child came hurrying up the steps.

"Loretta, you have been gossiping at the well!" cried the old grandmother from her elevation. "At least you might have taken your pitcher and filled it. We want water."

"Not at all," laughed Loretta. "You are mistaken, *madre*. I have not been to the well, but stayed talking to Antonio's wife"—laughing and looking at the sacristan. "I asked her for the hundredth time when he was going to put on Christian apparel; and the poor thing has come to that pass she said she had given it up; didn't know and didn't care. He was a good husband and that was enough for her. But what do you think? She said the See here was to be quite free, and not to be under Valladolid any longer. That would be a fine thing for our bishop, and a good thing for the husband, who would come in for something extra. Pray heaven it be true."

"But it is not true," returned Antonio. "There has certainly been such a rumour, and Luisa, woman-like, jumps

OLD ROOFS IN SEGOVIA.

to the conclusion that it is a settled thing. Do not imagine that what has lasted for centuries is going to be lightly disturbed. Your man will have to depend upon his good conduct and the bishop's favour for promotion."

"Promotion!" cried the grandmother; "who wants promotion? Be content. You have all you need; every want supplied. What more do you expect from life? Jewels and fine clothes? Jewels are for the good queen, fine clothes for Antonio"—pointing jeeringly to his smart-coloured suit.

Antonio took it in good part.

"It is my pleasure," he said. "I like this colour, which is warm and bright, like the blood that runs in the veins. Then everybody sees me coming. 'It is only Antonio,' they cry. 'Come in, Antonio; you are welcome.' My wife knows me a mile off, and is always ready with dinner when I have been out of a morning. My red clothes and red face hurt nobody—and I don't like changes."

"Every man to his taste," replied the grandmother. "If you choose to wear one leg red and the other yellow, and a green coat on your back, like a clown, and paint your face black like a sweep, it is no one's affair but your own. But come, Loretta, here is your pitcher. Go down to the fountain and don't spend all your time in profitless gossip."

The artistic piece of pottery appeared at the window, and to our surprise dropped from the first floor into Loretta's arms, who caught it cleverly and gracefully. The pitcher exactly suited the woman's picturesque style; and as she went off laughing, wishing us good-day and fair weather for our travels, her lovely child trotting by her side, we thought we had seldom seen a prettier group.

The old woman watched her pass down the steps and out of sight, a half-regretful expression in her brown Castilian eyes. "Ah!" she cried; "who would not always be young, and live in a golden atmosphere instead of grey? It is the one thing I have never got over—growing old. But I try to forget my years. I sing at my work, sit and spin in the sunshine, and never look at myself in the glass. By that means I cheat old age and am happy."

"You cheat more than old age," returned H. C. gallantly. "You are unjust to your looking-glass, which you deprive of a beautiful reflection."

The old woman looked pleased; evidently thought H. C. a man of taste and discrimination, and finally shook her head.

Our browny-red Antonio had gone off with his keys and his gratuity, well pleased with the world and himself; and as far as one could tell, poor, industrious, and contented, he need envy no one. We also departed, feeling that in spite of a disappointing interior, our time had not been wasted. These interludes, unexpected and unsought, brought us into slight contact with the people, and showed us a little of their tone and disposition, something of their mind and manners. The women seemed, as a rule, better than the men; more earnest, hard-working, and dependable. Spain given over into their keeping would be a more prosperous country than it is.

As we went down the steps and turned round by the church, the grandmother watching us out of sight, we met Loretta and her pitcher coming from the well. The pitcher was full, and she carried it gracefully, as they all do, resting lightly upon her hip. The rich red of the pottery, as we have said, harmonised wonderfully with her fair Andalusian beauty. Her child trotted and babbled by her side, a small earthly cherub brimming over with unconscious happiness.

"So you have obeyed the mother, and not gossiped at the well, Loretta."

"For a good reason," she laughed; "there was no one to gossip with. I found myself absolutely alone at the well, and it does not happen once in a hundred times."

"Then you had not even the merit of resisting temptation?"

"I am really not a gossip," she returned; "but who ever heard of going to the well and not exchanging words with

SEGOVIA.

one's neighbours? Whilst the pitcher fills we hear the news of the town. Life would be dull if we never used our tongues. It is only the mother's way. She thinks of her young days when she too went chatting and lingering to the well—and came to no harm, though many another did, perhaps. I know nothing about it. I had no chance, for I married my good man as soon as I was of sufficient age. He waited for me," she added rather proudly, "for he is fifteen years older than I; but there isn't a handsomer man in Segovia. Many a half-lady with a good dowry would have had him. This child, José"—turning to the cherub—"is his image in miniature. No Andalusian he, but a dark-eyed Castilian, like all his people. And he is the bishop's right hand. Ah! there goes Antonio—and his pretty wife Luisa with him. She, too, is going to the well, and he never lets her go alone. That is his one fault. He is a jealous man, madly in love with his wife, and thinks every-one must be in love with her too. There they go. Luisa carries her pitcher to the well empty; Antonio carries it back full. I have to do both," she laughed. "I would not see my husband carrying a pitcher. It is woman's work."

"Loretta, if you were not gossiping at the well, you are gossiping now. What will the mother say?"

"Oh, but there is a distinction," H. C. hastily put in. "With me she could not possibly come to any harm. I would defend her against a hundred foes"—in his best Napoleon manner.

"Foes?" said Loretta, looking puzzled; "there are no foes here. We are all friends and neighbours, and live at peace. Our little colony is quite a byword and proverb in Segovia. 'Happy as the San Millans,' they will tell you, for that is our parish, and that is what they call us."

She went her way with her pitcher and cherub, and we went ours. A little lower down we met Antonio and his wife also returning from the well. He was carrying the pitcher, the same artistically-shaped pottery that is here so general.

Antonio bowed with the air of a grand seigneur. The man was a strange mixture of simplicity, dignity, and the ludicrous. We stopped to speak to the wife—a small, pretty Castilian, with high colour, and flashing eyes—a sensible face that would battle well with the world, and take life very much as she found it. If Antonio in his dress reminded one slightly of Mephistopheles, there was nothing of the romantic and yielding Gretchen about Luisa.

A very different woman, too, from Loretta. She had not the grand Andalusian beauty of the latter, and was a far less striking figure. But pretty and feminine she undoubtedly was, with a very sweet-tempered expression joined to her sense and firmness—a woman to make home happy and well-ordered. Antonio had some excuse for his worship, if none for his jealousy. Her sense was common-sense—perhaps the most uncommon of all. It was very different from the romantic, ambitious mind of the fair Andalusian.

"We have been to the well, señores. This is my wife Luisa. I always go with her to carry the pitcher. She is not strong enough to bear heavy weights."

"It is not that," laughed Luisa. "I can carry my pitcher just as well as Antonio. No delicate mortal am I. That is not the true reason. He will not let me go to the well alone because he is jealous of others talking to me. It is his one fault, and heaven knows I give him no cause. I have eyes and thoughts only for him and the children, and keeping the home well. Foolish man!" laughing and looking at him with pretended anger.

Antonio's face was redder than ever. He winced under the accusation.

"Jealousy, they declare, is a proof of love, Luisa. Perhaps you ought to be glad of this mark of your husband's affection."

"Perhaps so," returned Luisa. "All the same I would rather be without it, for jealousy is dangerous. I often wonder what he would be if I were as other women, gadding about, laughing, flirting with every one I met—and no harm either."

Antonio looked volumes, put down his pitcher, placed himself in position, and made a movement of drawing a sham dagger. It was impossible not to laugh at the little browny-red man, who, like H. C., put on a Napoleon manner, ridiculously misplaced. He laughed at himself, but there was an element of tragedy in his tone as he said:

"I should kill you."

"You make my blood run cold," laughed Luisa, pretending to shudder. "And what good would that do? Without me you would die of grief. Or perhaps survive, and marry a second wife—a shrew, who would lead you a demon life. What a fine revenge!"

They were like two children in their happiness, and evidently no cloud came between. The wife's good sense saved them, for it was, as she had observed, a dangerous element, this jealousy, especially in the impulsive passionate Spanish temperament.

"There is our home," said Antonio, pointing to a house a little higher up the hill—a small, picturesque abode, with latticed panes, and a wonderful old red-tiled roof with projecting eaves and a dormer window. Ancient it looked, but not dilapidated or neglected. The windows were clean, and clean white curtains hung behind them. Evidently no slovenly housewife reigned there. One half the lower window displayed small wares; the other belonged to Antonio, where

STREET IN SEGOVIA.

he plied his tailor's trade—for Antonio was nothing more romantic than a tailor. He made his own red clothes, as well as the quieter garments of his neighbours.

"There we live," he said, "and whilst Luisa sells her goods on the one side, I work on the other. And so we just manage to pay our way. Our neighbours are not rich, and we are contented with small profits."

"We have all we want," returned Luisa, "and two lovely children to add to our wealth. If we were not contented we should not deserve to dwell in the happy colony of St. Millan's."

They, too, went their way, and we ours, almost sorry to leave all this St. Millan atmosphere and influence. From the few specimens we had seen, it was certainly a happy land.

We passed the fountain on our way down, and if deserted when Loretta went to it, it was crowded enough now. A chorus of female voices rose on the air; but we recognised none of them, and would not wait to be disillusioned of our St. Millan impressions.

We worked our way round to the river, and crossed the weir into the paradise of nature where reposed the ancient Mint with its grey-tiled roofs and small turrets.

The miller was at his door—tall, thin, grave-looking, with great dark eyes that shone out of his white, floury face. He asked if we would like to look over the ancient premises, after wishing us good-day.

"Rather wish us good-morrow," we replied. "To-morrow Segovia's sun will not rise for us, and we shall leave our spirit behind. Segovia has no rival."

"In fact, it will be a case of astral body," said H. C. But the miller had never heard of astral bodies.

"Nothing lasts," he returned. "In this world it is a constant coming and going. Everything is always changing Even in my little life no two days are alike. Sometimes I think I see a difference in the very corn I grind. The very machinery seems to work day by day with a new voice."

Then he took us over his mill. We trod within walls that had stood for ages. How much remained of what had been? Little or nothing. These days were very different from those when the coinage was struck here, and bags of silver and gold reposed in the deep, dark cellars. Now there were only bags of flour, and in place of coining instruments immense grindstones rolled heavily, crushing the grain. Rooms, floors, partitions, all had changed.

Everything was quiet when we entered, but the miller pulled a string, and immediately there set up a rumbling and creaking and groaning, a sound of chains and machinery such as one might have imagined in Dante's "Inferno." The rushing of the weir was completely drowned. The miller smiled at our bewilderment; one had to shout to be heard.

"There is something peculiar about the place," he said. "They built in the past as they do not build to-day. Always we have this strange reverberation and echo, as though we had hollow walls about us that absorbed all the sound and gave it out again with double force. But the walls are substantial; there is nothing hollow about them."

"How long has it been a mill?"

"I hardly know," replied the miller. "I have been here ten years, and before that I was at San Sebastian. We do not belong to Segovia, and though I have lived here so long, I know little about the place and people. We are friendly with our neighbours; but when I have done my day's work I am tired and like to be quiet, and my wife is an invalid. So far, life for us has not very much change. It is grinding

EL FARRAL AND THE OLD MIST.

corn all the year round, and watching the sunrise and sunset —and little else."

"Do you see anything of the old woman in the cloisters?"

"A little," he replied. "Poor thing! The tragedy of her life took place long before we came here, but one sees it all in her face. We get her to come to us sometimes. She will spend an afternoon or evening with the wife, and go back to her cloister quite cheerful and revived, only to look sadder than ever the next morning. We ask ourselves whether it is a kindness to lure her from her solitude."

"It must be so. The mistake was ever to allow her to take up her abode in that world-forgotten spot, where no strange footstep echoes from one week's end to another."

"The last time she came," continued the miller, "—it was Sunday evening and the mill was at rest—she told us her hours were numbered: in a vision or dream her lost ones had come to her with some sign or message to the effect that her pilgrimage was almost over; they would shortly be re-united. She seemed quite jubilant over it; we had never seen her so cheerful, so like other people. But on meeting her next morning, it was the same sad face as usual. We thought we would try and laugh her out of it. 'Have you had another vision to say the time is put off?' we asked. She shook her head. 'I realised it all yesterday,' she said, 'but to-day it seems as far off as ever. Nevertheless, I know it is near. You will see that before this day month my life's hope will have come to me. I shall no longer be here.' And it will be a happy release," concluded the miller.

With that he pulled a cord again, the machinery stopped, silence fell upon the mill. Once more we heard the falling of the weir. We bade him good-bye, and he accompanied us to the riverside, where the water flashed in the sunshine.

The leaves of the trees whispered and rustled, and they, too, glinted and gleamed as they caught the sun's reflection.

High up, the town walls stood out boldly. Groups of donkeys passed through the gateway of Santiago, trotting down the long white hill. The miller went back to his work and in a few moments we heard the roll of machinery grinding the corn. As we went our way, he put his head out at a window and waved us a grave salutation.

Outside the walls of the barefooted Carmelites, and just by the old bridge we met a detachment of the young uncloistered monks.

Insensibly there came the thought of our late fellow-traveller, the gentleman-monk who had renounced the certain pleasures and pains of the world for the uncertain rest and repose and religious progress of a Carthusian monastery. Where was he now? What doing? What thoughts—hopes—regrets were working within his soul? His very refinement must protest against surrounding influences. Few companions would he find amongst the cloaked and hooded monks of the Order. We felt moved to seek him out; warn him afresh of his danger; bid him return to the world and play his part. Wholesome pleasures and duties would give him greater strength and religious consolation than a colourless convent life. We would bid him read Fénélon, great and good amongst the great and best, who protested against this weak withdrawal from the world.

The young monks filed away, disappeared within their walls, and above us rose all the glorious outlines of Segovia.

The Alcazar crowned its rocky precipice, and below at the watersmeet the troubled streams rushed into their one existence. Over all, the sun poured his tropical rays--

THE ALCAZAR.

a majestic, matchless scene, upon which those distant cathedral outlines threw the charm and influence of absolute repose.

We climbed the long white hill and found ourselves—we hardly knew how—once more and for the last time in the church of Corpus Christi.

Service was going on; an Eastern perfume of incense hung about the lovely pillars and arches. Behind the screen hooded figures were dimly outlined in the obscurity. A soft murmur of penitential voices floated through the air, a Gregorian monotone, inexpressibly sad, seemed to die away in unseen recesses. More than ever we felt that life was never intended for this.

The body of the church was empty, and the scene was only the more impressive. Service was concluding. The old priest turned and lifted his hand in benediction. There was something beautiful about his face and expression, the well-shaped head and flowing white hair—a great exception to the generality of the priests one saw. A head fitted for a mitre. If our gentleman-monk had entered the church instead of the cloister, we felt that in time he might have become such an ecclesiastic as now stood before us with hand upraised, and voice that came from the heart, subdued from emotion.

Without sound, almost without movement, the hooded figures glided from behind the screen; lights were extinguished on the altar. The old priest passed through the doorway, and bowed to us as he went out—evidently meant as a token of fatherhood and brotherhood—and we, of the same Christian faith, but not of the same creed and ritual, responded.

We, too, passed out. Our moments in Segovia were

numbered. We had gone through a wonderful experience, a strange, eventful history. Never had the unexpected been so full of surprise and charm. If we closed our eyes we were dazzled by a marvellous assemblage of outlines stamped for

OLD NOOK IN SEGOVIA.

ever upon memory and imagination. We felt confused and bewildered as one gem after another rose up in vivid mental panorama—a succession of grand monuments and impressions. The outlines of the town were crowded with endless magic. Perhaps the beauty, and repose, and solemnity of the cathedral, its exquisite cloisters, haunted by the dignified figure of the bishop, placed itself in the foreground; but undoubtedly the most impressive scene of all, running riot in thought and fancy, was that from the south bank of the river—the bold, frowning precipice crowned by the Alcazar, the town-walls rising behind it, above which uprose the wonderful cathedral outlines. Nature and art could not go beyond this.

We entered our primitive inn for the last time. In the artistic kitchen the old woman and chef reigned together. She stayed her peeling to wish us a good journey and a happy life, whilst the chef stood up in cap and apron, and, like Antonio, bowed his farewell en grand seigneur.

"Ah, señores," quavered the old woman, "you are preparing to leave. I am sorry, and you will be sorry. You are quitting our beautiful Segovia for that ugly and wicked Madrid, where the devil lurks at every corner for his prey, and catches only too many victims. Don't let him catch you."

"Peace, woman!" cried the chef. "Madrid, señores, is an earthly paradise, and if I might make so free I would beg you to give it my best affections. There at least one can live and enjoy one's days; whilst as for Segovia——"

The old woman rose like an avenging power, and holding forth a claw-like hand clutching her knife, seemed about to plunge it into the heart of the chef. We felt we would not wait for the drama, and turned to the little group ready to escort us to the omnibus.

The shades of night had fallen as we crossed the square for the last time, and the cathedral rose darkly against the darker sky beyond; the streets were putting on their weird aspect as caves and dormer windows, Eastern casements and narrowing perspectives grew faint and unreal; the city walls seemed to be guarding a town pregnant with mysterious shadows and mighty whisperings of the past; the broad fountain was deserted, and the water ran in neglected waste.

We passed under the Roman aqueduct, and almost shrank from the crushing weight of stone upreared in all its majestic outlines and arches. We curved round by the sleeping houses, the closed and silent churches. Again we reconnoitred the solitary building whose doors had opened on our first arrival to admit the warlike youth with clanking sword and gun. To-night its dark and frowning walls might have held some mighty inquisitorial secret of life and death.

And then away from it all; the dream was over; Segovia was no more. But even the common-place railway-station possessed a charm denied to all other stations, for there, in large letters, one read the magic name, with its worldful of charm and delight. As we steamed away, we felt that if the world held but one Spain, Spain owned but one Segovia. We thought of Thorwaldsen, and how he wept when he had completed his chef-d'œuvre, because he could never surpass it

and we sympathised with him, and understood. Even the attainment of perfection has its sad side.

Through the cold and barren plains of Castile, now shrouded in night, we were soon journeying towards Madrid. But no picturesque monk was at hand to pour his confidences into listening ears; and, closing our eyes to the world around, we lived over again, in all their magic and reality, our days and experiences in Segovia. There, truly and indeed, in far greater measure than we had yet found it, dwelt the imperishable ROMANCE OF SPAIN.

CHAPTER VIII.

Crossing the boundary—Mountain ranges—A fruitful land—Old and New Castile—A contrast—Desolate plains—The Castilians—Hardy race—Best seen in the villages—Begging system—Tillers of the soil—Healthy influences—Dining with Duke Humphrey—Overcoming difficulties—The hopeful Castilian—Madrid—Modern influences—Luxury—Historical site—Noisy streets—Last and least interesting capital—Rejected by Goths, Romans, and Moors—Trying climate—Extremes of temperature—Rapid changes—Skies that charm—Pandemonium—Shrill voices—So many provinces, so many kingdoms—Religious decline—Discarded mantilla—A woman's voice—The flower-seller—Tuberoses—Sad story—Innocence suffering for guilt—In the dining-room—Babel of sounds—Old Spanish countess and her daughter—H. C. in a fine frenzy—History of an attempted elopement—A *billet-doux*—H. C. unhinged—Rapid flight—Madrid's commonplace element—The Prado—Massacre of 1808—Manzanares—Riverside washerwomen—Royal Palace—Armoury—Voices of the dead centuries.

The plains of Old Castile passed away in the darkness; we crossed the boundary-line and entered New Castile.

These two provinces are the central plateau of Spain, one-third of the entire country, lying high above the level of the sea. Mountain ranges diversify them; not heaven-soaring, like the Alps; not covered with eternal snows; in loneliness and solitude they live through the ages; but their outlines, stretching across the vast plains, are often beautiful, and may be traced far as the eye can reach.

They have a mission, also, in sheltering many parts of these endless plains. Thanks to these hills it is a great corn and fruit-growing country. The vine is abundant, and many and many an acre overflows, figuratively speaking, with the red and white juice of the grape.

Castilla la Vieja y Nueva, "the Land of the Castles," a name inherited from the Moors, like much else that is

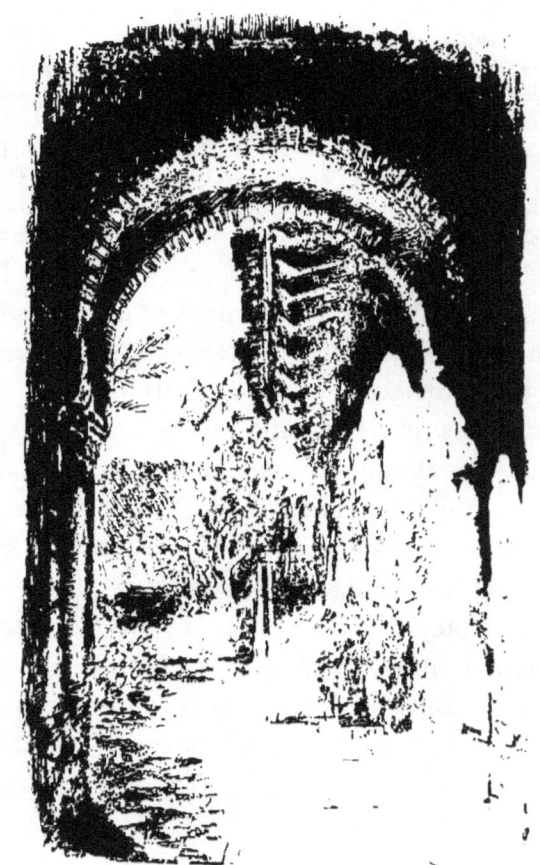

A BIT OF OLD SPAIN, NEAR MADRID.

beautiful and romantic, existed as far back as the year 800. Many of these old fortresses may still be found, some in ruins, others almost perfect; fortresses built after the manner of Roman citadels.

The north-west portion, sheltered by the Guaderramas, formed Old Castile, the Bardulia of the Goths. It was this part that attracted the ancients, and to-day is most rich in remains.

In these provinces of Old and New Castile will be found the finest vestiges of antiquity, and some of the most glorious cities of Spain.

Nothing presents a greater contrast than the aspect of the two provinces. The mountains rise in great diversity of form, and their valleys are beautified by immense forests, by rivers rich in trout. On their banks are the ruins of many a monastery, where in days gone by men lived, happy, it may be, in their monkish calm and narrow existence. In contrast are vast plains where the mountains are not seen and the whole country looks bare, desolate and mournful; nothing breaks their monotony, and mile after mile is passed without sign of human habitation. Neither hedges nor dry walls are visible; trees are not planted; it is not the home of wild flowers or of bird-life.

Yet these deserted plains are less forlorn than they appear. To a great extent they are cultivated, but with cereals which leave the earth barren for part of the year. The trees are all fruit-bearing; nothing is done to please the eye where the first consideration is profit and utility. The Castilians are poor, and live from hand to mouth, as the saying runs. Nevertheless, physically and mentally they are a hardy race — the backbone of the country—and if ever Spain is regenerated, the revival will begin here. The Castilian is said to be honest and true. In the towns he is certainly often very disagreeable, but there one rarely meets with the true specimen. The long unbroken line of ancestry is best seen in the villages of the plains, where only he will be found upright and unconsciously dignified. He thinks no one superior to himself, and in his own estimation equals the proudest noble. To foreigners he has a frank aversion. The town-dwelling Castilian is cunning and suspicious, with hand raised against his neighbour.

Madrid itself has the worst specimens. The capital has no humanising influence upon the people, but the contrary.

NEW MADRID.

Here the most degraded are found; but perhaps this is true of all capitals. Not civilisation, but herding together demoralises. The begging system, licensed by government, and made profitable, is a national disgrace, and the open system of exacting fees and bribes for the smallest service is almost as bad. They are all slow, unwilling, more or less idle, working in a half-hearted way, under protest.

But in the far-off villages it is different. The vast

plains are cultivated by the peasantry, who toil early and late. In Spain—a century behind the rest of the world—machinery has not been introduced; everything is done by manual labour. The tillers of the soil often have to go long distances to their work. Cottages are few and far between; the plains are far-reaching. They start before daybreak, and return after nightfall. Tired with their long day, they make a frugal meal, and then to bed. Of home they really see nothing, excepting on Sunday, their only day of rest.

Standing in groups about the villages, dressed in the long cloak that often sits upon them as gracefully as upon the noble, they look picturesque. Most of the people work in the fields, men, women and children, and not infrequently overwork into ill-health and shortened lives. All are simple, happy and primitive, easily contented. Wisdom has taught them not to expect the impossible. Fun and laughter, a light heart and a gay temperament are the characteristics of the dwellers in the plains; healthy lives and influences.

As a result, many an acre, many a mile of the plain country will be seen, at certain seasons of the year, gorgeous with the yellow flower of the saffron. This is in great demand; no kitchen is without a large supply, and it is said to cause the ugly yellow tinge that often distinguishes the Spaniard. Other crops grown in the plains are an abundance of Indian maize and *garbanzos*, or chick peas. The latter forms almost the staple food of the peasantry, and is supposed to have been brought into the country by the Carthaginians. This, also, is found in most of the Spanish kitchens, the foundation of many of their dishes.

The Spanish cooking is behind the age, and is only combined with the French in the larger towns. Dry bread is a luxury in comparison with rancid oil; and in many places it means literally dry bread, for butter is too often unknown.

In some remote parts, when the traveller arrives at a small *renta*, the most primitive of all inns, he finds nothing whatever provided in the shape of food. What he has brought with him he may prepare in his own way, with such accessories as are at hand. On the whole, travelling in the interior of Spain often means dining with Duke Humphrey. This, however, is one of the minor evils of the country. At these inns, on asking what they have, the answer will be that they have everything, but that means if you have brought it with you.

And a great amount even of such materials as these fondas, posadas and ventas have at command, are grown in the plains of the Castiles, New and Old. A little more capital and enterprise, a little more knowledge of farming and irrigation, and the half-barren wilderness would become a fruitful paradise.

They have yet to learn the art of overcoming difficulties. Water is scarce, and they do not know how to supply it artificially. Often for many months of the year it never rains; everything dries up and withers; the cultivator loses heart. Day by day he sees his means of existence growing less and less: a demoralising, hopeless experience. But the remnant saved gives him courage to go on year after year; always hoping that next year may prove better than the last, though the "seven fat years" never come. Yet they go on, and as we have said, are happy and contented, merry and full of fun. The mere fact of existence is a pleasure. Year after year brings the same result; they know exactly what to expect; and if

MARKET-PLACE, MADRID.

their privileges are not great, their cares and responsibilities are few.

Through this country we journeyed in the dark hours of the night, and about ten o'clock found ourselves entering Madrid, not sorry for once in a way to be spared a night in the train.

In the short drive to the Hôtel de Paris we realised that a different element surrounded us. The beauties of Segovia had given place to newer influences. Gas and electric light blazed in the streets; tall houses crowded everywhere without a single artistic or redeeming outline; cabs, omnibuses and tramways filled the air with sound; the place seemed full of life and movement. After the intense quiet of Segovia it was almost bewildering.

The hotel overflowed with light and comfort; we felt once more in the midst of civilisation, and were not sorry. One grows tired of roughing it in country inns, of coarse food, and clumsy waiters who move as though time stood still for ever.

Our rooms seemed almost wickedly luxurious, with windows opening to the great square—the Puerta del Sol. The only suspicion of romance or poetry about the hotel, was that it stood on ground once sacred, for here formerly was the church in which Murat committed some of his worst acts during his short reign of terror in 1808; and on the very spot above which the lift ascended, many of his victims were buried. Here too, in 1821, the Canon Matios Vinuesa was murdered. Thus the house has an historical site. The square itself is oblong and awkward, but all Madrid seems to meet here in constant, ever-moving crowds. The great gateway has long since disappeared, and with it all the pomp and pageantry, the regal and military processions that passed through it as the history of Spain developed.

To-night it was still far from deserted, streets were noisy, lights gleamed everywhere. But as far as could be seen, there was nowhere a vestige of antiquity; all was hopelessly modern.

The last of the capitals of Spain, Madrid is the least interesting, both in appearance and situation. Valladolid, Seville, Granada, and Toledo have all had their turn, and all possessed merits denied to Madrid. But it has now been the capital for three hundred and fifty years, and no doubt will remain so.

It was raised to dignity by Charles V. The town lies some 2500 feet above the level of the sea, and the air suited the gouty king, who, in spite of all objections, set up his Court in the midst of these barren plains.

The spot had been previously rejected by all the reigning powers, including the Goths, Romans, and Moors; its only advantage consisting in being the centre of the country. Lisbon, it has been well said, should have been chosen, for it has many attractions. Had this been done, Portugal would never have separated from Spain, and she would have had an element the less to contend with in her decline.

The climate of Madrid is also trying; the place is said to be unhealthy—intensely cold in winter, too hot in summer. The look of the people seems to confirm this. One constantly comes across invalids apparently in the last stages of consumption. Lying on its high plateau, the town is bounded on one side by the snow-covered Guaderramas, from which the snow disappears in the extreme heat of summer, but soon returns. The wind rushes over the

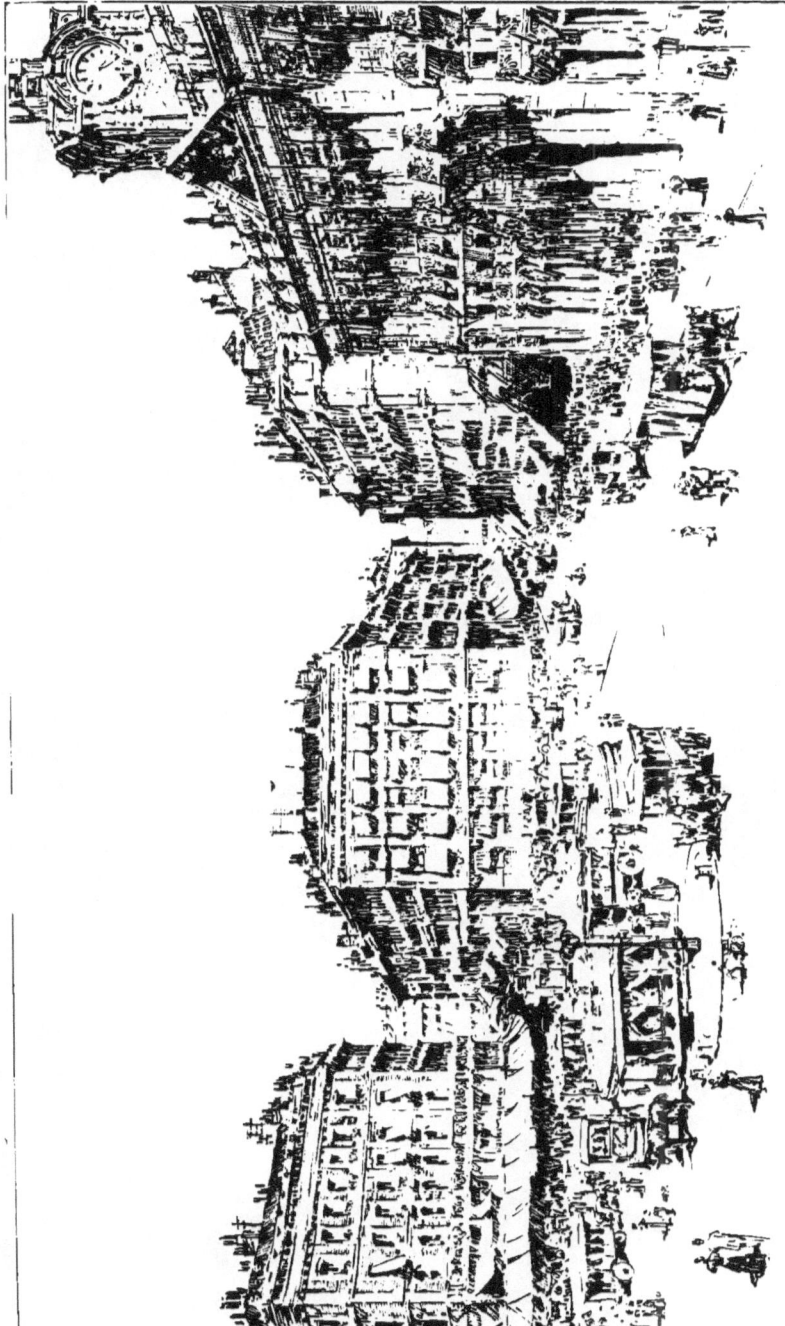

CHIEF SQUARE: HÔTEL DE PARIS IN THE CENTRE.

mountains and passes through the streets in ice-laden blasts. To the chilly, ill-developed Spaniard, this is fatal. He wraps his cloak around him, muffles up his throat in wool, mounts the peaked Capuchon, and makes himself fifty times more delicate than he need be. But it is of little use; the wind finds out the plague-spot, and does its work. In the course of a single morning we found the temperature passed from summer to winter, and again to summer, changing with the shifting wind. There is a proverb that the air of Madrid will not put out a candle, but will destroy a man's life :

"El air de Madrid es tan sutil
Que mata á un hombre, y non apaga á un candil."

That morning the wind would have put out not only a candle but a furnace. It rushed through the town with terrific force, though short-lived. The people hurried along, buried their faces in cloaks and comforters, and shivered; idle vagabonds, lurking at street corners in almost transparent clothes, turned blue. Three hours later we again rejoiced in midsummer. The evening was distinguished by a true sunset of Spain; the sky one blaze of colouring quite unknown to England, glorifying the whole town, window after window seemingly on fire. For once Madrid charmed us; but her skies, like those of Rome, are proverbially beautiful.

The climate at its best is perfect: a light, sparkling air, very exhilarating. The most favoured months are those of April, May and June; and again, October and November. Everything depends upon the winds, and from the rapid changes the Spaniard has some excuse for seldom parting company with his cloak: a garment, says the proverb, only worn gracefully at Seville.

Sunday was by no means a day of rest. Saturday night no one seemed to think of sleep or repose; at midnight the streets were still thronged, and at every few yards stood a man or woman with something to sell, each trying who could shout the loudest. The result was pandemonium; and again and again we discovered that the Spanish voice, male and female, is shrill and penetrating. That excellent thing in woman is indeed rarely found out of England. Many of these were selling a literature that would never have passed an English Lord Chamberlain—in the days gone by. The morals of Spain are not to be admired, and this, perhaps, is one of the least hopeful signs of the country. In great part the people live for pleasure. Of course there are exceptions, but the nation is tainted with the influences of the South.

It is remarkable how tone and character vary in different provinces, so that Spain may be said to consist of many small, distinct kingdoms, whose only bond of union is the same monarch and the same language. Each individual loves his province, looks upon it as his home and country, and considers the adjoining province an alien land, for which he has little affection or concern.

There was a time when all Spain was intensely, superstitiously religious; so far the country was united by a common sentiment and influence; but this is no longer so, and of all the provinces, perhaps the Castilians alone have remained devout, as they have remained the finest characters.

For this decline there are internal and external reasons. Within, the Bourbon rule has been disastrous; without, the waves of doubt and rationalism sweeping over Europe have not spared the Peninsula. Reaction was no doubt inevitable from the long and tyrannical dominion of monks and priests, who still possess great power, though a mere shadow of their former rule. The monkish sway of the Escorial is said to have contributed very much to the decline of Spain; and nothing realises that decline more vividly than a visit to the great building reposing on the slopes of that wide sierra, where empty corridors, a ghostly silence, and a death-in-life atmosphere for ever reign.

Apparently no one is less concerned with the downfall than the Spaniards themselves, and Madrid seems the least care-laden of cities. From early morning on Sunday to late night the scene was amazing. It was almost impossible to walk through the streets for the constant crush and crowd of people; but the picturesque element was wanting. Many of the Spanish women have put aside the graceful mantilla for hideous hats and bonnets, with fatal result.

All day long and after darkness had fallen the air was full of sound, the streets were full of the cries of those who sold. One voice, a woman's, rising above all others, piercing, sad, haunted us. The voice had rung out thin and clear on the Saturday night, and we wondered as to the melancholy history of its owner. For it was distinctly a voice with a history.

Early next morning it began again, and we went out and found that it belonged to a woman, pale, sad, to whom life was evidently a burden. She looked as though her days were numbered, and the rest so much needed was not far off and would be eternal. A slight hectic upon the white, worn 'cheeks, a certain brilliancy in the large, dark eyes, as of a consuming fire, seemed to say that consumption had marked her for its own. She was thinly clad. It was all very well this hot sunny morning, but the afternoon might bring its cold blast from the Guaderramas.

The woman was still young, perhaps five or six and twenty, but her face was suspiciously transparent. Where the strength came from for that ever-sounding voice was a mystery; but we felt that one fine morning she would wake up to find it gone for ever.

She sold flowers—white flowers that matched her appearance; long stalks of exquisite tuberoses, white and luscious, filling the air with sickly perfume, bunches for which she asked a few halfpence, but in London would have sold for three times as many shillings.

It was impossible to look without sorrow upon this frail flower-seller. We asked about herself as we bought.

"You do not seem strong; this life in the streets is hardly safe for you."

"It is nothing now," she returned; "nothing in warm weather. I almost enjoy it then, though sometimes ready to drop from fatigue. But the winter days and winds almost kill me. Sometimes I think they will kill me outright."

There was a certain shrinking modesty about the woman, rare in her class. Street life is too often fatal to any feminine quality. This woman had certainly been comely; even now her delicacy gave her a refined beauty not without charm. A thin shawl was about her shoulders. Her abundant dark hair was coiled in massive plaits round her small head, neatly arranged, the head bare of all other covering. A ring was on her small, delicate hand.

"You are married?"

"Yes," she replied; "and that is the cause of my trouble. I have a husband who half the time does not work, and when he does work, spends all he earns in drink. So night and day, summer and winter, I have to be out selling flowers, trying to keep a roof over my head and my children in food.

We have to work in Madrid—or want. There is no alternative. We receive no assistance. And "—with a flash of her large liquid eyes—" I would sooner starve than ask; sooner die than become one of those idle beggars who trade upon the sympathies of the public."

" Have you many children ?"

" Two," she answered. " My good old mother lives with me and takes care of them. Sometimes my husband goes off and I don't see him for a month together; then we have peace in the home; when he returns, I just make him welcome and never upbraid him or ask a question."

So all countries have the same record of sin and sorrow, domestic dramas and tragedies; the innocent suffering for the guilty. As we went away, the plaintive voice followed us, but the stream of people going to and fro took no heed. To them one voice was the same as another. Probably none ever stopped to inquire into the history of the flower-seller, or ask a reason for that undertone of sadness. But we never see tuberoses or meet their perfume without a vision of that sad voice and pathetic face.

The laughter and animation of a French crowd did not characterise these Spaniards. For the most part they seemed to find their pleasure in sauntering without much conversation.

This did not apply to the dining-room of the Hôtel de Paris—a babel of sounds at luncheon or dinner. Smoking was the rule. The presence of ladies made no difference, and in some instances they smoked also. At the small table next to our own sat an old Spanish countess and her daughter, the former painted and powdered, the flash of diamonds mingling with the glitter of beads. The daughter was tall, handsome, dark-eyed, dark-haired, with a complexion too pronounced not to be real. She was very self-confident, and probably the mother's lynx-eyed generalship was not without reason. The daughter sat exactly opposite H. C., and it was soon evident that his dreamy gaze had reached her heart. In other words, she fell desperately in love. No doubt for the one hundred and fiftieth time, but that only causes the last new fire to be all the more ardent. Fortunately it also burns itself out quickly, leaving the empty shrine ready for a fresh divinity.

This fair and fickle damsel, we say, fell in love. The language of the eyes was eloquent. H. C. gradually worked himself into a fine frenzy, and we threatened change of hotels at the first sign of encouragement. We had no desire to play second in a duel with the fair inamorata's father or brother, for we discovered that she possessed both—the father a crotchety old count, the mother a vain, frivolous, ill-tempered old countess. The two had agreed to differ, and went their several ways, the son remaining with the father, looking after his broad but not lucrative acres in the Asturias; the daughter and mother wandering about the world, both, for the sake of appearances, spending three months out of the twelve at home.

All this information was gathered and stored from the most reliable sources.

"Last winter," said our informant, "there was quite an adventure in the place. I was staying here at the time. Madame Y—— and her daughter were spending three months in the hotel. They occupy the best suite of rooms, but the daughter insists upon taking her meals in the public dining-room; she likes distraction and the admiration she receives, for, of course, they are well known, and really belong to our first nobility. There came to the hotel a French count—a parvenu, with a long title and a short purse. He heard that mademoiselle would inherit her mother's large fortune, which, by the way, is not so certain. I ought to know, for I am her father's cousin. The man was a scented dandy, but, I must admit, handsome. The two managed to become acquainted—it is not difficult where both are of the same mind—and one fine morning they were caught in the act of eloping. Monsieur le Comte had to make a flying exit from Madrid without his bride; the old countess, furious and really alarmed, locked up her daughter for a week, administered lectures, and finally took her off to her father's home in the Asturias, where they remained for three months. The whole thing has blown over, and here they are again, the mother's complexion more artistic than ever, the daughter quite ready for another adventure."

After such an account we felt on the brink of an escapade. It may therefore be imagined how our blood froze when one evening on rising from table the fair damsel dexterously dropped a billet-doux at H. C.'s feet as she passed him. A thunderbolt would have been more welcome. H. C. picked it up and read it through, paling and flushing in turns. The deadly missive was nothing more or less than a declaration and a proposal to elope the next day, with an assurance that southern winds should waft them to an earthly paradise where perpetual summer reigned. The lady had evidently a mania for elopements. It was useless to argue. H. C.'s poetical mind took fire; he retired to his room and we saw him no more. On knocking some hours after at his locked door, he requested to be left in peace—and the composition of love-sonnets. It was a matter for prompt action, and the next day saw us on our way to Toledo.

Q

But this is anticipating; we are still in Madrid.

We have said that the commonplace element reigned, as it reigns more or less in all capitals, in place of the ancient and artistic. Some capitals have at least a few exceptions— a wonderful old house, an old cathedral, vestiges to remind us of past days of beauty and greatness. Paris has Notre Dame; London, Westminster Abbey; Rome, multiplied splendours; Athens, the Acropolis; even cold and distant Trondjhem gives her contribution.

But Madrid has nothing. There is not a church worth visiting; not a single building, as far as we could see, with outlines of the Middle Ages. When she was first founded something might have been done, some grand Gothic cathedral arisen, worthy to rank with the glories of Castile. But Charles V. thought more of curing his gout than of building monuments; and Philip II. had no love for the beautiful.

Not that Madrid is in every sense of the word modern. Its records date as far back as the tenth century, when it was used by the Moors as an outpost of Toledo. But there has not remained one Moorish trace to bear witness to those days; and the Moors themselves held in contempt the small place rising in the midst of the plains. Yet the plains were not as bare then as now. Immense forests spread far and wide, and were the scene of frequent boar and bear hunting.

Nevertheless, with all its commonplace element there is something pleasing about Madrid; a certain enjoyable lightness, the life and vivacity of a capital not overwhelmingly large. The larger capitals become oppressive and crushing; crowds of streets and houses grow into a nightmare.

Madrid has nothing of this element. Its half million inhabitants are stowed away in a comparative nutshell.

Only when they all come out in a body for Sunday parade, does any sense of a crowd begin to haunt one. It is, indeed, very like a small Paris, especially in its outskirts, where new and well-built houses are daily springing up in the broad thoroughfares, and people dwell luxuriously in palatial flats.

Few towns possess a finer boulevard than the Prado, over two miles long, with its trees and statues. One of the most remarkable monuments is the obelisk erected to the memory of the people massacred by Murat. Surrounded by sad cypresses, it recalls the terrible story—perhaps the greatest blot in the life of this ambitious monster, who in 1808 arrived at Madrid, pretending friendship to the people, but in reality aspiring to the throne. The people would none of him, whereupon he seized and executed some hundreds of them on the Prado, hoping to establish himself by a short reign of terror such as Paris had undergone twenty years before. The details of this massacre, given by eye-witnesses, are too terrible to read. Victims were seized indiscriminately, and even children were not spared.

But Murat had reckoned without his host. England, passive during the French Revolution, which, indeed, was no concern of hers, would not leave weaker Spain to the mercy of a tyrant. Wellington was on the point of sailing for South America, instead of which he changed his plans, came down upon Spain, and Murat's short triumph was over.

The massacre has not been forgotten. Every year, on the 2nd May, the chief priests and rulers of the town go in procession to the obelisk, and from early morning to midday masses are offered up for the repose of the souls of the victims.

On summer evenings the Prado is a lively scene: fountains send forth a sound of running waters; gaily-dressed crowds saunter to and fro; every chair is occupied; the cries of the water-sellers are heard on all sides. Beyond this lies the park, with its broad, stiff-looking avenues and miniature lake.

The Manzanares, on which Madrid is built, is a small river here and there crossed by enormous bridges, a contrast giving rise to the saying that Spain is a country of rivers without bridges, and of bridges without rivers. Here it is hardly more than a mountain torrent, having its source in the Guaderramas, whose outlines may be seen twenty miles away. Small and shallow for a great part of the year, there are times when the torrent swells to an enormous volume, and comes rushing from the hills in such force that the very foundations of the bridges seem threatened. On its banks, long rows of picturesque washerwomen beat their linen with an arm that would honour a blacksmith. All over Spain these riverside women are bright bits of colouring in the landscape, chattering, good-tempered, with tongues that, like the stream, flow on for ever.

On as magnificent a scale as the bridges, the Royal Palace overlooks the Campo del Moro, part of which has been taken in to form the palace gardens. The palace itself is said to be one of the finest in the world, standing over thirty yards high, a square of four hundred and seventy feet. Architecturally it is imposing, but only beautiful by moonlight, when the plains lie sleeping in the silver beams. It is said that here stood the original outpost Alcazar or fortress of the Moors, burnt down in 1734. Philip V. then determined to build a palace that should more than rival Versailles, on the

PALACE BRIDGE OVER THE MANZANARES.

opposite hill of San Bernardino; and the plans were drawn out by Jubara on a scale of unequalled splendour. But Elizabeth Farnese, the queen, so opposed the expense of the scheme that the intention was abandoned and Jubara died of grief. Here Wellington stayed when he entered Madrid in triumph after the Battle of Salamanca in 1812. Only a short time before, Napoleon, placing his hand on one of the white lions of the principal staircase, had cried: "Je la tiens, enfin, cette Espagne, si désirée!" But he, too, had reckoned without his host.

The palace stands well above the Manzanares, which flows at a great depth below. Beyond this stretch the gardens of the Campo del Moro, and the far-reaching plain is relieved by patches of wood and forest, the distant, undulating Guaderramas closing the scene. It is all wild and barren, fine in extent, but melancholy and destitute of colour. No building in Madrid is more exposed to the elements than the palace, and in winter the wind comes sweeping over the snowy hills and across the harsh plains with such violence that the sentinels sometimes freeze at their posts.

Here, in the south-west corner, is one of Madrid's greatest treasures and attractions: perhaps the finest armoury in the world. This south gallery is the one solitary remnant of the old Alcazar. The collection is contained in one large room built in 1565 for Philip II., when he removed the armoury from Valladolid. The original building was burnt down in 1884; many objects were lost, but much, happily, was saved—the best of the armour, the gold Visigothic crowns, with all their historical interest, and the MS. catalogue of Charles V.

It would take days to thoroughly examine and exhaust

these treasures. The moment you enter the room you are transported into another and more ancient world; days of splendid tournaments, fields of cloth of gold, pageants more gorgeous than anything this civilised age dreams of. Days of Knights Templars, when war was a sacred mission, kings fought with lance and shield, and lay dead upon the battlefield.

All the suits before us had been worn by the noblest champions of Spain. Every age and every species of armour seemed represented. In the centre of the room figures in battle array sat their horses proudly and firmly, and the effect was curiously life-like. Magnificent suits, inlaid with gold, wondrously chased, must have cost a king's ransom; suits that had fought many a hard battle, graced many a tournament, caused many a heart to beat, many a fair cheek to pale. Banners hung from the roof; walls were lined with coats of armour, and armed knights stood in long rows on every side. The German and Italian armour was the most artistic and highly wrought; the finest blades were those of Toledo, which have never been equalled.

One suit worn by Philip II. bore the arms of England, in honour of Queen Mary. There were many suits worn by Charles V., some engraved with the Virgin, or the image of Santa Barbara, patron saint of the artillery. There were magnificent casques, swords, and shields, damascened and engraved after Benvenuto Cellini. In the centre of a group of equestrians, looking rather out of place, was the litter used by Charles V. when suffering from gout.

There was the sword of St. Ferdinand, conqueror of Seville, and also of Isabella the Catholic. Amongst other swords was that of Charles V., of Philip II., and — more interesting than all — of Boabdil, last king of

CHANGING GUARD.

Granada, round whose name lingers so much sadness and romance.

Near the door was a suit of armour said to have been worn by Isabel at the siege of Granada, and the name Isabel is engraved on the vizor. It was probably worn by her husband. There were also many children's suits of armour worn by the sons of kings.

Conspicuous amongst the helmets was that of Jaime el Conquistador, bearing the winged-dragon crest. Not least interesting were some curious saddles and leather shields used by the Moors; the latter made of skins held together by a cement of herbs and camel's hair, strong enough to resist a spear.

The whole collection is splendidly arranged and kept. At once you seem to fall back into the Middle Ages and all their chivalry. Endless scenes of battle and tournament arise as we wander to and fro, lost in dreams. Many descriptions of wars crowd the brain. We see plains filled with mailed horsemen, and hear the bugle-charge.

To make the illusion more perfect, the guard outside was being changed; bugles were sounding through the great court, one heard the roll and rattle of gun-carriages, officers giving the word of command, the trotting of excited horses. A battle might have been going forward.

And within these walls were endless signs and symbols of the wars of the past: wars which had made or marred Spain. These swords had been wielded by the greatest of the world. Those Visigothic crowns carried one back to the darker ages, before the Moors had come over and conquered the Peninsula and a new order of things set in.

The whole room seemed full of the voices and events of the dead centuries. The very guardians were more grave and sedate than guardians usually are, as though they too were influenced by these splendid relics. And as the moments passed unconsciously amidst this crowd of dreams and visions, we felt that, not in the commonplace streets of Madrid, not in her gorgeous palaces, nor amongst her people of to-day, but in this one solitary chamber, if anywhere in the capital, dwelt the ROMANCE OF SPAIN.

CHAPTER IX.

Madrid—Commonplace atmosphere—Blue skies—Frivolous shops—Modern Spanish art—Fan-language—Wasting the midnight oil—The picture-gallery — Rare treasures — Banished by Ferdinand VII. — Restored by La Portuguesa—Velasquez considered—Murillo—A comparison —" Surrender of Breda "—Raphael's " Salutation "—Spain's debt of gratitude—An early morning journey—Grey skies and mist—Villalba —Été de St. Martin—Nearing the Escorial—Distant view—Ugly and unimpressive—Spaniards' eighth wonder of the world—In honour of St. Laurence—A monk-king—Philip's rooms—Religious bigotry—Cruelty under the name of religion—Last weeks of life—Mental and physical suffering — The Escorial — Debased architecture—Many destinies—A friendly monk—Splendid library—Halls of philosophy—The church —Magnificent coro—Frescoes—The chapel solemn and impressive— Tombs of the kings—Curious custom at Galapagar—Ghastly ceremonial —A quiet guide—Primitive inn—Within the precincts—Crowd of picturesque beggars—Silence and emptiness—A gigantic tomb—Ichabod.

MADRID had the merit of being what she appeared, uncompromisingly modern and commonplace; an effect redeemed only by her blue skies and wonderful atmosphere. But she was full of bustle and movement and all the ordinary elements of life. There was an air of fashion about her; many traces of past greatness; evidences of wealth; as befitting the capital of a country great in extent if not in influence.

The shops were a display of frivolities. Pictures of modern Spanish art glared at one from innumerable windows, and like most of the art of the present day, whether Spanish or other, the effects were false. Here and there one praised the technique—more often than not a trick of the brush—but all other merit was conspicuously absent; there was no attempt at reproducing nature: a common fault of our day, and the most fatal. It was the virtue of the ancients—this faithfulness to nature—and one of the great secrets of their success; and when to this they added tones, colouring and conception, they became immortal.

The most popular shops were the fan-shops; proving that whatever the decline in art, there has been no falling away in the tender passion.

The Spanish women are not at all behind their sisters in this respect. They seem to spend all their pin-money in fans, for the shops had no lack of customers. With these the sirens dark and fair flit and flirt and cultivate a silent language; so that holding the fan one way means, "Do you love me?" and holding it another, "You are beloved."

A whole vocabulary of fan-language, published in a large volume, may be learned like the Dumb Alphabet or the Rules of Harmony, but it frequently leads to domestic discord. It is part of a fair senorita's polite education; studied chiefly in the retirement of her chamber, before a mirror which reflects a vision of dark eyes, pearly teeth, and rosy lips, bewildering to anyone who is anything less than a fossil.

They used their fans pretty freely in the streets, but H. C. had not their language at his finger-ends, and could not interpret their signs. So fair dames shrouded in mantillas—there were a few left—which displayed their forms to perfection, and left their charming faces half-hidden and half-seen—what can be more distracting?—fluttered their fans in vain. Some were in carriages, some walking—it was all equally incomprehensible.

He bought a book of the language, wasted the midnight

oil in studying it, grew pale and feverish; but by the time it was mastered we had left Spain.

We have said that Madrid is rich in her magnificent collection of armour. It is well known that she is equally rich in her Picture-gallery; and many a visit is necessary to appreciate its treasures. Few collections equal them; few are better disposed; but the rooms are badly lighted. Amongst these matchless treasures, we discover that Spain has had a past greatness, patronised the beautiful in art, and contributed largely to its development, founding a school of her own scarcely inferior to the best of other nations.

The gallery lies outside the town, near the east side of the Prado, a classical-looking building, fronted by a portico supported by six Doric columns. At the French invasion it was partly destroyed; for it is the glory of every enemy to destroy all that is beautiful and all that can never be restored.

After the invasion it remained half-ruined and neglected until the reign of Ferdinand VII. Upon his marriage with his second wife, La Portuguesa, Monte Alegre, a Spanish consul in France, was recalled and obtained great influence over the weak monarch. The palace was refurnished in French style with French rubbish; and its priceless pictures were consigned to the lumber-room. Here they remained until the queen removed them to the half-ruined building on the Prado.

The splendour of the pictures at once attracted the attention of Europe, the gallery was completed and became famous. Ferdinand obtained credit for the whole thing, was held up as a lover and patron of the fine arts, declared to be an enlightened monarch. But the only part he had played in the matter was to take the pictures from his own walls and banish them to his garrets.

The collection was begun in the sixteenth century, in the days of the Renaissance, under Charles V., who certainly loved and patronised the fine arts. It was an age when beauty was appreciated, though the shadow of decline was already falling. The fine arts were still things to live with—influences none would be without who could afford to have them. If kings patronised art, all others followed their example.

In those days artists were well considered, all honour was paid them. The guests of kings, they were treated with greater distinction than nobles. Genius was recognised as a divine gift, raising its possessor to heights even monarchs might envy. Philip IV. a century later reigned in Naples and the Low Countries, when what has been called the Second Restoration of Art took place.

And so by degrees the Spanish collection was formed. It is now one of the finest in the world, rich in the works of Raphael, Titian, Rubens, Tintoretto, Paul Veronese and Vandyck. Nowhere else are the splendours of the Spanish School so evident as represented in the works of Murillo, Velasquez and Ribera. In fact, Velasquez can only properly be seen and appreciated in Madrid, the gallery containing sixty-two of his finest examples. He is especially popular in these days, his style and manner appealing to the present fashion of working.

But Velasquez was a mighty master, who yet, had he not been so great, would have remained unknown. He conquered by the force of genius, and his pictures command a fabulous sum. Nevertheless, with the exception of a few of his works, in spite of his incomparable greatness, he is hardly pleasant to live with, although his composition, tone, colouring and technique, have seldom been surpassed.

We recognise his strength and genius when visiting the Madrid gallery, and wonder at the extraordinary energy and industry of the master. But nearly all great men have been endowed with unusual energy; and it has been said that genius is only another word for an infinite capacity for taking pains—a great mistake. Genius is surely inspiration heaven-bestowed upon the few favoured mortals sent to be a light in the world: the power of creating. Its possessors, it is said, are born to sadness and sorrow, and this too often seems to have been the case; but probably these elements are necessary to bring out all their possibilities—and who would not pay the price to rank amongst the immortals?

On the walls of the Madrid gallery, Velasquez certainly proves his right to the wreath. Vigorous handling and splendid colouring are his, rather than grace and beauty. He is true to nature, wonderfully life-like, but his subjects are sometimes very unpleasant. One gazes with wonder at the power with which he has represented the dwarfs of Philip IV. They are life itself, but revolting; it is the grotesque in art, and we pass to less forbidding compositions.

Of these there are any number of examples; and presently one comes to the generally admitted conclusion that Velasquez was essentially not a religious painter. Into his sacred subject he puts all his earnestness, but his inspiration is secular; the devotional and the spiritual are wanting, as they have been wanting ever since his day in the painters of all nations.

The spiritual appears only in the early masters. None but those who live a life of devotional contemplation and look upon their mission as sacred can produce the spiritual.

R

Fra Angelico, it is said, painted upon his knees, and one is not surprised at the result of his work. But the Fra Angelicos of art soon passed away, never to return. The spiritual has died out and there can be no greater mistake than to attempt it. The one who has approached most nearly to it in modern times is Mr. G. F. Watts. Sir E. Burne-Jones, with all his splendid qualities, could not paint the devotional. His faces are beautiful but wanting in soul. The strong, manly, earthly nature of Velasquez, too much in touch with the influences of this world, certainly did not realise it.

His earliest work in the gallery, the "Adoration of the Kings," was painted when he was only twenty years old; the grandeur and importance of the subject proving the boldness of the youth in attempting what was far beyond his age; the mastery of detail, the splendid handling of the brush, declaring his extraordinary genius. Everything is present but the sacred atmosphere; therefore the picture is a failure. So with his "Crucifixion": a subject many great masters have attempted, few succeeded in. Perhaps none has been more criticised than Velasquez. He brings immense earnestness to his task; his effects are genuine, his conception fine, his darkness real, the gloom impressive; there is a solemnity upon all; the drawing is magnificent; but the face bears nothing of the divine; the arrangement of the hair is grotesque, the picture is terribly unpleasant; again one turns away with relief.

On the other hand, in more worldly subjects he is hardly surpassed. Looking at such work as the "Surrender of Breda," we feel that here he is almost unapproachable. It is gazing at life itself. Of the numerous figures every one might have sat for his own portrait: Spaniard, Italian,

Fleming, each is endowed with his national characteristics. The countenance of Spinola, who took Breda in 1682, is wonderful for vigour and fidelity, standing out from the canvas a thing of life as he bends over his fallen enemy, Justin of Nassau, all the kindliness of his nature in his expression, all the generosity of a noble conqueror. Into this picture Velasquez has introduced his own portrait, and did well; a noble and manly head, full of dignity, gained in part by his association with Court life, in part from his innate character.

For much of his time was spent at Court. He was a great favourite with Philip IV., a constant patron of art, and himself an artist—in spite of all his social vagaries and shortcomings. It speaks well for Velasquez that he did so much good and earnest work in the face of all the temptations of the idle and dissipated life by which he was surrounded, but in which he took little part. His heart was evidently in higher things. Nevertheless, but for the offices he held he would have painted more and possibly have reached a still higher level. Thus we find that the religious subjects with which he began his artistic career presently disappear and give place to subjects entirely secular though never trivial. Where he paints the repulsive, as in the repulsive dwarfs, it was by command of the King, not of his own free will.

Some of the influences of his life were favourable to his higher development. As a child, his genius made itself evident. He loved Nature, and loved to copy from Nature. Later on he was much influenced by Ribera and such of the Italian masters as Spain possessed. Upon these his earliest manner was founded, always retaining a distinct individuality of his own. No artist ever lived who was less a copyist.

He was always essentially naturalistic, with an amazing freedom of touch; and in these Madrid pictures, nothing strikes one with more surprise and admiration than great effects produced by simple means. Nothing is due to claptrap elements; he was independent of and above them.

Everything about his work is genuine, earnest and sincere. Gifted with great virtues, he has scarcely a fault. His details are extraordinarily perfect; he was equally great in action and in still-life; greatest of all perhaps in his portraits: so excellent in these, one feels to be gazing at the human face, not its mere presentment. If he failed anywhere it was in the want of a certain refinement. His was a nature that could not polish. This was due partly to a want of imagination; and it is this very want of imagination which makes him so life-like: he could only reproduce what he saw. All his accessories, armour, drapery, landscapes, could not be surpassed in accuracy. His animals are as true to life as his people. His magnificent colouring is harmonious and transparent; but the sober tone of many of his pictures would not appeal to all.

Like many other great masters, he had three distinct periods. Rubens influenced him much in his second manner, for Rubens was living in Madrid as Ambassador from England in 1628. Yet nothing is more remarkable than the contrast between the voluptuousness and gorgeous colouring of Rubens and the sober tones of Velasquez, in which the sensual finds no place. He was also much influenced for a time by his studies at Venice and Rome; the latter bringing about his third and last manner, in which he returned in some degree to his first.

Velasquez married early. He was much attached to his young and beautiful wife, and this no doubt helped to keep him clear of the shoals and pitfalls of Court life. His father-in-law, Francisco Pacheco, was a great writer on art, one of the few true judges of his day, and Velasquez owed much to his guidance. His life passed happily and tranquilly, but he worked incessantly, devoting every moment of his spare time to painting—moments too few and far between.

He had many copyists and imitators; and many works in the various public and private collections of Europe attributed to him, are not his. Perhaps Velasquez was never more thought of and more popular than in the present day; for, as we have said, his style appeals to the technique and mannerism of the modern school.

Next to Velasquez the painter best represented in the Madrid gallery is Murillo. No greater contrast could exist between two great masters: the one distinguished for grace, refinement and religious sentiment, as much as the other excels in bold and manly vigour, breadth and freedom of work; the one elaborated, highly finished, as polish upon ivory, the other rugged and unstudied, producing his effects by the simplest means.

The two great painters of Spain were friends and contemporaries, Murillo being seventeen years the younger. Like Velasquez, he was chiefly influenced in forming his style upon the works of Ribera and the Italian masters though the results were so widely different. He also had three periods or manners, but they are rather transitions than changes, and the unpractised eye will less easily trace them than the distinct styles of Velasquez. The latter was more original, less conventional; more correct in drawing, perhaps really more true to nature; but he had not the innate refinement of Murillo, and altogether failed in giving to his Madonnas and sacred characters that air of purity and innocence which in the case of Murillo almost takes the place of absolute spirituality.

Murillo had far more imagination than Velasquez, and hence with the world in general will ever be more popular, as he is with the Spaniards, who think him the greatest artist the world has produced.

His genius awoke early, and when still a boy his pictures were sold in the market-place of Seville, his native town. Here he passed the first years of his life, and had already made a name for himself when he went to Madrid to study the masters in the Royal Collection. He never quite shook off their influence, probably because they appealed to his cast of mind, imitative rather than original; excelling in his own way but founding no new school.

Thus after long study of the two painters, Velasquez stamps himself distinctly as the greater of the two, because the more vigorous; with greater depth and breadth; whilst Murillo possesses a charm denied to Velasquez.

He was also less divided in his work. Velasquez passed his days at Court; Murillo, though encouraged by the King, spent little time basking in the royal sunshine. Well for him, perhaps. Velasquez had the strength of mind to "care for none of these things;" Murillo, with greater softness and refinement, would have yielded to unhealthy influences. As it was, after his one visit to Madrid he returned to Seville and devoted life to his art; painting an enormous number of pictures thoroughly and conscientiously, to the best of his power.

The Spaniards called his first manner *frio*, or cold; his second *calido*, or warm; whilst his third manner was only distinguished from his second by greater freedom of touch, a slight *mistiness*, with which he never could have been quite in sympathy, but wherein the influence of Velasquez is unmistakable. He also owed much to Titian and Rubens, yet his colouring is distinctly his own. He was particularly fond of a warm brown, found in nearly all his pictures, very pleasing and refined, so that we at once identify him. His colouring was transparent, harmonious and full of charm. The convents and churches of Seville and of Spain in general were his great patrons and directed him to the religious branch of his art, in which he excelled. In Madrid and Seville he is largely and well represented, but scattered about the world are many so-called "Murillos" he never even saw, much less painted. He had many pupils and many imitators: and it says much for the original genius of Velasquez, that while Murillo could be so closely imitated as to make the copy almost doubtful, a copy of Velasquez is at once apparent, and borders on the absurd.

But for religious sentiment, few pictures in the world, none in the Madrid collection, could equal the "Salutation" of Raphael. Few pictures have ever so closely represented the divine element. In spite of its having been much injured and restored, of having been transferred from panel to canvas, it immediately arrests and holds the attention as one of the great treasures of the world; that perfection in art hardly to be surpassed by human skill; a picture that, in one's possession, would be curtained, not to grow too familiar with its beauty. Before this one remains long, wondering that the spiritual can be so closely rendered; realising that in such subjects art has reached its highest and best.

There is much else of the beautiful, the splendid and the marvellous, in the Madrid collection; and in this at one end of the town, and in the Armoury at the other, the Spanish capital possesses two treasures worthy of many visits, much thought and study. But in these pages there is not space to enlarge upon the charms of the gallery; nor is this chapter intended to be a disquisition upon art. A perfect picture, like a landscape, must be seen to be realised and appreciated.

As for the Madrid gallery, we felt that the mornings of a whole month would be well employed in studying the best of its contents. Spain owes a debt of gratitude to those of its kings who brought these treasures together. Whatever their shortcomings in other ways, they proved themselves true lovers of the beautiful, and enriched their capital and country with a collection that has few equals. Thus in these two buildings the chief charm of Madrid exists, and some will say that it needs no other.

Therefore, as far as the town itself was concerned, we left no great regret behind us when one morning we took train for the Escorial, that monument and record of the past which once swayed so powerfully and so disastrously the fortunes of the Peninsula. The skies were grey, the landscape was half obscured by mist, as we journeyed in the heavy, uncomfortable carriages that special company delights in. Nor did we lose very much through that early morning mist, for the country has few fine points about it, though they improve as we make way. We are in New Castile, and in New Castile lies the Escorial, though described as in Old Castile. The plain is fertile, but not distinctive, until, approaching the Escorial, the mountains stretch over the country in fine, broad, far-away slopes and undulations.

At Villalba we found ourselves in a narrow valley, through which runs the little river Ulzama, reflecting the shadows of an ancient monastery, one of the many deserted ruins

PALACE OF THE ESCORIAL.

scattered over Spain. Through this valley Wellington's army marched in 1813.

This was our last station before reaching the Escorial. After passing it, the landscape widened, outlines grew broad and expansive. We looked down upon a great plain, bare and barren. In winter the hills are covered with snow, keen winds sweep over the country, the cold is intense and searching. Fortunately for us, winter had not set in ; though November, we still rejoiced in warm days ; even on this grey morning the sunshine made itself felt behind the clouds—a true été de St. Martin. This is rare in the north of Spain, and any hour might bring "pale, concluding winter" on our track.

Nearing the Escorial, we saw that the great building lies in the plain, or rather, upon the slope of a chain of mountains which fall away in immense, far-reaching undulations, whose outlines stand out clearly against a background of sky. To-day the grey skies only seemed to harmonise the more with the deep tones of the landscape, barren tracks and great solitude.

At the station, however, was neither silence nor solitude. No sooner alighted, than we were besieged by an army of guides, only to be shaken off with difficulty.

The village—more than a mile from the station—lies on the hillside, and needs a steep climb to reach it. There are two villages of the Escorial, the Upper and Lower—the latter near the railway ; the former picturesque and well-built on the mountain slopes, consisting of some three hundred houses amidst which the royal structure rises with its domes and turrets, a gigantic mass of yellowish grey stone, imposing from its size, repelling by its ugliness. One feels what a waste of money is here ; how beautiful it might have been ; what an architectural dream should have arisen in these sad and solitary mountain slopes at a tithe of the cost—all lost for want of taste and judgment. But it is imposing, as all immense piles are imposing. What else makes St. Peter's at Rome so famous?

The Spaniards considered the Escorial the eighth wonder of the world, and it was certainly an almost impossible task for this people to accomplish. Philip II. built it partly in memory of his father, who had wished, during his lifetime, to found a royal mausoleum which should hold all the future kings of Spain. Partly, also, in memory of the battle of St. Quentin, the accomplishment of a vow he had made to St. Laurence, on whose day the battle was fought. For this reason it has been said to be planned in the form of a gridiron—St. Laurence having been grilled over a slow fire by Valentianus in the year 261.

The Spaniards claimed for themselves the honour of winning the victory, but without his allies Philip would have fared badly. Philibert of Savoy, D'Egmont, Flemish infantry, German cavalry, and one thousand English under Lord Pembroke—these won the battle for Spain. The French lost three thousand men, with their colours, baggage and artillery, whilst four thousand men were made prisoners. Had Philip pursued his advantage, he might have ranked as one of the great conquerors of the world. But he was never a warrior at heart and delighted in peace. Even the crowded capital was hateful to him. His pleasure was to withdraw from the haunts of men, and he was never so happy as amidst the solitudes of the Escorial. His temperament was artistic, and it is strange that a man of taste should not have built a finer memorial.

The first stone was laid in 1563, and the last in 1584.

From that time Philip made it his habitation. For exactly fourteen years he lived here a life of seclusion, half king, half monk, wholly recluse, governing the world, not by his presence but by orders carried out by his generals and ministers. He died and was buried within the walls, exchanging the living tomb for the actual. The rooms he

PHILIP'S SITTING-ROOM IN THE ESCORIAL.

inhabited still remain as they were. Here he lived, and here the end came after a long and painful illness. They are bare and cold. An oblong room, paved with bricks, the walls naked and whitewashed, lighted by a solitary window looking on to the gardens. Here the great nobles of Spain, the ambassadors of Europe, would assemble to receive the orders of this strange but powerful monarch, who appeared never otherwise than of sad and anxious aspect, and whose intolerant bigotry often led him to cruel deeds. From this silent and chilling apartment he ruled the world.

At one end it opens on to two small rooms equally comfortless. One was his bedroom, rude enough to satisfy even the "Iron Duke," the other his study. Both are closets rather than rooms, and are lighted only by the larger room. The furniture he used—his desk, his gout-rest (he was a martyr to gout)—remains as he left it. A small room or alcove opens on to the church, in full view of the great altar. Here, when too ill to attend mass publicly, to glide in with his brother monks and take his accustomed seat in the Coro, he would cause himself to be placed, and here, in his last days, tortured by pain, he was daily carried, daily joined in the services of the church. In this alcove, looking on to the altar, he died on Sunday, September 30, 1598, at the age of seventy-two.

The last weeks of his life are a frightful and terrible record. His sufferings were agonising, and to these physical pains mental torture was added. As death approached, his vision seemed to clear to the mistakes of his life. Religious bigotry had led him to many acts of cruelty and bloodshed, and he felt that these would not be his best passport to the world to which he was hastening. It was the old story of tyranny under the cloak of religion. However justified this may seem in days of health, the hour comes when everything is seen in its true light. So with the wretched Philip, who nevertheless had acted in accordance with the spirit of his age and without violating his conscience.

But if Philip's own apartment was bare and narrow, he lavished magnificence enough upon the rest of the immense

PALACE OF THE ESCORIAL.

building. Seen from a distance, it is undoubtedly imposing. There is a certain majesty and dignity about it as it reposes on the slopes of the hill. Its situation, however, had one unfortunate result—it made Madrid for ever the capital of Spain ; there could be no longer any question of removal.

The Escorial sleeps, we say, in the great plain, on the hill slopes. In the distance stretch the chains of the Guaderramas and the Gredos—those hills that look down into Old Castile, as though protecting the romance and chivalry of the country.

As we approach the great building and examine it more closely, we are more and more disenchanted. Its style is bad ; it has scarcely a single outline or trace of beauty ; imposes only by its size, its area of about one thousand yards, numberless portals and niches, and twelve hundred windows. There is no look of antiquity about it to charm the eye. It is built entirely of granite, and is chilling in tone ; the blue slates and leaden roofs are crude, cold and commonplace. The style is Doric, but small details are swallowed up in the immense size. Above all rises the great dome, centre of the temple.

The enormous building had many destinies. It was a palace, a temple, a treasury, a mausoleum or pantheon, a museum, a monastery, has many courts and cloisters, many halls and rooms, chief amongst which must be placed the library, splendid both from its size and contents. When we entered it was almost empty. A monk—one of the brothers —was going round with a visitor, explaining the rich contents of its cases. His hooded cloak and sandalled shoon and corded girdle harmonised wonderfully with his surroundings. He might have been another St. Jerome—chief of their Order—fresh from study and contemplation. The

s

room is arched, beautifully subdued in light, a rich, solemn and reposeful tone over all. It is 194 feet long, 32 feet wide, 36 feet high. Bookcases line the walls, magnificent in design. The floor is of costly marble, and marble tables in the centre of the room hold cases of rare treasures—illuminated MSS., gemmed bindings, rare documents; the devotional books of Isabella the Catholic, of Charles V., and Philip II. Amongst them is a splendid Alcoran, and a Book of the Revelation which belonged to the Emperor Conrad. One volume, splendidly bound, with bronze corners and massive silver clasps, contained, in gold letters, the four gospels, the prefaces and epistles of St. Jerome, and the canons of Eusebius of Cæsarea.

The great central portal was formerly opened only to royalty. Through this, living or dead, it passed within the walls. The portal admits into an enormous court, on one side of which is the library, on the other the Halls of Philosophy, where the monks of old discussed and settled points of morality and theology. Near these Halls is the Camarin, once a cabinet for pictures, now containing a small altar used by Charles V., an alabaster statue of St. John the Baptist, an altar cloth that formerly belonged to Thomas à Becket, various instruments of torture, and some MS. writings of the great St. Teresa of Avila, that wonderful little town we shall presently visit. At the end of the corridor is the entrance to the church.

And the church is that portion of the building which most arrests attention. Passing in from the great court, where a few monks are hurrying to and fro, you find yourself under the flat roof of the dark ante-chapel. Above is the magnificent Coro. The roof supports the whole weight of this Coro, and is said to be a marvel of architecture. Philip II.

CORO OF CHURCH.

would not believe it safe, and ordered Herrara, the architect of the Escorial, to support it with a centre column. Herrara constructed a column of paper, and the king, jumping upon the floor of the Coro, was satisfied. Presently the paper column disappeared, but the king is said never to have noticed its absence.

The Coro is large and magnificent. The dark, rich-looking stalls—one hundred and twenty-four in number—are carved out of seven sorts of wood. At one end is the great lectern on which stand choir-books no one man could move. There are five frescoes representing the martyrdom of St. Laurence and the history of St. Jerome. A matchless rock crystal chandelier is suspended from the ceiling, brought from Milan in the seventeenth century. Behind the Coro we were shown the famous white marble image of the Saviour, given to Philip by the Grand Duke of Florence, and said to have been carried from Barcelona on men's shoulders. It is the work of Benvenuto Cellini, sculptured in 1562, but was disappointing.

In the Coro alto are the two hundred and eighteen books of the choir, some of them of parchment, illuminated by Andreas de Leon. Here Philip II. would take his seat with his brother monks—a long string of grave, silent, cowled men who had forsaken the world. Here they would enter, a long procession of one hundred and twenty-four figures, and silently join in the mass, able to look over into the chapel below. Here, it is said, Philip was kneeling when he received news of the Battle of Lepanto—that tremendous victory which was to decide whether Europe should fall into the hands of the infidels, or they give place to the Christians. Philip, it is affirmed, heard the news unmoved, and remained in his place until mass was over.

The chapel itself is full of solemnity, quiet and simple. No trivial ornament offends the eye, no tinselled altar. You pass out into an enormous and impressive building, 320 feet long, 230 feet wide, 320 feet high. In some respects it is more imposing than St. Paul's, because less distributed into aisles and arches. In its conception, it is undoubtedly the crowning-point of the Escorial. There is a majesty about it due to its fine porportions, for its architecture, like that of St. Paul's, is more fitted to a heathen than a Christian temple.

This sense of proportion is at once felt. The pavement, of black and white marble, is very effective. The magnificent high altar is reached by a flight of red marble steps. Marble, varied and costly, enters into the whole interior decoration. It is a vast space, in which one's footsteps are lost. One cannot but feel admiration for Philip II., who, whatever he might have denied himself, was unsparing of magnificence in other ways. We marvel that so mighty a building should exist in this far-away mountain retreat.

Near it is the great marble staircase leading down to the tombs of the kings—the Pantheon—a staircase so florid and decorative that it might conduct to a banqueting-hall rather than a death-chamber.

The room itself, not very large, is octagonal. It is gorgeous and splendid with marble and gilt bronze; jasper, porphyry, and other precious compositions mingling their colours. The atmosphere is silent, subdued and solemn from its destination. In the eight sides are twenty-six niches, where repose, visible to the eye, the magnificent black marble sarcophagi containing the kings of Spain, the reigning queens, and the mothers of kings. There is a fine but simple crucifix by Pedro Tacca. Every sarcophagus bears the name of its owner in gilt letters. The chamber is placed exactly under the high altar, so that the officiating priest elevates the Host immediately above it. The niches are nearly full. When there is room for no more, one

A SPANISH GARDEN, NEAR THE ESCORIAL.

wonders what will happen. Will it mark an epoch in the history of Spain? Will the country cease to exist, absorbed into other nations? Or, on the other hand, will it spring into new life and vigour, begin a long and illustrious career, and become once more great amongst the people of the earth? If so, a new and larger Pantheon must be built, tomb-house of the kings to be.

Philip II. had nothing to do with this gorgeous chamber. He had built the Escorial as a monument to his father, but the actual tomb itself was nothing but a plain vault. Then came Philip III., his silly son, who began the Pantheon, and it was completed by Philip IV.

On their way to the Escorial the royal bodies rest the first night at Galapagar, a village high up in the mountains, four thousand feet above the level of the sea. Here, the next morning, an officer of state approaches the coffin and asks if it is the royal pleasure to move on. Silence gives consent. A ghastly ceremonial, reminding one that in death, king and peasant are equal.

The Escorial itself is nearly three thousand feet above the sea, and was built out of the granite mountain on which it stands. Even amidst such mighty surroundings it looks huge and imposing, an enormous mass of grey-stone work, strongly contrasting with the barren slopes that surround it on all sides. Only where the village lies is to be found a handful of verdure and cultivation.

On first arriving at the station we had walked up the steep slope through a splendid avenue of trees. The omnibuses, with their freights, struggled round by the roadway, thinking it hard work in spite of the efforts of their four horses. We had escaped the guides, who are more or less unnecessary, but in the centre of the avenue found one so quiet and "unpersisting," that we had not the heart to refuse him. He spoke English, and was useful in guiding us systematically through the intricacies of the great building.

At the village we found the inn, primitive yet not uncomfortable. Upstairs, a really good table-d'hôte déjeuner was going on. Behind a counter two Spanish females dispensed their bounties, adorned with raven tresses and flashing eyes. The assembled guests were a mixed crew of various nations,

ARCHWAY LEADING TO THE ESCORIAL, AS SEEN FROM THE INN.

and the waiter moved about with that gloomy and protesting air that is the especial privilege and characteristic of Spanish servants. There is now said to be a newer and better inn. Opposite our inn, we passed under an archway on to a long paved terrace. On one side one wing of the building stretched away to a great distance; on the other a long row of picturesque beggars were seated near the wall. They seemed interminable, and we wondered how they had all assembled in this quiet, distant spot; men and women all differing from each other, all more or less in tatters. These were waiting doles from the convent. On the terrace stood a monk talking to two of these beggars, who were endeavouring to move his heart and extract coins from a probably empty pocket. They formed a striking group. The whole assemblage, indeed, was striking and singular, and the repose of the place, the gravity of the building and the grandeur of the mountains, seemed to lend a temporary dignity to the very mendicants themselves.

The royal palace lies to the east of the church, and is considered to represent the handle of the supposed gridiron. Sketch the building in outline, and with a little effort of the imagination it bears this appearance. The rooms are small, lined with very fine tapestry made at Madrid. The walls of four of the rooms are covered with extremely fine inlaid work, a gigantic labour of time, skill, and expense. The palace alone is said to have cost nearly £300,000. Most interesting of all were the elaborate frescoes in the long corridor painted in 1587 by Gravello and Fabricio, representing the battle of La Higueruela and the defeat of the Moors: copied for Philip II. from an original in the Alcazar of Segovia—which perished in that terrible fire. The crowd of figures, the innumerable horses and horsemen, the life and movement of the whole scene— all this is very wonderful and remarkable.

In visiting the Escorial nothing strikes one more forcibly than its silence and emptiness. It has become in very deed

BEGGARS AT THE ESCORIAL.

a gigantic tomb, a mere echo and shadow of the past. Its courts and corridors, palace and library, are not less empty than the bare rooms once inhabited by Philip, not less silent than the Tomb-Chamber. A living tomb it is to all intents and purposes; visited by a few stragglers from the outside world, who come and go and leave no more sign or record behind them than the shadows that linger in hall and room. Here and there a monk flits through the corridors, hastening on some errand of mercy, some office of devotion, some special penance for a trivial fault committed. Once the monks were numerous, all-powerful, rich in this world's goods, ruling with iron hand and narrow, bigoted mind, the destinies of Spain; tending to her downfall. Now on every wall is visible the word Ichabod. Her glory has departed. The coffers are empty; the council-chamber is closed, silent and deserted; the monks of old have long mingled with the dust of the earth. Records remain. Records of tyranny, of terror, of inquisitions; of secret midnight horrors, when prayers of agony for mercy fell upon deaf ears. These perhaps were never heard within the walls of the Escorial itself—who knows?—but within those walls dwelt strong men and firm wills and sinister purposes, that held in their hands the guiding of human destinies, even though separated by leagues and seas and kingdoms. All is over; everything perishes and comes to an end. The evil that men do lives after them; but they with their little brief authority pass like meteors across the sky, and die out, and are no more seen. Tibni dies and Omri reigns. Every dispensation has a similar record, every son of Adam must go through the same experience.

Here, too, very emphatically, within these silent walls of

the Escorial, where the shadows and echoes of the past confront one at every step; where picturesque monks still move through the corridors like ghosts with silent footsteps; where the kings come to sleep their last sleep, and take their last long rest; here in this wonderful and mystery-laden atmosphere dwells much of the ROMANCE OF SPAIN.

CHAPTER X.

The Tomb-Palace—Secluded monks—An invisible college—Scene changes—Toledo—A hasty journey—The Russian count—H. C.'s successor—Luxury of grief—A choice luncheon—A vision of the plain—Bridge of Alcantara—New inn—Serenade—Spanish love-songs—Lady Maria again—Flirtation—In the dining-room—Shooting party—Curious apparition—Ancient Briton—Drinking healths—Going out in the darkness—First impressions—A late chemist—The great square—Old arcades—Outlines of Alcazar—A *cul-de-sac*—Shudderings—Room of the Secret Inquisition—In front of cathedral—Dim outlines—In the cloisters—Haunted—The archbishop—Deserted streets—Lost again—No watchman to the rescue—Black vacancy—Old square again—Midnight and total eclipse—H. C.'s terror—Toledo by daylight—Disappointing—Wynds and steeps—Moorish traces—Cervantes' courtyard—A bit of Old Toledo—Santa Cruz—Given over to the students—Cells—Young demons—Puerta del Sol—Nunnery of Santiago—Puerta Visagra—Two sets of walls—La Cava—San Servando—Wild slopes of the Tagus—A small hermitage—Bridge of San Martin—A fine view—Departed glory.

WE turned our backs upon the Escorial and felt we were leaving a silent world full of the ghosts and shadows of the past. Having still some time on our hands, we wandered over the sombre hills and undulations.

Far as the eye can reach, nothing appears but green and rocky country, excepting when, looking back, we see reposing on the hill-slope the silent and solitary Tomb-Palace. Only in the small section of the monastery and college—closed to strangers—dwells any life or movement, and even here it is subdued. Why they keep themselves so retired it is hard to say. The monks or brethren are not vowed to silence. If you meet them in the corridors, they will stop and speak and freely answer questions; will show you over the library and Chapter House, explaining everything with a certain *camaraderie* of tone and manner very unusual in a monkish order. The college is of secondary rank in point of education, and one sees and hears nothing of the pupils who lodge and board in this mysterious establishment. Ask the monks why they do not show this part of the building and they reply that there is nothing worth seeing. Perhaps they are in the right. Within their own doors, safe from the intrusion of the outside world, they have freedom in captivity.

The train rumbled out of the tunnel and came up to its time, wobbling from side to side like a fat Dutchman. A long wait of nearly half-an-hour and we were off again. The outlines of the Escorial grew faint and faded, and we presently found ourselves once more in Madrid.

The scene changed. It was not long before we were again contemplating old-world outlines in Toledo which charmed us, though not as we had been charmed with Segovia. Toledo possesses ten times the fame and reputation of that fair city, and only a tenth of its merit.

At the last it was a hastily arranged journey, to save H. C. from the fate that had overtaken the French Count the previous year. When, many days later, we returned to Madrid, we went to the same hotel. Some would say it was a rash proceeding, but we knew better. Such human nature as that fair lady possessed is to one thing constant never. We felt she would have found her consolation, and so it proved. The very day we left there had come to the hotel a Russian Count—they are always Counts or Barons, these foreigners. He had small beady eyes, balanced by a fierce moustache which went up and down ferociously when he talked and ate, whilst his little eyes glared just as though he were grinding the bones of an enemy and enjoyed the *bonne bouche*. He was not on the whole bad-looking, and Russian fierceness is often mere outward expression; internally it is amiable, given to hospitality. He looked a gentleman, too, and we thought must be a real, not a sham Baron.

"There is your successor," we said to H. C. that last morning at luncheon. "Mark my words—if we return here you will find that Mademoiselle has transferred her affections. I shouldn't wonder if they become engaged."

H. C. looked depressed. He made no answer, but for a moment glared viciously. Had he been Irish or Corsican, we should have seen no more sunrises, and the Russian Count would likewise have fallen a victim to the rapier. But, on returning to Madrid all had come to pass. The lady was persistent, the gentleman susceptible; the bait took, and the great fish was landed. There were no tender regards for H. C., who was passed over without recognition. The pair were actually engaged, so rapidly had matters progressed. In point of family it turned out that both were entitled to a seat above the salt. The Russian was a member of the ancienne noblesse, not a vulgar parvenu. His future mother-in-law felt her ambition gratified, and her jewels and beads glittered more resplendently than ever.

But this is anticipating. As yet we have only arrived at the morning of our departure for Toledo.

H. C., sad and gloomy, threw himself back in a corner of the carriage, buried himself in cushions and curtains, and took to sighing. We crossed the Manzanares, and at one moment thought he would have plunged into its depths, for he put his head out of the window and looked down

T

with a sort of insane glare. But unlike Peepy Jellaby, where his head went his body would not follow, and the head had to be drawn in again. He was enjoying the luxury of grief, hugging it to his bosom; determined that for him all happiness in life should be over. This lasted a whole hour, at the end of which, the brow unclouded, he brought out from under the seat a small basket we had not hitherto noticed; opened it, took out a bottle of choice Lafitte, some delicate sandwiches of *pâté de foie gras*, did justice to both, and then saw life under a new aspect. The wound was healed, and Richard was himself again.

We travelled through uninteresting country, fertile plains without any remarkable feature or great historical interest. It took four or five hours to accomplish the journey of some forty-six miles, and we changed trains twice. Everything on Spanish railways is slow and deliberate, as though life went on for ever and time was eternal. Approaching Toledo, richness of vegetation distinguishes its famous *vega*. It is difficult to get a distant view of the city, for the surrounding hills conceal it, in spite of its crowning a precipitous rock some two thousand feet above the level of the sea. But within two or three miles the hills suddenly seem to roll back, and the town stands out in all the splendour of an impregnable fortress. The situation is very wild. The river banks are steep, broken, and rocky, and the stream running between them is now calm and quiet, now a boiling, hurrying torrent. Pile after pile of uneven rock towers upwards; the ancient walls circle round rich in tone, magnificent in bastions and gateways; within them a multitude of houses, churches and religious institutions. It is a mighty vision rising out of the vast plain.

The omnibus leaves the station and crosses the famed

ALCANTARA BRIDGE.

bridge of Alcantara, with its wide and lofty arch : a bridge guarded at one end by a gateway of the time of Charles V., at the other by a larger gateway, battlemented and semi-Moorish. Above, one notices the apses of the old church of Santiago, standing out prominently. Passing to a small walled courtyard where in days gone by swords flashed, and the shout of warriors and the tramp of horses echoed down the stream, we begin a steep, steady climb. On the left rise the time-defying Moorish walls, some of their towers and bastions dating back to King Wamba and the seventh century; to our right the rugged slopes lead to the plain. The lower town outside the walls is a vision of picturesque roofs, churches and gateways; a sharp turn and we pass through the ancient horseshoe Puerta del Sol, one of the most perfect examples of Moorish architecture. Our first view of Toledo gives no special impression; houses hem us in on every side; the rattling omnibus winds its way through narrow mazes to the great square, and soon after reaches the hotel.

Until recently Toledo was so badly off for inns that only those capable of enduring any amount of discomfort thought of putting up for the night. The usual plan was to leave Madrid by an early train and return by a late one, and with this most people were satisfied.

All is now changed. A new hotel has arisen, one of the best in Spain, which is not famous for its inns any more than its railways or the civility of their officials. This new inn has only a few drawbacks. It is so expensive that everyone on arriving should make an arrangement, especially as to the price of rooms: a usual custom throughout Spain; and one is apt to pay dearly for the omission.

In the large centre court, with a high glass roof and no

ventilation and some very great drawbacks, people sat and drank coffee. Round it ran upper galleries leading to the bedrooms, from some of which the morning view was very fine. Over the wide plain the Tagus ran its course, the silver stream flashing in the sunshine, whilst here and there a small craft rested upon its surface. Far away in the distance were the faint and charming outlines of the Gaudalupe Sierra. This was the view from H. C's. windows. From our own we had nothing but a vision of chimney-pots, ancient roofs and outlines. Each had its charm; our own full of human interest. At night lights glowed from the ancient casements that stood out like an Oriental city down the long narrow thoroughfare.

Late one evening an opposite casement opened, and a vision of beauty, faint, shadowy and refined in the darkness, appeared, holding a guitar. A lovely female voice rose in the stillness of the air and with exquisite expression sang some Spanish love-songs. There were impassioned parts when one trembled for the instrument; other passages where the guitar sank to a whisper and the voice pleaded in softest strains. This went on for nearly half-an-hour, when the vision withdrew and the casement was closed.

During the singing the sky had seemed illumined, the stars flashed applause; now the darkness was Egyptian, the silence that of the tomb. We were puzzled and mystified, wondering what this serenading could possibly mean, until we suddenly remembered that H. C. had occupied our room that day for a whole hour alone, pretending he was writing a long letter to his aunt, Lady Maria; whilst in the court below we were planning with the guide how to make the best of the time. He was making the best of his time by carrying on a flirtation with the opposite window; and no letter to Lady Maria was ever posted from Toledo. Hence the serenade. We enjoyed it from a refined and musical point of view; but the perfidious one for whom it was intended was fast asleep out of sight and sound, dreaming no doubt of flashing eyes and forward manners left behind in Madrid. The hotel lies four square, and his room faced west, ours north. But again we are anticipating; we had been a whole day and more at Toledo when the serenade thrilled the air.

The night of our arrival we were glad to find dinner still possible, and comfortably seated at one end of a long table were well and attentively served. At the other end—it was a very long room and the table stretched far down—a party of men sat smoking and drinking coffee. All were young, varying in age from twenty to twenty-five; and all were Spanish noblemen staying there for shooting and hunting. One of them was closely connected with the owner of the hotel, a marquis who had built the place partly to establish a favourite dependant; but the latter proving ungrateful, it was now under new management. One of these young men we say was related to the marquis, and we found that we owed a good deal of extra attention and comfort to his presence. When they left, the *table-d'hôte* fell off, servants grew negligent, discipline was relaxed.

To-night the scene was almost weird. The centre of the room was in comparative darkness, whilst each end of the table was lighted by shaded lamps. The Spaniards had one or two candles for lighting cigars, and these and the red shades showed up their faces in the surrounding gloom with ghostly effect; all were animated, laughing, talking, gesticulating, never still for a moment. Several were handsome, but only one looked intelligent. The others seemed to have no thought or wish beyond sport; their whole conversation was upon this one topic, on which they rang the changes with amazing facility.

Presently a waiter spoke to one of them — the more intellectual—who at once went out into the court. Standing close to the room door was a tall, strange-looking man, with handsome face and long hair, and a sheepskin garment slung over his shoulders. He looked like a resuscitated ancient Briton, tall, spare, powerful. His rank was evidently humble, but from his familiar manner with the Spaniard, he was as evidently privileged. A short, friendly conversation settled the next day's movements, when the two entered the room; the ancient Briton was greeted all round, drank to their health in a bumper of claret, and took his departure. His sturdy footsteps echoed through the paved court, and the interrupted mirth went on again. We afterwards found them polite and kindly, ready to do all in their power to add anything to a stranger's sojourn in their country, and it is only amongst such as these that true courtesy exists.

About ten o'clock we went out into the darkness for a first impression of Toledo, a darkness to be felt; even the outlines of the houses were almost invisible. The chief streets were badly lighted, others not lighted at all, shops were closed. A late chemist was putting up his shutters, and little streams of red and green light came from the windows. We asked him the way to the cathedral, feeling that there our steps should be first bent. His directions were complicated; but we presently found ourselves in the chief square, lighted by a few electric globes, where they shocked one even more than in Burgos. One expects these old-world towns to stand still, and we resent innovations; would like the inhabitants to go about in fifteenth-century costumes, with manners

STREET LEADING TO CATHEDRAL.

to correspond; but whatever towns may do, people move more or less with the times.

The electric light to-night was just sufficient to show up the old arcades round the square, leaving the interiors in gloom. High up, the outlines of the Alcazar were faintly visible against the dark blue sky and flashing stars. Every house was closed, the place deserted; we alone woke the echoes. Not even an old watchman was in sight, and we do not remember to have seen one in Toledo. They are always welcome, always interesting, these watchmen, with their voices breaking in upon the night silence; bringing with them a breath of the old world, which, with the shades of our ancestors, has become history, and passed away for ever.

We turned down the chief street. Not a human being in sight; not a stray dog or cat; no siren at an open window serenading the stars—or H. C., who was yet unknown. That came soon enough, as we have seen.

Then chance or instinct directed us into one of the thousand dark narrow thoroughfares which make Toledo even in broad daylight a complicated maze. Even to-night we had a slight feeling of disappointment, an idea that Toledo would not prove equal to its reputation; but we banished the thought as we stumbled on in the darkness. The street was badly paved and we were going down hill. In every archway a ghost seemed to lurk; the place was in reality full of ghosts: ghosts of all the centuries that have lived and died since Toledo sprang into existence.

Once, near the cathedral walls, where two ways met, we came to a standstill. Behind us was a short *cul-de-sac* with a great doorway at the end, and as we looked a shudder passed through us, cold water crept up and down our back.

What could it mean? What strange, uncanny influence was at work? Had a murder been committed there?

DOOR OF THE INQUISITION.

Were we standing upon the very spot where the bones lay hidden, and were we destined to restore them?

We knew the next morning. That very doorway, in the days gone by, had admitted the members of the Secret Inquisition. Tortures had taken place within those walls; the shrieks and groans of the victims had cried to heaven for vengeance, whilst the ghastly judges looked on approvingly at another turn of the screw or round of the rack, until death ended the scene.

To-night it looked gloomy and mysterious enough for anything. Silence reigned. Suddenly the great tongue of the cathedral boomed the hour, and we started as though all the ghosts of the centuries had spoken. It ought to have been the witching hour, but only eleven slow, sonorous strokes rang out. The vibrations died away upon the air, and once more silence reigned. No night bird had been disturbed; no moping owl—night's shrieking harbinger—flew out to complain to the moon—perhaps because no moon was visible. But the iron tongue had guided us. In a few moments we found ourselves passing under the bridge leading from the cloisters to the archbishop's palace, standing on the small irregular square before the cathedral.

Here only can we form any idea of the great building whose fame has reached to the ends of the earth. It has no outward beauty to boast of, and is so crushed in by surrounding houses that the sacred element is lost. For any sense of reverence and the fitness of things we must go to the interior.

The massive tower was dimly outlined against the sky, and beyond it an effective dome: the only two prominent features of the exterior. In the darkness they looked exaggerated, and seemed to touch the clouds. Details were lost, but thanks to the night the general effect was good. The doors, closely barred and locked, suggested the awful loneliness and silence within. We traced the bridge leading from the cloisters to the palace, and pictured the venerable Archbishop—primate of all Spain—passing through and pacing solitary cloisters and deserted aisles in the darkness, contemplating the fleeting character of all human hopes and plans: a thousand unseen ghosts whispering in his ear that great as he was, the wings of Time are never folded, and the day was not far off when he would be as they.

Under a sudden impulse we passed up the staircase and crossed the bridge to the upper cloister. Everything was quiet and silent, dark and gloomy. In the quadrangle below the shrubs were gently stirred by the night breeze, with such a sound as ghosts might make. The outlines of the large, beautiful pointed windows were faintly visible, and beneath them in the deep gloom of the lower cloister we heard the measured sound of a footfall—slow and grave, as though its owner were lost in thoughts of eternity. Was it indeed a ghost haunting these tomb-silences? In the darkness every now and then we caught the outlines of a tall, venerable figure, cloaked and hooded as a monk who had done with the world, its pains and pleasures. Afterwards we knew that imagination had not deceived us. The Archbishop had quietly left his palace to pace the cloisters in earnest thought; a frequent habit; perhaps to solve some problem from the Vatican, or weigh some new point in the Church's doctrine; or, it may be, to merely contemplate the much attempted, the little done in his short life, as in all lives.

Then the iron tongue boomed out again the half-hour. It was time to find our way back to the hotel, where the door-keeper was no doubt trying to think charitably of us. For Toledo it was evidently late beyond excuse. We turned from the cloisters into the almost equally deserted streets, and feeling rather lost and helpless, trusted to instinct. We soon found instinct nothing but a broken reed, as we passed through endless windings, in every dark corner of which the assassin's dagger seemed upraised and flashing.

"Here we are at last," said H. C., as the windings suddenly came to an end.

There we were indeed, outside the town walls, gazing upon black vacancy. Below us lay the lower town in darkness and repose. We listened for the cry of a watchman, but it never came; there was no help at hand. To raise one of the huge knockers adorning so many of the Moorish houses and rouse a sleeping inhabitant might well prove our last act on earth. We turned back, trusting once more to chance, wondering whether we were destined to walk the streets until morning.

Suddenly, we never knew how, with inexpressible relief we found ourselves in the great square, the outlines of the Alcazar looming out mysteriously. As we stood a moment —in joy at being lost in the wood no longer—the great cathedral bell rang out the hour of midnight. At that moment out went all the electric lights, with ghostly effect. Again cold water crept up and down our back in a hundred waves. H. C. gave an exclamation of terror, thinking his last hour had come, and his conscience was heavily laden with broken hearts and vows writ in water. It was not ghosts, however, but the praiseworthy economy of Toledo. A few moments more and we were in front of the hotel— closed and dark as the rest of the sleeping town. A porter only half awake opened as charily as if we had been assassins or bandits from the mountains, and never did belated travellers more cheerfully hear door close behind them.

The next morning rose bright and clear, and we went out with the guide for our first daylight impression. Toledo is too intricate in its ways and windings, too full of interesting objects, to waste time in exploring alone. Again we found ourselves in the great square, scene of our recent midnight adventure—picturesque with trees, whitewashed arcades, and green-shuttered upper floors. There are many lovely bits in Toledo, but we soon discovered that the general effect is disappointing. One expects so much from this ancient place, with its world-wide fame.

A great deal of it is modern and commonplace. The city is irregularly built, narrow streets or wynds being thrown about without rhyme or reason, steep and ill-paved, the greater part without any distinctive feature. Here and there you find a street of old casements, a fine doorway, or a front untouched; but these are the exception.

The wynds are so tortuous and confusing that at the end of a week one feels scarcely more at home in Toledo than after the first day. This was purposely done to perplex the enemy when attacked, make it easy of defence, and keep it cool in summer. The houses are heavy, often nothing but a blank wall with a solitary door of admission.

Many are undoubtedly Moorish, but the Moorish element does not predominate and is chiefly seen in the walls and gateways, of which Toledo may well be proud.

Though disappointment kept pace with our footsteps, we nevertheless felt there was much in Toledo to come for—an abundance of interest, a crowd of wonders; but each and all had to be taken distinctly and separately; there was no general effect, as in Segovia.

We stood in the centre of the square, admiring its picturesque irregularity and ancient arcades. It is historically romantic, often mentioned by Cervantes in "Don Quixote," and here the great writer lived for a time. The house he inhabited under the arcades was an inn, and is

CERVANTES' COURTYARD.

one still, and its courtyard is one of the most charming bits in Toledo.

A large square court, with doors opening on all sides: one the kitchen, another a drinking-room; a wide, fine old staircase leading to the upper floors, where an open passage ran round. Pillars upheld an open corridor above, protected by a wooden balustrade, over which Cervantes himself must have leant and thought out many a chapter in his great work. Above this again smaller pillars supported the old tiled roof which slanted upwards. Ancient wooden rafters, great beams black with age, formed the ceiling supporting the upper corridor; all delightfully old, centuries old, taking one back at once to the Middle Ages; everything, as it seemed, ready to fall to pieces and pass away.

Adjoining this old inn was a great Moorish archway, another of the best bits of Old Toledo; the house above it ancient and dilapidated, a slanting roof, tiled and overhanging, throwing deep shadows upon the white walls beneath bathed in sunshine. Above the roof rose a small open turret, the iron framework holding a bell. On each side were houses with ancient casements and overhanging eaves, and lengthened waterspouts like so many gargoyles, the whole looking as though it had never been touched for centuries. Here, indeed, was a little bit of Toledo as we had dreamed the whole town would be, taking us back to the days of the Moors. Through its wonderful outlines the old square formed a separate and charming picture, with its arcades and waving trees, the magic of the blue sky over all.

Just beyond this old-world vision on the right lies the splendid building of Santa Cruz, enclosed within large iron railings and great iron gates, founded in 1504 by the great Cardinal Mendoza of Santa Croce, and completed by Queen Isabella. It was first destined for a foundling hospital, then gradually changed into a seminary for boys and girls, and is at the present moment used as a college for military students

DOORWAY OF SANTA CRUZ.

boys from the age of fifteen— worthy successors of those
youthful heroes who set fire to the Alcazar, and probably

LEADING TO SANTA CRUZ.

danced before the flames. Since then they have been
transferred to Santa Croce, with additional supervision, to

which the birch would be a good thing well applied. We were shown two long rows of solitary cells extemporised just within the entrance; wooden erections resembling school cubicles. In these, refractory boys are separately confined, sometimes for days together, with only their work for company. A chair, table, and hard bed made up the furniture of the little room.

"Are they ever empty?" we asked our military guide.

"Scarcely ever," he answered, laughing. "The young demons are difficult to manage; but though they dread the cell more than anything, even that does not stop their mischief."

The portal of Santa Cruz is rich and beautiful with its double semi-circular arch supported on each side by two twisted columns. Through this you pass into a charmed world—enormous rooms or halls bare and deserted, wide and lofty, that in the matter of decoration have fallen into partial decay. The ceilings are magnificent, the whole place is palatial. The church consists of one long nave lighted by an octagon cupola.

An inner doorway admits to a large court or cloister, which also seems time-worn and neglected, a staircase of rich carving and splendid design leading to the upper gallery. Beyond is a second small court abounding in trees and shrubs, the exquisite green contrasting vividly with the surrounding arches—such a secluded spot as a Moslem might choose for his harem.

Passing downhill beside the garden of the Miradero, where every tropical plant seems to grow, we reached the Puerta del Sol outside the wonderful town walls. The gateway is a tower of strength, a perfect example of Moorish architecture, with its four horse-shoe arches. Above the arches is a

PUERTA DEL SOL.

blind pointed arch, and yet above this a lozenge bearing the ecclesiastical arms of the city.

A PATIO IN TOLEDO.

At our feet lies the lower town; a little to the right the church and nunnery of Santiago, where dwell fifteen nuns of noble birth, wearing the white dress and red cross by which one recognises the Order. It is difficult to gain admission, but the lovely patios or cloisters with their pillars and porcelain tiles repay any amount of perseverance.

In the church of Santiago—which has nothing to do with the convent of that name—is the disused pulpit of San Vicente Ferrer, but the colouring has worn away from its rich stone panels and delicate stem. The church has a fine tower with some remarkable brick arcading, and we notice its picturesque apses when crossing the bridge of Alcantara on our way from the station. Beyond the convent flows the Tagus, and all the surrounding scene is strikingly beautiful.

A little further on we come to the comparatively new Puerta Visagra. The ancient gate of that name is now blocked up, through which Alonzo is said to have passed when he entered Toledo in triumph. The new gate was built in 1550 in the outer walls.

Toledo has two sets of walls; the first, built by Wamba in the seventh century, forming the inner line; the outer walls built in 1109 by Alfonso VI., the walk round them one splendid record of antiquity after another. The city seems guarded with fourfold strength. We look down into great depths. The vast plain stretches far away to the horizon. Nearer is the bridge of San Martin, its Moorish gateways standing out magnificently. Close by are the baths of La Cava, overshadowed by an old ruined tower in which one still traces remains of exquisite Moorish arcades. This was once the favourite bathing-place of Zoraida, daughter of Count Julian; and here, when bathing, tradition says, she was seen by King Roderick, the last of the Goths, who fell

BRIDGE OF SAN MARTIN.

in love with her, captured her, and thus became the last of his race.

To the east, not far from a valley of grey rocks, are the ruins of the castle of San Servando, that in the thirteenth century played a great part in the history of the country. What remains of it is now used as a powder-magazine. Again, beyond this, to the north-east and near the bridge of Alcantara, are the ruins of the summer residence or castle of the Princess Galiana. Here, it is recorded, Charlemagne was regally entertained, fell in love with the princess, and she with him. Galiana was everything that was charming, beautiful and good, but a heathen. For the king's sake she embraced Christianity, followed him to France, married him, shared his throne, and proved in every way an exemplary queen.

Of this once magnificent castle little now remains but crumbling grass-grown ruins, a mere rubbish-heap where the street arabs play at hide-and-seek. One tower still exists. A small door in the grim grey wall led to the melancholy interior, a crumbling staircase to the upper platform from which sprang the tower. It is now inhabited by poor people, and a small child nursing a still smaller child sat in the narrow doorway. The room was black with dirt and smoke; yet they seemed decent folk.

From the tower the view was wonderful. Far and near we traced the course of the great river of Spain, romantic and wild, that runs in swift volume from east to west through the very centre of the Peninsula. Scarcely any country has the record of a great river so little used. Sad and solitary, it takes its lengthened course through Aragon and Castile, running westward into Portugal. Its waters are not navigated, its banks show little vestige of life beyond ruined castles and here and there a decayed monastery. Toledo is one of the exceptions.

We turned back into the little room whose grimy condition was partly owing to peat burning. The woman was neatly dressed, the children were well cared for. Her husband was employed at the waterworks below, as his father had been before him, in the first days of the works, a quarter of a century ago. Before that time Toledo was supplied with water brought in by donkeys. We looked round at her walls and suggested that here too a little water would be well applied.

"I have often said so, but my husband has no time to think of it," returned the woman. "The place is dark, and it does not much matter. It is a hole to live in, and I want to leave it and go into the town. But my man will not hear of it. He likes to sit and smoke on the top of the tower, and says he can breathe there—he could not breathe in a street— his lungs trouble him."

When we left the tower the spirit moved us to take the long walk to the bridge on the southern bank, past the waterworks where the good woman's husband earned his daily bread. It was quite true that until a few years ago the donkeys were the water-bearers of Toledo. No springs flowed from its rocky foundations. The Romans built a great aqueduct, but nearly all traces of it have disappeared. Then the Moors erected a great wheel which forced up the water through pipes; for they were a scientific people who understood a good deal of everything. Water with them was essential to religious as well as daily life. It has been well said that where the Greek put up a statue and the Christian a crucifix, the Moor dug a well. Here the water-clocks were made by Az-Zarcal the Moor, for the calcula-

GATEWAY TO BRIDGE OF SAN MARTIN.

tions of Alonso el Sabio the astronomer, and they became so famous that Daniel Merlac journeyed all the way from the University of Oxford to see and use them in 1185.

Amidst the wild and rocky slopes of the Tagus we found the hermitage of La Virgin del Valle: a small deserted habitation, now little more than a chapel amidst the hills; beside it a lodge, in which a woman sat spinning.

The chapel wall overhung a deep precipice of rock and bank, and far down flowed the gleaming waters of the Tagus. On the other side rose the wonderful rock crowned by the city, the massive Alcazar always towering above all.

We left the woman spinning and went our way towards the bridge of San Martin, now on a level with the river, now circling over the hills: passing through a wonderful valley of rocks, grey and lonely, where women were washing linen at a small rivulet, near them some picturesque Moorish mills in the hollow. Beyond all this, we came to the ruined castle of San Servando, and the projection that is said to have been the Tarpeian rock of Jewish executioners, and soon found ourselves opposite the fine old gateway protecting the bridge of San Martin with its colossal arches. Standing conspicuously on the very summit of the rock was the church of San Juan de los Reyes, built by Ferdinand and Isabella and dedicated to St. John the Apostle. Its north wall is decorated with the chains and shackles of prisoners liberated at the taking of Granada; Catholic kings and others, who sent them to the Votive Church as a thankoffering; relics grim and ghastly but interesting. From here the cathedral comes into view, and Moorish steeples, towers and bastions add to the marvellous outlines. The ancient city walls are everywhere visible, not stiff and formal, but winding with the pic-

X

turesque irregularity of the rock they guard; and taking
them as a whole they are perhaps the most wonderful walls
in the world, with their eastern tone and colouring. There
is also a distinct sadness over all, which almost seems the
very keynote of the scene; a sadness suggesting past days,
mighty men and departed glory.

We gazed long and silently. Then passing through the
old Moorish gateway with its horse-shoe arches and noble
bastions on to the bridge, we looked down upon the flowing
water and listened to its song; and to our ears the burden
was ever the same—a burden now centuries old: "Here,
too, dwells the romance, the true ROMANCE OF SPAIN."

CHAPTER XI.

Toledo—Past history—Present condition—Departed glory—Deserted streets—Closed churches and convents—Cathedral—Rich treasury—General effect—A splendid eagle—Interesting screen and stalls—Capilla Mayor—Cloisters—Religious and domestic elements—Santa Maria la Blanca—Wonderful interior—El Transito—San Juan de los Reyes—Chains and shackles—Old cloisters—Cristo de la Luz—Once a Moorish mosque—Toledo's strong points—Scattered charms—Moorish houses—The fourth Alcazar—Burnt by students—Sacked by troops—Rebuilding—A matchless scene—Stronghold of the past—The song of the river.

THE history of Toledo dates back to ancient times. According to tradition the sun at its creation was placed over Toledo, and Adam was its first king. Other sayings bear upon its remote origin.

The exact age is unknown. Toledo, Segorbo, Sagonto, and various other towns, were the principal centres of the district of the Celtiberi and Carpetani, now called by the more romantic and familiar names of Old and New Castile. They belonged successively to the Egyptians, Phœnicians, Rhodians, and Jews. Toledo is derived from Toledoth, the Hebrew "City of Generations," and is said to have been the place of refuge of the Jews when Jerusalem was taken by Nebuchadnezzar.

When Toledo was captured by the Moors, the city was filled with Hebrews, who revenged themselves upon the Goths for past persecutions by helping the Moors to victory. Their turn for persecution came also.

Ages before this, in the year 195 B.C., Toledo had been

taken by Marius Fulvius, the Roman conqueror, and the Roman reign lasted until the year 414 A.D. Then came the Visigothic Domination, lasting three hundred years, to be succeeded by the Moors, who reigned from 711 to 1492.

Before the Christian era, Toledo was powerful and privileged. The strongly-fortified city was allowed to coin money bearing its own arms, and was already celebrated for its "white," or steel blades. During the first three centuries of this dispensation it steadily prospered under Roman rule. In the year 400 the first Christian Council was held at which nineteen bishops presided. Succeeding Councils became governing assemblies composed of seventy-three rulers, who held their conferences in the Church of St. Leocaldia—now called Cristo de la Vega—and elected their own kings.

Enrico, in the year 483, founded the Gothic monarchy; but Leovigildo, in 586, was the first king to rule over the whole of the Peninsula, and establish the Gothic throne at Toledo. This lasted until internal dissensions put an end to the dynasty. Don Rodrigo was the last of his race he who fell in love with Zoraida whilst she was bathing in the Tagus, and by running away with her gave the final blow to his power. The Moslems stepped in, and the reign of the Moors began.

They were not days of peace for Toledo.

For three hundred years it was the scene of constant internal warfare on the part of the Moslem chiefs, who occupied it as a dependence of the Great Empire of Cordova. In 1012 the Governor of Toledo, a delegate of the Caliph of Damascus, revolted, and declaring that he recognised neither in Spain nor out of Spain other sovereignty than that of heaven, was proclaimed king.

When Ferdinand the Great died, his sons became Kings of Galicia, Leon, and Castile. Alfonso VI. had taken refuge in Toledo, where he was well treated by the reigning king, Yahyah. The latter had become unpopular, but Alfonso was liked. He was a Christian, Yahyah Mahomedan. The Moslems had begun to reverence Christianity, and the Moz-Arabian sect was increasing. When Don Sancho, King of Castile, was assassinated under the walls of Zamora, Alfonso, under the direction of the Cid, united the crowns of Castile, Leon, and Galicia.

Four years before this, in 1081, the Mozarabians revolted, joined themselves to the Jews, and appealed to Alfonso for protection. Yahyah retired to Valencia with his followers and his immense wealth, and Alfonso was proclaimed emperor.

Toledo now became the outpost of Christianity for the kingdoms of Spain, defending them against the Moslems of the south. This continued for nearly four hundred years. Twice in that time, in 1197 and in 1295, large Moslem armies besieged Toledo in vain. Next, in the fourteenth century, it was the scene of that terrible civil war between Pedro of Castile and his brother Henry of Trastamara, which the battle of Montiel brought to an end. Other quarrels arose. The Moslems had grown ambitious and dissatisfied, and the little kingdom was divided against itself.

Civil wars would no doubt have continued to devastate the country, when towards the end of the fifteenth century, Ferdinand and Isabella stepped in to the rescue.

Isabella, Queen of Castile and Leon in her own right, married, in 1479, Ferdinand, afterwards King of Aragon. They had come to Toledo in fulfilment of a vow, to found the Franciscan convent of San Juan de los Reyes. Here a daughter was born to them, afterwards known as Mad Joan. Their son, however, was full of promise, but his death just as he approached manhood changed the fate of the kingdom. Toledo was in a state of religious intolerance, the Christians had lost the upper hand, persecution was rife, and in 1485 the Inquisition began its horrible work under the bigoted rule of the Catholic monarchs. Victim after victim passed through that awful doorway, at which we had involuntarily shuddered in the midnight darkness. After the conquest of Granada, the Moors were expelled, the Inquisition scattered the Jews, and the town was almost ruined and depopulated.

This time it was final. From that day Toledo quietly and steadily declined. Even her religious influence she has retained only in a measure. "Toledo," says one of her historians, "has to-day become nothing but the archives of our sovereigns, the noble pantheon of our glories. Her great workshops exist no more—those laboratories from which Padilla was able to draw twenty thousand armed men in a single day. Political revolutions have reduced to nothing the rich revenues of this wonderful town, from which the clergy alone drew the enormous revenue of forty million reals. All classes have become poor, without a single trade or industry that holds up any hope of wealth in the future."

So Toledo has withdrawn into an aristocratic exclusiveness and placed herself in some sort of antagonism with Madrid. She is jealous of her rival. It is hard to serve where we have reigned. Poor and proud she shuts herself up with her sulky humours. Of late years, if there has been any slight lifting of the load, it is in the direction of improved agricultural resources. A little more life has sprung up in the

LOWER TOWN.

surrounding country, but there is abundance of room for improvement.

Through this town, so historical and ancient, so full of beauties, yet disappointing, we wandered day after day, trying to master its curious streets and wynds. It bore so many traces of the past as to seem a dead world; so many of the present that its chief thoroughfares were but of yesterday.

In many of the old streets we had outlines of Moorish casements, overhanging eaves, tiled roofs, and balconies of old wrought-iron-work that filled one with delight. The wonderful cathedral lies in the very centre of the city, surrounded by a multitude of houses, churches, and convents, once rich and flourishing. Now half the churches are closed; many are in ruins, some have disappeared, and houses have been built on what was once consecrated ground. Many of the convents are deserted.

Of the thirty-four hospitals only four remain, with a very struggling existence. It has been well said that "the voice of the Goth echoes amid Roman ruins, and the step of the Christian treads on the heel of the Moor:" for Romans, Visigoths, Saracens, Christians, have all reigned in Toledo, all had a long day, and left distinct traces behind them. The narrow wynds are solitary; carriages can only pass through the wider thoroughfares, which are few and far between, whilst immense houses, once the palaces of the rich and great, are silent and empty, or have been turned into habitations for the poor.

The cathedral is said to have been first erected to the Virgin when she was alive, and if this could be proved, it would stand as the earliest of Christian churches. Under the Moors it became a mosque, until Bernardo, first archbishop, turned them out. In 1226 it was pulled down by Ferdinand, whose religious zeal waged war against the mosques as Don Quixote warred against the windmills. The new cathedral commenced with great magnificence, and without a trace of Moorish influence, was finished in 1492, taking two hundred and sixty-six years to build. For five hundred years, one hundred and fifty artists were employed in decorating the interior, all the rich bishops in Spain contributed to the expenses; and in spite of plunder and desecration Toledo's mother church still abounds in treasures.

No other cathedral probably equals it in this respect. Altar after altar is decorated with masterpieces of painting. Tone, colouring, richness of decoration, beauty of composition—all are there: some of the finest examples of the Spanish school. Gold and silver relics are equally numerous. During those five centuries they must have worked with heart and soul for fame and heaven. The west front was restored about the latter part of the eighteenth century, and has suffered in consequence.

The building is planned on an enormous scale, and in the best style of the thirteenth century. Its architecture is pure Gothic, with traces of the transitions that took place during the two centuries and a half the work was going on. Almost all beauty lies in the interior, but the three west portals are very fine; the central doorway in the richest fifteenth century style, covered with Gothic ornamentation, figures of angels, saints and prophets. The great door itself is loaded with bronze embossed work, bearing many inscriptions.

The entrance most used is the north transept. We pass

through a splendid ironwork grille leading to the fine fourteenth century doorway, richly sculptured and decorated, and entering, look through a forest of aisles, pillars and arches, lighted by high windows, filled in with rich stained glass. The enormous size—four hundred and four feet long by two hundred and four feet wide—is hardly realised: consisting of a central nave with double aisles supported by eighty-four pillars, each formed by a cluster of slender columns. Capitals and mouldings are pure examples of French twelfth and thirteenth century Gothic, a period never excelled in architectural merit. The magnificent rose window over the west doorway contains the finest and oldest glass, a glazed arcade running beneath it.

Splendid as it is, the general effect is disappointing, without solemnity or repose, that calm and soothing atmosphere which we have already said is the first necessary element in a religious building. Yet it is full of wonders: in height and size overpowering; the pointed windows possessing extreme brilliancy and depth of colour, and dating from the fifteenth and sixteenth centuries. Towards evening the tinted shafts of light stream across the darkening aisles until one feels lost in a glorious rainbow vision.

Both under and upper stalls are gems of fifteenth century carving, crowded with grotesque ornaments, historical, allegorical and religious; details representing scenes in the campaigns of Ferdinand and Isabella, then occupying the attention of the civilised world: faithful records of the period. One special scene—the surrender of the Alhambra—might well have broken the heart of its owner.

The lower stalls date from 1495; the upper from 1543, consisting chiefly of single figures of saints, enriched with many details. The old Gothic stalls are influenced by the Renaissance.

In the middle of the Coro stands the lectern: perhaps the finest brass eagle in existence, fighting, with outstretched wings, a dragon under its feet; for eyes it has large red stones that glow like fire, and stands upon a great canopied pedestal bearing many statues, the twelve apostles amongst them. Six lions carry the whole.

In front of the lectern is a black wooden image of the Virgin, of great antiquity. The screen round the Coro, external and internal, is of extreme interest and merit. The nave screen consists of an arcade filled with rich tracery. There are also many brass and iron screens, some massive and bold, but not rich in the delicate details that charm most in ironwork. The nave has no triforium, but a middle-pointed clerestory. The chancel has a low triforium with cinquefoil arches and coupled shafts, beautiful and effective. Beneath the chancel is a crypt containing the remains of St. Ursula.

The chapels seem countless, and the Capilla Mayor is large enough to form a church. Enclosed by a splendid ironwork screen, it contains many royal tombs, including that of Alonzo VII. Cardinal Mendoza also lies here; that prelate who was called Tertius Rex, and so influenced Ferdinand and Isabella as to virtually share their throne.

In the Chapel de los Reyes Nuevos repose many kings and queens, including Catalina, wife of Enrique III., and daughter of our own John of Gaunt—that prince of whom it was written that " Hell felt itself defiled by his presence."

The Chapel of San Ildefonso is interesting in its rich Gothic influence, middle-pointed and elaborate: a saint who was Archbishop of Toledo, and died in 617. The Virgin is

EAST END OF CATHEDRAL.

said to have appeared to him in his lifetime, and to this Toledo owed all its ecclesiastical greatness. A Gothic shrine erected over the spot is ornamented with open gilt-work. Close by is the slab on which the Virgin's feet alighted, encased in red marble and railed off from profane touch. The stone around has been worn away with the kisses of the faithful.

Countless relics and treasures dating from the twelfth to the eighteenth centuries are formed of gold, silver, ivory, and rock crystal, many of them studded with jewels. The Gothic Custodia was finished in 1524 and weighs 11,000 ozs., whilst the cross above it is said to have been made with the first gold brought to Europe by Columbus. An immense amount of magnificent tapestry decorates the cathedral walls and chapels on certain occasions. The vestments are miracles of handicraft new and old. All these treasures the guides of the cathedral exhibit with a pride and fervour in which the vulgar hope of reward seems to have no place. Such at least was the evident nature of the delightful old man who took us from chapel to chapel and from room to room: rooms overflowing with gems of antiquity. The walls are decorated with works of the old masters, and some of the ceilings are gorgeously painted by Luca Giordano.

The splendidly proportioned cloisters are full of grace and elegance, gay with flowers and shrubs that grow tall amidst a background of pointed arches. But the tracery of the lovely windows has disappeared.

A splendid staircase leads to the upper cloister, also reached by a staircase from the Archbishop's palace joined by a short covered gallery. This upper cloister seemed a mixture of religious and domestic elements. Small doors lead to priests' habitations, and to those of one or two of the vergers. A woman came out of one of them full of household bustle, two small children clinging to her skirts. One or two little acolytes were playing about. A priest walking up and down in meditation seemed undisturbed by

CATHEDRAL CLOISTERS.

the domestic drama. All was crowned by a slanting roof of great tone and beauty.

One of the most interesting relics of the past, but at some little distance from the cathedral, is the Church of Santa

Maria la Blanca, in the Jews' quarter, built in the twelfth century.

The exterior is a mere barn, but passing down the few steps leading to the interior, we find ourselves in a new world: a forest of octagonal pillars supporting eight horse-shoe arches in each of the five arcades; seven ranges of pillars, forming five naves or aisles. The capitals are moulded in stucco; each elaborate and each a different design, composed of branches, leaves, garlands, intertwined with punctured fir cones, chiefly of the old Byzantine style. The ceiling is a mere support of rafters said to have been made out of the cedars of Lebanon, whilst the soil on which the church is built was brought from Mount Zion.

A certain melancholy air of abandonment and ruin about the interior rather added to its charm. The central aisle with the gloomy depths of the east end was a weird, effective picture, of which the keynote was mystery. The spandrels above the arches, filled in with arabesques, added to the richness of decoration; and above them, below the roof, was a wall arcade. In the outer court one still sees the deep wells at which the Israelites washed, and these are said to communicate with vast subterranean passages. Within a stone's throw run the rapid waters of the Tagus, and we look down upon all the wonderful view over Moorish walls, bridges and castellated forts.

Near this deserted mosque, this ancient synagogue, stands another, most interesting, less ancient, much larger and finer: El Transito; built in the fourteenth century by the treasurer of Don Pedro the Cruel, with much of the interior well preserved. The honeycomb cornice, recalling so many passages of the Alhambra and of some of the mosques of Cairo; the rows of Moorish arches supported by coupled

Y

shafts of coloured marble; the splendid ceiling—these features are specially striking.

SANTA MARIA LA BLANCA.

Passing upwards by Santa Maria la Blanca, the eye rests with a certain pleasure on the florid San Juan de los Reyes, which stands just above it. Here Ferdinand and Isabella intended to be buried, but their tombs are in the cathedral at Granada, with which city their fame is more closely linked. The splendid Gothic portal was almost ruined by the invaders, who spared nothing and burnt out the quarters of the monks, using the chapel as a stable for horses.

The west front has no merit. Curious and interesting are the chains and shackles of the Christian captives hanging upon the north wall. The interior consists of a single nave of four bays, the arches supported on columns covered with rich arabesques. Springing from the gallery on each side is an openwork rostrum like a small pulpit facing the high altar, with the initials of Ferdinand and Isabella interlaced. Here, overlooking the kneeling congregation and officiating priests, the Catholic monarchs attended mass.

The cloisters—once marvels of beauty—are still so in their exquisite Gothic outlines, the refined tracery of their pointed windows. Unlike the cathedral cloisters, much of this tracery remains, but they are being barbarously restored, and the once beautiful tone of age and decay has given place to a pale whitewash. Only when night falls, and the outlines are subdued, and the silvery moon pencils the delicate shadows of the windows upon the pavement, can we realise what these cloisters were in the days when monks and priests walked the silent passages, and felt themselves better and holier for the quiet splendour on which they looked.

Through a labyrinth of wynds in the heart of the city, to the Calle del Sol, and near its magnificent old gateway, we find the Moorish mosque of Cristo de la Luz—one of the most ancient and interesting objects in the whole of Spain.

Its date is uncertain, but it is the earliest of the Moorish buildings. Some of the capitals are Visigothic, and must date between the fifth and eighth centuries; probably old material re-used by the Moors in the building. The interior is divided into nine sections by four round pillars, about a foot in diameter, and from the capitals of these pillars—all of different designs—spring sixteen horseshoe arches. The vaults above are formed by the intersecting ribs, with charming effect. On the walls are paintings of saints of the thirteenth century, singular and primitive. The interior is very small, but remarkable, possessing the peculiar influence of all Moorish buildings—strength combined with imagination and refinement.

But the little Moorish mosque had to go with the times, and became Christian. Here, in 1085, Alonzo VI. heard the first mass after he had conquered the city, marching at the head of his warriors through the old Puerta Visagra. It was the first church he passed on his way, and he entered. The interior is only some twenty feet square, yet the work is so wonderful and ingenious that it looks much larger. Just a hundred years later it was given to the Templars, and to suit their requirements the present brickwork apses were added. Inside and out, the church is full of interest.

Thus Toledo is both ecclesiastical and warlike in effect and tradition. Towers and steeples are all more or less built of picturesque brick—without buttresses—with arcades one above another, with open Moorish windows, in which the trefoil often appears, and in which the bells are often hung, their graceful forms adding to the outlines of the tiled roofs above them. Most of the churches have apses at the east end. Unseen, none can imagine the beauty of brickwork such as this. The thin bricks have a thick mortar joint between them, and the result is a splendid and varying tone, to which the softening hand of time lends its influence.

CLOISTERS OF SAN JUAN DE LOS REYES.

Apart from this, the town can boast of very little general impression. Its charms are scattered. There are many old Moorish houses, most of them dating from the twelfth to the fifteenth centuries—houses chiefly built by the Jews and Moors, and by Moorish architects—all following the same plan—a long, dark passage, ending in a front door studded with immense nails, and a huge knocker, or handle. The patio has the usual open passages on all sides, supported by wooden or stone columns, and nearly every court has one or two wells, with exquisite ironwork. Most of these houses are undecorated, but a few remain of great richness and magnificence. Of these, the walls of the chief room are lined with encaustic tiles, like a dado; the remainder is plain up to the cornice, but the entrance archway is ornamented with foliage, arcading, and delicate tracery. The ceilings are sometimes rich, and of the massive *Artesinado* style, to which the great height of the room—often 35 or 40 feet—lends itself. There is a brilliant harmony of colours—an art in which none were more at home than the Moors—red and blue predominating. These houses give a special interest to Toledo, but, as we have said, they are few and far between.

Of the larger secular buildings, none were more vast, none so prominent as the famous Alcazar. Its destruction by fire yields only in importance to that of Segovia.

Toledo has had four Alcazars in its time. The first was supposed to have been placed on the site now occupied by Santa Cruz. It was the Prætorium of the Goths, and here Alonzo VI. took up his quarters after expelling the Moors. Another Alcazar was built by the Goths near a gate of the inner walls erected by Wamba.

A third was inhabited by Alfonso VIII. in the thirteenth

century, and much of it still stands with its fine portal. The fourth and present Alcazar crowns this vast rock, 2000 feet above the level of the sea. This was the Amalekite Kassabah, once nothing but a small fortress surrounded by ramparts, added to and embellished by Alonzo VI., and inhabited by Alfonso VIII. and his successor.

Charles V. undertook the construction of the present building, completed in 1551, and, therefore, comparatively modern. In 1710 Toledo was taken by the Portuguese, under the Archduke Charles, and the soldiers, helped by the German, Dutch and English, burnt the Alcazar and watched the blazing pile. What escaped of its magnificent panellings was broken up into firewood, and burnt in the military kitchens. Thirty years later, in 1744, Charles III., King of the Asturias and Castile, restored the ruin. The building was converted into an immense silk-weaving factory, of which the workers were paupers. Next came the French in the occupation of Toledo, who turned out the paupers, destroyed the silk-looms, confiscated the funds, and transformed the Alcazar into a barrack.

Not satisfied with this, and with having half ruined the city, Soult's troops set fire to it on taking their departure. This was completely restored, only to be finally burnt to the ground in 1886 by the military students, who set fire to almost every portion of the building, so that nothing remained but the outer walls. A certain halo of romance still clings to these walls, for here, in 1665, the widow of Philip IV. was imprisoned during her regency, and some of the details of her life closely resemble the life of Mary, Queen of Scots.

Once more the Alcazar is being gradually restored. Its proportions are vast, many of its architectural details superb.

CRISTO DE LA LUZ.

Once more its stables will be capable of holding hundreds of horses. The magnificent staircase—said to have had no rival—will again lead sumptuously to the upper galleries, immense rooms and corridors opening out in all directions. Its ceilings are being elaborately painted and decorated. The great quadrangle, beautiful with arcades supported on slender columns, resembles a vast cloister. But all signs of antiquity, magnificent colouring, priceless panelling, in which the Middle Ages alone excelled, can never be reproduced. The ancients, dying, took their secrets, power and genius with them, and they are lost to us as the centuries themselves.

Thus, right and left, north and south, Toledo is full of separate and individual points of interest, of unrivalled charms. If all these could be detached from their surroundings, and brought together in a magic circle, they would form a city of glorious effects such as the world has not seen, and will never see. Scattered, their influence is weakened and Toledo suffers. Only after many days do we realise that we are really dwelling amidst imperishable monuments of a time when men worked for art and perfection.

From the heights of the Alcazar we look upon a matchless scene. A great cathedral, which has long ruled the ecclesiastical destinies of the Peninsula; a host of church towers and steeples, proclaiming the past wealth and devotion of the town, rising out of a crowd of red and grey roofs. Surrounding us are the city walls, almost more beautiful and interesting than all else. From every point we see rising battlemented Moorish towers and formidable bastions, witnessing to the strength and power, and love of beauty in detail and outline, which ever distinguished the Moors.

These, in truth, transport us back, in the twinkling of an eye, a thousand years in the world's history. We lose ourselves in dreams of antiquity. Our gaze wanders over the wide plain, and in a vision we see Alonzo with his army of followers approaching in battle array; hear the tramping of horses, the wild shouts of victory, are dazzled by the flashing of armour, the glinting of white Toledo blades. The gates fall back and Alonzo marches through the city, halting before the little church of Cristo de la Luz, and entering, returns thanks to Him in Whose hands are the issues of life. Did the conqueror, even in that excited and triumphant moment, bestow one thought upon the beauties of architecture by which he was surrounded, and which remain to this day? Did the prayers and praises then offered up return to him in the blessing of an impulse bidding him be merciful and just as he was great and powerful? Here the oracle of history is silent.

Still gazing from the Alcazar, we feel that the scene is little changed. Centuries may roll over the face of the earth and it remains the same. The outlines and undulations of the everlasting hills are fixed and firm. Seed time and harvest, spring and autumn, summer green and winter snow, are eternal in their recurrence. These shall never fail.

Surrounding this wonderful stronghold of the past, we look upon the gleaming, rushing river; through the vast plains trace its silvery, winding, sometimes turbulent course. If the ancient walls it guards take us back one thousand years in the world's history, these waters tell you that, in their experience, this has passed as a watch in the night. It flows on for ever. As it ran in the days of the Romans and the Visigoths, so it runs to-day; its voice ascending as the voice of many waters. And ever, as the past grows older and more sublime, its song increases in volume and emphasis, and the burden is ever the same :

"Here, here indeed, in matchless beauty and in myriad form, dwells the romance, the true ROMANCE OF SPAIN."

CHAPTER XII.

Regrets—Early morning—The Escorial once more—Wild scenery—Avila—First view of the walls—A city of the past—Back in the Middle Ages—Melancholy inn—Civil host—Cathedral—Another world—Wonderful interior—A church militant—A 15th century Solomon—San Vicente—A Romanesque vision—Magnificent porch and doorway—San Pedro—Vespers—Dim religious light—An effective choir—Locking up—Overlooking the valley—Convent of St. Thomas Aquinas—Dominican brother—Interesting church—Tomb of Prince Juan—St. Teresa—A freezing experience—Welcome refuge—Philosophic watchman—Heretic also—The last of Avila—Night journey—Salamanca—Sleepy porter—Maddening bells—In the past—Old and new cathedrals—Charm of situation—Famous old bridge—Banks of the river—Washerwomen—H. C. for once resists temptation—General effect disappointing—Curious illusion—Uncomfortable quarters—Strange room—Grinning skeleton—Mocking laughter—Valladolid—Bearish post-office—Old square—Unfinished cathedral—Santa Maria la Antigua—Simancas—Curious little town—Historic plains—Mad Joan—Mediæval castle—Spanish archives—Old custodian—Quaint and original character—Face to face with the past—Golden moments—The imperishable Romance of Spain.

So, after all, we left Toledo with regret. As the train steamed towards Madrid, the hills again seemed to fold themselves about that rocky vision rising out of the vast and silent plain, and we saw it no more.

Madrid acts as an excellent foil to all these old-world towns. The wonder is that, so near the capital, many are so little spoiled. That modern atmosphere to which we now and again returned threw out all those ancient outlines in greater glory, as shadows bring out the beauty of sunshine. We felt this on each returning visit, and perhaps never more so than the day we left it for Avila.

It was early morning. The sun had not long risen above the horizon, and a mist lay over the land like a white cloud, which gradually lifted and disappeared. Our journey took us past the Escorial, and once more we saw the mighty pile sleeping on the wide slopes behind it.

Here we entered upon a remarkable bit of railway, passing through no less than forty-four tunnels. The scenery was wild and mountainous, and gradually ascending to a height of nearly five thousand feet, became almost sublime. Below us reposed vast plains, intersected by chains of barren hills, sheltered valleys, and here and there a laughing stream. With scarcely a human habitation visible, it seemed a deserted world.

Out of this wild solitude, reposing on precipitous slopes north of the sierra, Avila came into view, looking like an imperishable fortress, full of strength and dignity. Once more we felt that we had captured a prize. Yet few visitors seem to trouble Avila. We were the only passengers left on the platform by that morning train, and before we had been many minutes within the walls, quite a tail of little boys followed and stared as though we had been curiosities.

Walking up the steep hill leading from the station, we were again face to face with walls that have seen century after century roll away. They had not the old-world charm of Segovia, the crumbling, irregular, romantic appearance of Toledo, but were sharp and perfect as though built only yesterday. It was difficult to realise that more than eight hundred years had passed over them; and that, exposed to winter winds and summer heat, three thousand five hundred feet above the level of the sea, they had escaped the ravages of time and atmosphere. They are lofty and massive, forty feet high, twelve feet thick, battlemented throughout, with towers at short intervals. Of these there are no less than eighty-six and ten gateways. The walls altogether conceal the town, leaving nothing visible but the tower, pinnacles, and short spire of the cathedral. Every gateway is formed by two of the towers being brought nearer to each other, carried up to a greater height, and connected by a battlemented arch—giving an impression of great strength.

In days gone by Avila must have been impregnable. The little town commands the surrounding plain, which here begins to be fertile; a great corn-growing country right up to Leon, where you find yourself within a hundred miles of the Bay of Biscay. On all sides stretch chains of mountains, across which to-day an icy wind was blowing, tempered by the brilliant sunshine. No town in Spain so fortified, none so compact. It possesses some ten thousand inhabitants, and within the walls the air of a dead city almost adds to the charm of this wonderful little mediæval place, which has scarcely a rival. It is by no means dead, but so few people seem to go abroad, that in some of its streets grass grows between the stones. Silence and repose are its characteristics.

Arriving, we looked long upon the grey granite walls, regretting that time had neither toned nor softened them. Passing through one of the gateways, we found ourselves in the very heart of the Middle Ages of the world. But the charm here was not so much in outline and perspective, for many of the thoroughfares were almost commonplace and modern. It was in the numberless relics one met on every side. Houses with quaint windows; an immense amount of stone-carving; pillars and arches innumerable; churches almost more beautiful than those of Segovia—in the possession of which Avila stands out conspicuously above

INTERIOR OF CATHEDRAL, AVILA.

other towns. The present town was rebuilt in the year 1088 by Don Ramon of Burgundy, son-in-law of Alonzo VI., conqueror of Toledo. No finer site could have been chosen. It lies high above the level of the sea, a stronghold of the mountains, and in days gone by was important in times of war.

The walls were commenced in 1090, and in the first year eight hundred men worked daily upon them. The whole was completed in nine years.

Our inn was large, rambling, and melancholy, the landlord civil and conscientious. It was one of those gloomy houses that might have been haunted by a ghost or other supernatural mystery, and with such an atmosphere could not fail to be interesting. One felt it had stood for some hundreds of years and seen many dramas and tragedies.

The house was in the small square, opposite the cathedral. Not a creature was visible from the windows; but this, as we have just said, only added to the general charm and effect of the place. Much life and movement amidst these splendid monuments of the past would have robbed them of half their character.

The cathedral was commenced in 1091, and took sixteen years to build, as many as one thousand nine hundred men working upon it at one time. The chief character of the building is twelfth or early thirteenth-century, as far as one can judge. The west front is late Gothic, and has nothing remarkable; the interior is the marvel. To enter the west doorway is to pass at once into a world full of beauty, solemnity, and mystery. In this it very far exceeded Toledo and Burgos. A great richness and multiplicity of detail, magnificent fittings, all blended so harmoniously that the sense of repose was not disturbed. Lights and shadows abounded; here and there the gloom was solemn in the last degree; equally so the mystery. Over all was an exquisite tone: the pure colour of the stone of which it was built softened by age, and by the high windows through which the light penetrated; a deep claret, rich and warm, in itself a great charm and adornment.

BASTION AND EAST END OF CATHEDRAL, AVILA.

The narrow, lofty nave had a single aisle on either side. Looking downwards, the east end was lost in obscurity. Arches and buttresses threw deep shadows which faded in darkness. The clerestory had double rows of windows, broad and round-headed, with richly chevroned arches, but the lower windows were blocked, forming a blind triforium. The light coming only from the upper windows added much to the shadowy effect.

A great beauty in the church was the east end. Double aisles surrounded the choir, the groining of which is carried on slender shafts of extreme beauty; the pillars round the apse consisted of a bold single column with three detached shafts facing the aisle. The exterior of the apse forms one of the towers of the city walls, a feature probably possessed by no other church in the world; making it in very truth a "church militant." Amongst the many fine monuments is the tomb of Alfonso Tostado de Madrigal, Bishop of Avila about 1450; his effigy in carved alabaster representing him in the act of writing, the delight of the good man's life, who was considered the Solomon of his age. Altogether the cathedral is a refined, artistic conception, a dream building; perhaps only equalled by Barcelona, another of earth's rare visions. Amidst the cathedrals of the world, we place Barcelona first.

But Avila was full of dreams, turn which way we would. We never lost sight of the vestiges of antiquity; not in ruins, but strong, substantial, time-defying. Everywhere the high walls with their battlemented towers were visible; it was impossible to get away from them. Every turning opened up some surprise, if only an ancient church. It would be hard to forget our first view of San Vicente without the walls. We had just left the silent cathedral, and passing through the great Puerta del Peso, down hill to the left suddenly came upon the Romanesque vision: a pure, beautiful reality, tropical in tone, outlined against the blue sky.

The outward effect is very different from that of the

cathedral. The one is solemn and sober in colour, as though it had dwelt under northern skies; the other might have come straight from the plains of India. It is dedicated to San Vicente and his sisters, Sabina and Cristeta, who suffered martyrdom on the same day, in the year 303, on a rock visible in the crypt below the eastern apse.

The church is cruciform, with three round eastern apses of Norman architecture, and a central lantern with pointed windows. The towers were never completed, but are almost more beautiful in their unfinished state. They do not open into the church, but are united by a lofty pointed arch of magnificent proportions, which forms a sort of porch to the double doorway of admission. The porch has a vault of eight cells, and is of extreme beauty in its simplicity of detail and outline: massive and full of dignity, throwing into strong relief the richness of the transitional doorway; by many good judges considered the finest doorway in the world. It is double, with a small round arch over each entrance, whilst a large and noble round arch encloses the whole. Nothing can exceed this doorway in splendour of ornamentation. Statues of saints are in either jamb below the great arch, which rests upon shafts with richly carved capitals. The whole formed of beautiful and delicate stone, looks ready to crumble away, yet has remained solid through all the centuries. Here we have the perfection of an art lost to the world.

Strange that San Vicente should have been built outside the walls, exposing it to all the fortunes of war. But San Pedro is also without the walls, and is very similar to San Vicente, though not quite so dream-like and refined. Yet it is splendid and imposing in its simple, massive Romanesque and severe interior. All the arches are round

SAN VICENTE.

with uncarved capitals, giving a general effect of heaviness and solidity not often equalled.

We entered it a second time when vespers were being sung and the evening shadows were falling. A few candles upon the altar, and here and there in nave and aisles, intensified the gloom. The small congregation knelt near the chancel, with faces dimly outlined. A choir of women and girls were singing hymns, and their voices rang through the vaulted ceilings, echoing in the darkest recesses of the round apses, floating about the high lantern over the crossing. The whole building seemed filled with melody.

Presently all streamed out, altar lights were extinguished, shadows died away, and lingering until all but one solitary candle at the far end threw out a faint gleam, we were suddenly brought back to the world by a sound of locking of doors. Then we glided from behind the columns like ghosts, and intercepted the verger on his way to the sacristy. Ghosts could not have frightened him more, and he was only too thankful to shuffle back, unlock the door, and dismiss the intruders.

Before this, when the afternoon was still young and the sun high and brilliant, we had walked round the massive walls and looked out upon the surrounding plains.

Southwards we traced the course of the Adaja, a long, pale, silvery stream here and there flashing in the sunshine. Far on the horizon the hills rose in wavy undulations, where many a secluded valley lies in laughing happiness, watered by slumbering trout streams. People come from Madrid to these valleys and plains and breezy downs in the heat of summer; and in winter many a dark-eyed, dark-skinned sportsman may be seen wearily trudging homewards at sundown with his bag of wild fowl, having, perhaps, during the day shot down a stray wolf, left quivering upon the red-stained slopes.

In the valley to our left stood in quietness and seclusion the church and convent of St. Thomas Aquinas.

Crossing a picturesque old bridge and following the white dusty road, a few minutes brought us in front of the great building founded in 1482 by Ferdinand and Isabella with funds said to have been furnished from confiscated Jewish property. Long a cloistered convent, it is now also a seminary for training young Dominicans, who are chiefly sent out to the Philippine Islands, like those of Fontarabia.

A Dominican brother in cloak and cowl and sandalled feet opened and bade us wait in the cloisters whilst he sought a guide to take us over the church. We found the cloisters large and interesting, in spite of being late Gothic and poor in detail, but steeped in an atmosphere of silence and mystery. Wandering, we came to a second and smaller cloister, also extremely picturesque, and were looking out upon the shrubs and creepers that grew in the enclosure, upon the outlines of the church rising above them, when we turned at the sound of a quiet footstep, and our monkish conductor, keys in hand, approached with a salutation—a monk, subdued, pale and thoughtful looking, older than the doorkeeper, and evidently of greater authority.

We followed him into the church, as architecturally interesting as the convent was the opposite. The Coro is placed in a west gallery over an elliptical arch, an arrangement which makes the entrance solemn and impressive. The nave is composed of five bays, and this gallery fills up the two western bays. The Coro has seventy stalls in flamboyant tracery, with richly-carved canopies. At the east end, the high altar is raised upon a similar arch, an

WEST DOORWAY, SAN VICENTE.

arrangement suggesting mystery and sacredness, a greater distance between priest and people.

The effect was admirable, especially from the Coro, where one looked across at the high altar, with all the lower nave lying between. The greatest ornament of that nave is the tomb of Prince Juan, Ferdinand and Isabella's only son, who died at Salamanca in 1497.

It is of white marble, one of the most beautiful tombs in the world, the full-length figure of the prince resting upon it, full of grace and religious feeling : a great work finished in 1498 by Domenico Florentesi. Here in this peaceful valley, under the shadow of walls and fortresses in his day already ancient, the prince sleeps his long sleep, he on whose life so much depended, and by whose death the crown of Spain eventually passed to Austria.

We left it all and turned towards the town, passing on our way the Carmelite convent and church, containing relics of St. Teresa and the tomb of her brother, Lorenzo de Cepeda. An apple-tree in the nunnery garden is said to have been planted by her. She was born in Avila, where a church is erected over her birthplace. From the age of seven her ambition was to go to Africa and suffer martyrdom. At the age of twenty she became a nun and founded seventeen convents of barefooted Carmelites. She died on the 4th of October, 1582, and is one of the leading saints in the Spanish calendar.

Our stay in Avila was numbered by hours. Having no conception of its splendours, we had formed our plans, and arriving in the morning, left late at night. Gladly would we have devoted days to this charmed atmosphere, which, like Segovia, is a rare treasure-house. Many an old palace reposes in silent dignity ; every street has a relic of the

Middle Ages to redeem the prosy atmosphere of to-day; its churches are marvellously well placed, and in close contact with the magnificent walls, form unfading pictures in the memory.

But we had other experiences in Avila.

The sun went down whilst we were listening to the sweet voices of the choir in San Pedro. An intense coldness had crept through the aisles, keen as though we had suddenly passed to Siberia. This proved nothing to the cold on leaving the church. Darkness had fallen and a wind blew sharp and cutting. A great-coat, and over that a thick rug, made no difference whatever; it penetrated through all. The blast rushes over the snow-capped Sierra, and crosses this little town three thousand five hundred feet above sea-level. Many of the inhabitants looked pale, sickly and consumptive, and no wonder. Midday had been glorious summer, this was worse than the bitterest winter we had ever felt. It rushed through the narrow streets, and the poor Spaniards, men, women and children, shivered as they drew their cloaks about them. The children, for the most part having no cloak to draw, looked pinched and miserable. Soon not a soul was to be seen.

We gladly turned into the hotel at the dinner-hour, and never was scalding soup more acceptable. The room was ill-lighted, the appointments were rough, the few people at table were rough also, the savoury meats appealed to anyone rather than to Englishmen, the waiters were clumsy and stupid. Yet we were thankful for the shelter. The food was ambrosia, and the poor wine was the truest nectar, restoring one's frozen circulation and bringing one back to life.

After this we braved the elements once more, wandered about, and revelled in the old-world outlines of cathedral, churches, walls, gateways, and palaces, now wrapped in all the mystery of night.

From the darkness presently a lantern gleamed, a tall form clothed in what looked like a dozen great-coats loomed out; a deep voice called the hour and the weather. We had found another old watchman, who altogether harmonised with the scene, and apparently we had the world to ourselves. The hour was growing late; everyone in Avila seemed to have gone to rest. At the first moment he turned his light upon us and looked suspiciously, wondering perhaps whether we were brigands from the neighbouring hills. We could not be mistaken for anything but men of peace, and the flash was withdrawn.

"A cold night, noble sirs, to be out in. I see you are strangers," said this Diogenes.

"And strangers we would remain, if this is a specimen of your climate."

"A fair specimen of what we must go through for the rest of the winter," said the watchman. "Presently it will be worse than this, though to-night is keen. As you see, I am well clothed, or I could not play the watchman."

"But surely you are not wanted in this small town? These walls must be sufficient safeguard against the powers of darkness?"

"I am of that opinion, but proclaim it not," said Diogenes. "Why should I cry down my occupation, and so play the part of a fool? It is an ancient custom, worshipful gentlemen, and the town will have it so. There might be occasions, too——"

"Such as to-night, when you come upon two prowlers, and flash your light upon them."

"I crave your highnesses' pardon," returned our watchman, who seemed to possess the Spaniard's love for titles. "In truth, this is a quiet town, and seldom do I meet friend or foe on such a night. One would not turn out a dog in it, and that anyone should be abroad for pleasure——"

"Passes man's comprehension. But, good Diogenes, we are men of peace, whilst thou art a mighty man of valour Administer to thyself something warm and comforting"—slipping a silver charm into his capacious palm, whilst a ruder blast than ever caused us all to shiver. "Surely, Avila possesses few such sons, and it behoves you to be careful of your life."

"Your highnesses are noble indeed," returned Diogenes. "Would that I could more often flash my light upon such wanderers. If I were a devout Catholic I would burn a candle and say a prayer to St. Teresa in your honour. But, alas! they tell me I am no better than a heathen, because I will not believe in candles and relics—a finger of San Salvador, a toe of St. Nicholas. Santa Maria! There is my religion"--pointing to the sky and the stars-- "and I say a prayer as I walk the streets in the night hours to Him Who made the world. I don't believe in priests, saints, and incense—and so they call me heretic."

We were standing near the wonderful church of San Vicente, which rose a black mass against the night sky, a halo of romance surrounding its faint outlines, of which we knew the full beauty and splendour. Beyond, towered the walls with one of the massive gateways, of which we could dimly trace the battlements. The old watchman—one of the biggest men we had ever seen—came into these surroundings with a touch of life that harmonised with them to perfection. He bade us good-night, a fair voyage, and a return to Avila, and we watched him slowly move away with footsteps that ought to have made the earth tremble, his voice rolling like a diapason as he disappeared down the echoing streets.

Then we ourselves turned in the opposite direction, and passing near the ecclesiastical bastion crossed the quiet cathedral square. Up came the hotel omnibus, lamps gleamed and flashed. The scene was weird and telling, but we were glad to escape inside from the cutting blast. Two passengers honoured us; one, an officer of some sort in uniform, the other, the postman in charge of the mail-bags. The door was closed; the civil landlord attended us to the last, wished us a good voyage, and begged the favour of our recommendation. With a sound of artillery we rattled through the streets, passed beyond the walls, and down the steep hill.

At the station a small crowd of rough country people waited, with not a feature of interest about them. Keen as ever was the wind as we stood in patience, and with joy at length saw a fiery red eye looming out of the blackness of darkness. The train puffed and snorted up to the platform, swallowed up all the waiting passengers, and moved on with its burden. For us, Avila was of the past, and we felt we were leaving a vision we should not easily find again.

We reached Salamanca about four in the morning. It was still dark, but the intense coldness of Avila had disappeared. The hotel omnibus rattled through streets of which we saw nothing. A sleepy porter, with electrified hair and shuffling gait, opened, after keeping us waiting whilst he made up his mind whether to answer the summons or turn again in slumber. He had just sufficient sense left

2 A

to show us to rooms, where we soon journeyed to the land of dreams, only to be awakened at daylight by a barbarous clashing of bells.

This was to remind the faithful that they must not expect peace in this world. The air seemed full of the sound of bells, as though all the churches had suddenly gone raving mad. The noise never ceased, and at last we got up, dressed, and looked out upon the scene. It was Sunday morning. In front was a small square, one of the offending churches on the left. We watched the bell swinging furiously to and fro, as though rung by a legion of imps. To us, who had hoped for a short repose, it was torment. At eight o'clock all the bells obligingly stopped for a time, their disturbing work accomplished.

Salamanca goes back to remote ages, and was an ancient city of the Vettones, but here, if anywhere, time has withheld his beautifying hand. Lying amidst the Iberian hills, it was supposed to derive its name from Elman, god of war. Plutarch relates how Hannibal raised its siege, and how the Spaniards, failing to pay their indemnity, Hannibal returned to sack the town. The men were to come out unarmed, but the women followed with concealed weapons, and when the plunderers rushed in to their work the women armed the men with swords, and they turned and routed the enemy.

The Romans made it a military station. Under the Goths its prosperity increased, and money was coined here. Next came the Moors, who were not likely to let so rich a prize escape, and very much injured it. In 1055 it was re-conquered by the Spaniards, after which for many ages the town had comparative peace. In the days of Ferdinand and Isabella it rose to yet greater distinction. Early in the present century, during the French invasion, it was

SALAMANCA FROM THE RIVER.

almost ruined; twenty-five convents, and as many colleges, were destroyed, their ancient timbers and carved panels serving as firewood. What Salamanca might have been but for this, it is difficult to say. Wellington came, but too late to save it. Four miles out of the town the famous battle was fought on the 22nd of July, 1812. In that battle the French lost twelve thousand men, the Allies five thousand, of whom three thousand were English. It was said that "Wellington defeated forty thousand men in forty minutes." He was made a marquis, and a sum of £100,000 was given to him to purchase estates. The French lost heart. Soult raised the siege of Cadiz and forsook the south of Spain. Napoleon was with his armies in Russia, and he, superstitious with all his courage, began to lose heart also and to think that the tide of his fortunes had turned—as indeed it had.

In early days Salamanca was governed by a Rector, who held the office for one year with despotic power. As a university town it was most flourishing in the fourteenth century, when it had ten thousand students. In the sixteenth century it numbered only five thousand. At the French invasion it suffered still more, and now has only about one thousand four hundred. At Salamanca the cruel and bigoted Philip II. married Maria of Portugal in 1543, and few envied the unhappy queen.

Salamanca of to-day is not that of the past. Its streets are uninteresting, though it has many a fine old bit, and some large and important buildings, most of them in a bad Renaissance style. One of the most interesting is the house of the shells, with quaint windows and ancient ironwork. The two cathedrals are imposing—the old and the new—the one small and compact, the other somewhat overpowering in size; the one an architectural gem, the other extremely disappointing.

HOUSE OF THE SHELLS, SALAMANCA.

The old cathedral was founded in the twelfth century, soon after the town had been retaken from the Moors; the new cathedral dates from the sixteenth. The one adjoins the other, so that one party wall suffices for the two. The first was built by Geronimo, confessor to the famous Cid and his faithful Ximena, after he became Bishop of Salamanca. Mass was first celebrated in the year 1100, and in the new cathedral in 1560.

The older building is Romanesque, plain, and massive, and remains very much in its original state. It is cruciform with three eastern apses, and a beautiful and effective dome over the crossing, raised upon two stages of refined arcades, some of them pierced with windows.

The roof, of glazed tiles, is octagonal and rises to a point, a rare but striking detail. Outwardly this is raised upon arcades of pure Romanesque work, with a pinnacle-turret at each corner. The main arches of the interior are pointed, those of the windows semi-circular; the capitals are richly carved, and the west porch is deep and fine.

A flight of steps led up into the new cathedral, built on a somewhat higher level. To pass from one to the other was to leave an old-world dream for a commonplace atmosphere. The old cathedral only brings out more conspicuously the poverty of the new, which possesses no beauty and produces no effect.

Salamanca's great charm is its situation. Outside its walls runs the fine river Tormes, spanned by one of the famous bridges of the world, composed of twenty-six arches, and full of the beauty of age. This river, rising in the Sierra de Gredos, flows single and solitary for one hundred and thirty-five miles, then joins a second river, and the two flow in one broad stream at the feet of the ancient university town, reflecting its splendid outlines.

Standing on the further bank, the city rises majestically

above the flowing water, and the arched bridge composes wonderfully well in the foreground. From this point of view it is a splendid picture of dilapidation, age and decay. The walls appear ready to crumble away. Houses, apparently

HOUSE OF THE SHELLS, SALAMANCA.

in the very last stage of existence, look as though the first winter wind would bring them to the ground.

Above these outlines the joined outlines of the two cathedrals rise in fine contrast, anything objectionable in the way of detail being subdued and softened. One sees only an assemblage of domes, towers and turrets standing out clearly against a background of pure sky. Again we feel that here is something to charm; a picture and a recollection to carry away, unique of its kind. The almost tropical colour of the stone used for the cathedral and for many of the houses adds very much to the warmth and effect of the whole.

In contrast with all this is the grey tone of the old bridge, over which troops of mules with their owners in gay holiday attire—for it is Sunday—are for ever going to and fro. On the bank of the river a long line of washerwomen—at least two hundred of them—are hard at work. From a deep recess of the bridge to which we have moved, they form a line of wonderfully bright colouring in the landscape, and laughing, chattering and working, seem happy as the day is long. One of them looking up catches H. C.'s admiring gaze—given, it must be admitted, to the general, not the individual effect. She laughs aloud, passes the word down the line, and immediately about a hundred spring up, heads all the colours of the rainbow, shout him a good-day and boldly challenge him to the waterside. He wisely resists the invitation and is spared the fine.

Passing into the town, we come here and there upon picturesque bits of old and dilapidated houses, with red-tiled roofs and eaves and dormer windows, many an ancient and artistic bit of ironwork, and balconies where rags are hanging out to dry or flowers are blooming, according to the fancy of the owner. It is outside her walls that Salamanca is distinctly beautiful. Within, the charm fades into a heavy, lifeless effect, with a few mediæval outlines. Church after church is disappointing, street after street commonplace. At sundown the great square, with its arcades, is the popular promenade for all who can spare the time—a sauntering crowd. But the square is comparatively modern, which makes the ancient market-place, with its quaint and curious arcades, thrown by the sun into deep slanting lights and shadows as he travels southwards, far more interesting.

At the end of one of them we looked upon a most curious,

OLD HOUSES, SALAMANCA.

most dramatic effect. The long arcade with its pillars and arches reposed in gloom, and out of the far-off, deep obscurity a cross seemed suddenly to shine, brilliant, startling and mysterious, almost supernatural, as a vision from the unseen world. But the explanation proved simple enough when we passed under the arches. It was owing to the partial opening of some great doors, through which broad streaks of daylight penetrated in the form of a calvary, a little more opening or a little less, and the effect would have been lost.

Our quarters in Salamanca were not refined or comfortable. It was a curious house with various staircases and long rambling passages, in which one for ever went astray. Once we turned into a wrong room, which might have belonged to Faust or one of his followers. Evidently some-one lived here all the year round; the room was not given up to mere birds of passage. It was a combination of the domestic and the horrible. Photographs of people in public and private life crowded the mantelpiece and the walls. A skeleton grinned horribly at us from a corner, and as we looked and trembled, it seemed to rattle all its bones and glare at us from vacant sockets, and move its jaws up and down. "Such as I am, so will ye be!" These awful words seemed to ring out from that voiceless throat and float about the room. On the table was a death's head and cross-bones, and near them an open book. Was this the abode of another St. Jerome, contemplating death and mutability in the midst of life? But St. Jerome would never have decorated his cell with photographs of dancers in bloomer costumes; and the book was not a devotional treatise for the healing of the soul, but a learned Latin disquisition on herbs for the restoration of the body. Evidently the owner of this strange abode was a doctor.

We made a propitiatory bow to the skeleton, and as we hastily closed the door, thought we heard shrieks of mocking supernatural laughter thrown after us by the awful apparition.

Into every part of the house and its dark corridors there

penetrated the horrible fumes of rancid oil issuing from unseen kitchens, where the chef seemed for ever engaged in unceasing labours. To our room they brought tea made with tepid water, and in the deep caverns of the tea-pot we counted exactly five-and-twenty tea-leaves. One morning, waking up in the agonies of headache, this decoction was produced as a cure for all ills. We desperately ordered boiling water, made a strong infusion of tea-tabloids presented to us before leaving England by a dear and thoughtful Samaritan — and convalescence followed. That pungent odour of rancid oil was never absent, and combined with the indifferent fare of the dining-room and the unusual stupidity of the waiters, made the inn anything but a pleasant resting-place. It had not even the redeeming quality of antiquity, or the atmosphere of mystery and tragedy that we had found at Avila.

Altogether we were not sorry to leave this Salamanca from which we had expected so much and received so little, and departed one fine day for Valladolid. Here, too, we had a right to expect much, for centuries ago it was the capital of Spain, and once upon a time it was rich and powerful; but unfortunately the period was architecturally debased—so perhaps, after all, we should again be disappointed. Still, we must dree our weird; it was written in the book of fate that we should go; and we went.

We left one afternoon, and arrived about eleven at night. The streets were in darkness, the hotel was closed, but a servant keeping vigil conducted us to rooms large and gorgeous in comparison with those we had lately inhabited. The hotel proved many degrees better in all ways, and was kept by civilised French people, who tried to bring the best of both countries into their management.

MARKET-PLACE, SALAMANCA.

Valladolid is an important town in the north of Spain, with a good deal of quiet movement about it. The atmosphere is not artistic, but commercial and uninteresting, and although the narrow streets are sometimes picturesque, the prevalent tone is one of neglect. Not that the people are poor, but they are thrifty; and having no eye for the beautiful, are indifferent to outside appearances. Like most people who work hard for their money, they exercise a wise economy; but they are not famous for civility, and the post-office officials were without exception the most bearish in the whole of Spain. On applying for our letters they demanded a passport, and because we had none, refused to deliver. We protested; they were insolent. As a last resource we appealed to our landlord, who thereupon accompanied us to the post-office, and to whom they were equally uncivil, but finally yielded to his formally written guarantee of our good faith and respectability; the whole done with an ungraciousness of tone and manner without parallel. We were told that the insolence of these officials was proverbial, and had much injured the town.

The old square, grand and imposing with its arcades, reminded one of Toledo and Salamanca, but is more ancient and picturesque. This, too, is the favourite promenade of the people, and here every evening they congregate for the daily saunter, without which mild recreation the Spaniards apparently could not live.

In days gone by all executions and bull-fights were held here, and of the two exhibitions perhaps the former was the less inhuman. Now they have built them a splendid bull-ring beyond the precincts, and here the people pay their prices and take their pleasure. As long as the bull-fight keeps its place in Spain it is hopeless to expect anything from the people.

In this square Berenguela took the crown of Castile from her head and resigned it in favour of her son Fernando III., otherwise St. Ferdinand, King of Leon, who immediately proved his fitness to reign by conquering Cordova and Seville. This took place before the whole assemblage of the town and all the Castilian nobles, on July 1st, 1217. Here in 1415 the good Alvaro de Luna was beheaded by his false king, Juan II., whose forty-four years' reign was not marked by one personal act of dignity or greatness. Almost all that was worthy had been the work of Alvaro, who for thirty years out of those forty-four had been Juan's wise councillor. Had he served his king less well, he might have lived the longer; but he died bravely, as one whose life has been devoted to good deeds. In this square Charles V., in state and majesty recalling the days of Jewish pomp and grandeur, pardoned the Comuneros, whose chief seat of action had been our fair Segovia, and so finally put an end to the rebellion. And here his bigoted, cruel and narrow-minded son, Philip II., in October 1559 held the first *auto-da-fé*. Thus the Plaza Major is interesting for many ancient and historical reasons.

Ecclesiastically, Valladolid is not favoured. Its cathedral, begun on a magnificent scale, was never finished, and is a mere colossal fragment, consisting simply of a nave and four bays with aisles and chapels; the nave two hundred and fifty feet long and one hundred and fifty feet broad. According to the original plan it was to have been cruciform, with four lofty towers, rivalling the dimensions of Toledo. The whitewashed interior with red-tiled vaults is not impressive, but might easily be made so, whilst the interior is frightful, with its shapeless buttresses and solid blocks of masonry. It was begun by Philip II., who transferred his

ARCADES, SALAMANCA: DRAMATIC VISION, AS WE SAW IT.

energies to the Escorial and neglected Valladolid—and so it will probably remain. These are not the days for building great churches in Spain.

Not far from the cathedral is a smaller but more interesting church, that of Santa Maria la Antigua, with its beautiful steeple and open cloister running along the north wall. So far it reminded us of some of the lovely churches of Segovia. Santa Maria dates from the year 1180, the period of so much that is excellent in the Peninsula. The interior is very fine, with its groined roof and round Norman columns. The steeple—Valladolid's greatest and most conspicuous ornament—rises three stages above the roof, each stage having arcaded windows with semi-circular arches resting on slender, beautiful shafts. The low square tower or roof is covered with green and red pointed tiles, in the form of scallops, dazzling in the sunlight. Other churches there are and many buildings, some of late Gothic and much merit, with a wealth of ornamentation, which must have cost endless time and patience; all more or less characteristic of Spanish art.

It was not for all these things — the College of San Gregorio, with its rich fifteenth century façade; the Church of San Pablo, rebuilt about the same time by Torquemada the inquisitor; the decorated church and monastery of San Benito; not for the house of Cervantes, where part of " Don Quixote " was written, or the abode of Fabio Nelli, the Mæcenas of Valladolid, with its Corinthian court and striking doorway; not for the Casa del Sol, where dwelt and died the learned Gondomar, who was Philip III.'s Ambassador at the Court of St. James; nor for the striking and beautiful patios that enrich many a quiet street—not for all this that we held our sojourn in Valladolid memorable;

but for our visit to Simancas, which lies seven miles out of the town, and where most of the Spanish archives are deposited in an endless series of rooms.

The drive was not remarkable, but once arrived we were in a new world, and at the same time a very old and primitive world.

The wonderful little town lies on the brow of the hill overlooking the plains of Castile with their splendid pine forests plains which conjure up remote history. Here in 934 the Moors were defeated by King Ramiro, from which, however, they soon recovered. Five centuries later it defended the weak and miserable Enrique IV. against the League. And here, in 1602, O'Donnell, the Irish rebel, fled after the defeat of Kinsale, and died. What Simancas is now in appearance, it might have been in those early days. It is surrounded by its old walls with remarkable gateways, and the streets are steep and narrow, crooked and irregular. Everything appears to be going to wreck and ruin, a grey-brown tone over all. We saw no other place like it in Spain. Apparently it had fallen into a long enchanted slumber. The streets were quiet and deserted. Here and there a few women sat outside their doors, working with the needle. We passed through court-yards that might have been farm-yards, unpaved, inches thick in mud, surrounded by walls with overhanging mediæval eaves. At every turning we came upon delightful old houses with dormer windows and wonderful roofs that apparently had been untouched for centuries.

This formed the charm of the place. It was a mixture of town and country; an overgrown village; a small dead world, melancholy to the last extent to live in, to the last degree interesting to visit. We had the place to ourselves;

DOORWAY OF SAN PABLO, VALLADOLID.

no one interfered with us or took any notice. The few sewing women looked up calmly from their work, bade us "good-day" in subdued tones, which seemed to say they had done with the world and had nothing left to hope for, and went on with their task.

At the base of the hill, below the walls of the town, ran the river, crossed by a fine old bridge with seventeen arches. Beyond lie the plains and forests, whilst seven miles off to the left we catch sight of the misty atmosphere and church steeples of Valladolid. To the right, across the historic plain, there still rise the grey walls and roofs of the nunnery of Santa Clara, crowded with interest and romance, taking us back to the momentous days of Ferdinand and Isabella. Here in 1555 died their sad-fated daughter, Mad Joan, at the age of seventy-six. She had been an insane captive for just upon half a century, first at the instigation of her father, then of her son, Charles V. But it was a cruel captivity. Her life was melancholy, her room a small dungeon without windows, into which the sunlight never penetrated, and where she had no chance of recovering her reason. It has been said that she spent her days in watching her husband's coffin, who was buried at Santa Clara before being removed to Granada; but this has been proved untrue—as far as anything can be proved that happened three hundred years ago. Her mental disturbance must have been deep-seated, for it descended to her children's children. Charles V. took a dislike to the world and died a monk at Yusti. His son, Philip II., was even more deeply tainted, and buried himself in the Escorial with all his gloomy thoughts, religious superstition and cruel bigotry. A century later it reappeared in Charles II.; after whom the Bourbons came upon the scene.

But the great attraction of Simancas is its wonderful, moated, mediæval castle, in which the archives of Spain repose: a splendid and imposing old fortress flanked by

DOORWAY, SAN PABLO, VALLADOLID.

towers, with walls impregnable and time-defying. The moat is crossed by two old stone bridges. This great pile rises magnificently against the clear blue background of sky; one of those ancient castles surrounded by an atmosphere of romance and chivalry; a witness to days when military tournaments only gave place to the sterner realities of the battle-field.

In a quiet nook near the castle lives the custodian—a grey-headed old man, who appeared with ponderous keys, and took us from room to room, from floor to floor, with the greatest delight. He seemed to have every detail by heart, and took the greatest pride and intelligent interest in the various histories and records. Here he pointed out papers relating to the defeat of the Spanish Armada; there records of Christopher Columbus going forth to discover new worlds. With the great Elizabeth he seemed to have been personally acquainted, so intimate was he with her reign, whilst Napoleon and Wellington he looked upon as mere ordinary heroes of a commonplace yesterday. He overwhelmed us with details and descriptions, and we listened and examined only too willingly.

It was a dead world, a past and romantic atmosphere, all come to life again. Scene after scene rose vividly before us; deeds and records affecting the whole universe and all time; landing us now in Egypt, now in Africa, now on the burning plains of India, now in the most chivalrous days of Spain: days of the Romans, the Visigoths, the Moors; of the Kings of Castile and Asturias; days when all the sad records of the conquest of Granada, the defeat of Boabdil, the loss of the Alhambra were events of an hour.

The documents co-existent with all these events brought us face to face with them, and the flying moments were golden. Countless papers were closely packed in forty-six rooms, and they could not have a more romantic stronghold. The castle in bygone ages belonged to the Admirals of Castile, but after it was bought by the Kings of Spain,

Cardinal Ximenes was seized with the happy idea of turning it into a repository for the national archives; whilst Charles V.'s secretary organised the whole matter. It has occasionally been proposed to remove them to the Escorial, but it would be sad indeed to rob Simancas of its chief interest.

The Castle itself, with its massive walls, numberless rooms, arched ceilings, staircases and corridors, ancient windows looking into silent courtyards, and picturesque turrets commanding the vast plains, is full of a strange, indescribable influence. Few places had interested us more, but it was an interest essentially distinct from any other. As our footsteps echoed through the silent and deserted rooms, every nook and corner seemed crowded with ghosts, and in the presence of these endless records of the flight of time we felt that we were ourselves but shadows. On every post and lintel, over every doorway, the words seemed written in letters of fire: "To-day we visit the tombs of our friends, to-morrow other friends visit ours." "This is the true life," said Jacobo di Dante from the other world, "not yours."

We made the most of our golden moments in this old and wonderful castle; the sun declined and still we lingered. And once again there seemed to ring through all these silent rooms, more emphatically than we had ever heard it before, in clear, distinct tones from which we could not escape, which haunted us long after, and haunt us now as the picture rises before us in all its charm and beauty: "Here verily and indeed dwells the romance, the true, undying and matchless ROMANCE OF SPAIN!"

BY THE SAME AUTHOR.

Price 10s. net. With 88 Illustrations.

IN THE VALLEY OF THE RHONE

SECOND EDITION.

EXTRACTS FROM THE PRESS.

"A series of lively and entertaining sketches of travel beautifully illustrated by numerous drawings of interesting places and scenes in the neighbourhood of the Rhone. . . . A pleasant, handsome book, attractive alike in subject, treatment, and illustration."—*The Times.*

"We have left the best to the last. 'In the Valley of the Rhone' is one of those delightfully illustrated antiquarian and archæological books of travels for which Mr. Charles Wood is becoming well known to us. He and his companions found many unknown gems of architecture and quaint relics of Roman and Byzantine days in their journeys, but lest this antiquarian lore, which is never intrusive, might possibly become monotonous, it is lightened with a kindly and gently humorous account of the life of to-day in strange old-world towns and almost unknown districts. For he is an artist in manners and customs, as well as in description, and a long line of monks and hotel-keepers, nuns and peasants appear before us; in a word, all those picturesque figures that make travel in Southern France the pleasantest of all pilgrimages to the artist and the man of culture. One is uncertain whether to admire most the descriptions of architecture and scenery, or the inimitable dialogues; on the whole, the latter being the rarer gift, we must value it more."—*The Spectator.*

"The Rhone from source to sea, from the glaciers of the Oberland to the shores of the Mediterranean, is a fascinating subject, and Mr. Wood has given us an enjoyable volume. To the old tourist it revives many pleasant memories, and it abounds in useful information for the veteran as well as the novice. Often, as in his 'Letters from Majorca,' Mr. Wood reminds us of the lively æstheticism of Stevenson in the Cevennes; and like Dumas, who had gone over all the ground before him, he has the happy knack of easy dialogue, and of discovering or inventing original characters. We never care to take him very literally, and for that we like him none the worse. He does not photograph individuals: he idealises in types—human and canine. Take his dog-talk. His interview with Bruno, the youthful St. Bernard, touches our innermost feelings. . . . So Mr. Wood goes about castles, cloisters, and sheepfolds, confessing the custodians. They are all remarkable men and women. They have attained to phenomenal ages and can recall extraordinary experiences. . . . The engravings which embellish his pages are a revelation of out of the way nooks and corners, even in cities so familiar as Avignon and Arles: of church porches and superbly decorated façades in towns which have been dying by inches. . . . Mr. Wood can romance, but he has the spirit of poetry, and there is a charming mediæval day-dream at Aigues-Mortes of sinister name, where St. Louis marshalled all the chivalry of his realm, and whence he sailed on his ill-fated expedition."—*Saturday Review.*

"The author is a capital companion, cheery and appreciative. . . . A pleasant book of travels."—*The Daily News.*

"This is the sort of book that makes one get out a Continental Bradshaw in order at once to find the best way of following in the author's footsteps. Mr. Wood's pleasant writing is easy reading. . . . He has a happy knack of meeting with odd people and queer incidents, while he has an eye for the picturesque, whether in mountain, stream, or ancient ruin."—*The Morning Post.*

"... The author has put into the text a variety of details which are far too often entirely overlooked by hasty travellers. ... Words of wisdom on this district are so rare that every one who wants to go there ought to read this volume before he starts ... It is full of useful hints."—*St. James's Gazette.*

"... The impressions that Mr. Wood records are his own, and recorded in his own fashion. He looks at everything with his own eyes, not with those of his predecessors, and his style is pleasant in its simplicity and lightness. The personal element in his experiences will interest many, and all his readers will rejoice in the many pictures which adorn his narrative. 'In the Valley of the Rhone' is indeed a handsome volume, and will, we are sure, appeal successfully to a large public."—*The Globe.*

"The author commences his narrative with his arrival at Montreux, from which place he made an excursion to the Rochers de Naye, of which he gives a charming description. ... Mr. Wood's book is full of anecdote and interesting descriptions of the places he visited and the people he met."—*The Field.*

"... In no sense a commonplace guide, Mr. Wood proves a cheerful companion, devoid of the asperities of the British tourist, and appreciates accordingly the people amongst whom he moves. His book is illustrated profusely and well, and forms an attractive volume."—*Review of the Week.*

"... The author is observant, and has omitted no incident of his interesting tour."—*The Outlook.*

"... Mr. Wood is able to get on the most friendly terms with people of all ranks and classes, and gains, and shares with his readers, the confidences of peasants and priests, nuns and post-boys, and thus we make many interesting and delightful acquaintances. ... For old street and church architecture and the remains of Roman and mediæval times he has the eye of the artist and the archæologist. The illustrations are numerous and excellent."—*The Scotsman.*

"The future visitor to the Rhone Valley cannot do better, if the land be strange to him, than take as a preliminary a little journey in the company of Mr. Charles W. Wood. He calls his book 'In the Valley of the Rhone,' and there could be no more delightful companion."—*Yorkshire Post.*

"Mr. Wood's book is not a guide-book in the accepted sense of a Murray or a Baedeker, but this outcome of his impressions and experiences is of inestimable value to intending tourists in a lovely and most attractive valley, while even to those who cannot hope to spread their wings so far, the charm and grace of his tale of travel are productive of much pleasure. ... The book is a very happy mixture of description, narrative and history, and is written in a style now vivid and sparkling, now confidential, while the excellent line and half-tone illustrations add considerably to its charm and interest."—*The Manchester Courier.*

"The picturesque and historical Valley of the Rhone has afforded another opportunity to Mr. Wood, whose fresh descriptions of places and people always seem to keep to the same standard of excellence, and throughout the 439 pages there is scarcely a page one would wish to skip. Mr. Wood has an undoubted gift for this particular branch of writing. He imparts his historical knowledge pleasantly, his gaiety of spirits is infectious, he is equally quick to seize on the amusing points of a situation as to vividly sketch to the eye of the imagination the exquisite scenes that appeal to him."—*The Western Morning News.*

"Mr. Wood has the light touch that makes such a record bright reading from first to last; and yet we feel that we are learning all about the history and antiquities of the region, and by the help of a very fine set of pictures, are ourselves for a little while transported to the sunny south, and loath indeed to leave it."—*London Quarterly Review.*

MACMILLAN AND CO., LIMITED, LONDON.

www.ingramcontent.com/pod-product-compliance
Lightning Source LLC
Chambersburg PA
CBHW032019220426
43664CB00006B/296